11/9
7/5

The Rise and Fall of the Dillinger Gang

The Rise and Fall of the Dillinger Gang

JEFFERY S. KING

CUMBERLAND HOUSE
NASHVILLE, TENNESSEE

Published by
Cumberland House Publishing, Inc.
431 Harding Industrial Drive
Nashville, TN 37211-3160

Cover design: Gore Studio, Inc.
Text design: John Mitchell

Library of Congress Cataloging-in-Publication Data

King, Jeffery S., 1940–
  The rise and fall of the Dillinger gang / Jeffery S. King.
      p. cm.
  Includes bibliographical references and index.
  ISBN-10 1-58182-450-5 (alk. paper)
  ISBN-13 978-1-58182-450-6 (alk. paper)
  1. Dillinger, John, 1903-1934. 2. Criminals—Middle West—Biography. 3. Gangs—United States—History—20th century. I. Title.
  HV6248.D5K56 2005
  364.152'3'092277—dc22
                                                                2005024570

Printed in the United States of America

1 2 3 4 5 6 7—11 10 09 08 07 06 05

To my mother,
Margaret Lydia King

Contents

Acknowledgments

Many people from such institutions as the FBI, National Archives, Library of Congress, state and local public libraries, state and local historical societies, and the online organization Partners in Crime have helped me greatly.

I am particularly grateful to Mary Ann Johnson, Herb Levine, Rick Mattix, Jeff Maycroft, Michael Webb, William Helmer, Rick Cartledge, Ellen Poulsen, Steve Nickel, Tony Stewart (JohnnieDillinger@aol.com), Ron Rosner, E. Shirlene Newman of the Washington, D.C., Public Library and Thomas Mann of the Library of Congress. Thanks also to my excellent editor, John Mitchell, and my publisher, Ron Pitkin.

Introduction

As the Roaring Twenties faded and America slipped into the Great Depression, several inmates of the Indiana prison system began an acquaintanceship that would in coming years lead to violence and death. One of those incarcerated, Indianapolis-born John Herbert Dillinger, a minor criminal who in his youth had displayed a talent for both baseball and mischief, had served time in both the Indiana State Reformatory at Pendleton and the state prison at Michigan City from 1924 to 1933. While behind bars, he met an unsavory crew of characters—among them, Harry "Pete" Pierpont, John "Red" Hamilton, Homer Van Meter, Charles "Fat Charley" Makley, and Russell Lee "Boobie" Clark—all of whom would become members of a violent outlaw band that historians would call the Dillinger Gang.[1]

Soon after his parole in May 1933, Dillinger organized an efficient criminal crew that spread terror throughout the Midwest during the next year, killing as many as sixteen people and robbing perhaps as many as two dozen banks. He escaped from jail twice and was declared "Public Enemy Number One" before he was killed by federal agents in front of a Chicago theater on July 22, 1934. With the exception of Russell

Clark, who received a life sentence in the Ohio State Penitentiary, all of the major members of Dillinger's gang met violent deaths before the end of 1934.

The 1920s was a period of great prosperity and optimism in the United States, but the enactment of nationwide Prohibition in January 1920 was one of the country's major failures. Although banning the manufacture, transportation, and sale of "intoxicating liquors" was supposed to create a more moral society, Prohibition's primary legacy was a vast increase in organized crime, as criminal syndicates sought to provide the illicit spirits demanded by a large segment of the American public.

Public apathy about the rise of organized crime, in tandem with new technology that was replacing the horse with the automobile and the six-gun with the machine gun, ultimately led to a crime wave in America during the twenties. Many outlaws and gangs throughout the country were able to operate successfully, in part because of primitive criminal-identification techniques and a lack of newspaper photography. Although newspapers often reported their crimes, thieves and killers could walk the streets with near impunity since few people had ever seen what they looked like. This, coupled with the unprecedented mobility provided by the proliferation of the automobile, plus the uncoordinated efforts of police agencies, meant that bandits were rarely caught.

Criminals often made pursuit and apprehension difficult by traveling to other states, where they could not be arrested because they had committed no crime in those jurisdictions. The Newton brothers, Harvey Bailey, "Baron" H. K. Lamm, and Eddie Bentz robbed banks, company payrolls, and even trains almost at will during the 1920s without being identified or caught. However, they never became household names. Kidnappings were largely ignored by law enforcement, for they usually involved criminals kidnapping other criminals for ransom.

It wasn't until the middle twenties, when there was an explosion of underworld violence in the large cities of the East and Midwest, especially Chicago, that the average citizen begin to realize something was terribly wrong. While there always had been corruption in state and local governments, gangsters were now able to use the vast profits they reaped from illegal alcohol to buy the protection of many previously honest state and local police, politicians and judges.

By the time of the October 1929 stock market crash, the rampant violence and corruption had turned American public opinion against the more notorious bootleggers and gangsters. This shift in public perception would lead, in 1932, to the conviction and imprisonment of the nation's best known and arguably most powerful underworld leader, "Scarface" Al Capone—on charges of not paying federal income tax on the profits generated by his sprawling criminal empire.

As the United States slipped into the throes of the Great Depression, state and local governments could not cope with either the crime wave or the massive unemployment and poverty spawned by the nation's economic collapse.[2] Exacerbating the problems were droves of immigrants and others seeking work who flocked to the nation's urban centers, straining cities' already meager resources. Law enforcement by local police became increasingly difficult as kidnappings of wealthy citizens for ransom soared and bank robberies became so common that many communities formed vigilante committees to stem the criminal tide.

By the early 1930s the mean national income had fallen by more than half since the stock market crash, and 13 million people were unemployed. Many were homeless, numerous banks had failed, and bread lines were everywhere. Although crime occurred throughout the nation, the problem was most acute in the Midwest and Southwest. Many considered Oklahoma to be the most dangerous place for lawmen.

The task of law enforcement at all levels—federal, state, and local— was made more difficult by the fact that many Americans sympathized with some of the more notorious outlaws and their gangs, viewing them as underdogs in a fight for survival during dire economic times. Many Americans thought of themselves as underdogs facing similar challenges and thus derived a degree of satisfaction from seeing poor and desperate individuals—people not unlike themselves—becoming rich, even if they were doing so illegally. They liked it when those they perceived as latter-day Robin Hoods triumphed over corrupt police and greedy bankers.

Midwestern cities such as Chicago, St. Louis, and Kansas City were hotbeds of crime in the early part of the decade. Chicago had provided heartland America with politically protected organized gambling and prostitution for decades. The City of Big Shoulders, like most other major urban areas, offered a plethora of amenities for criminals, including "fences" who could sell stolen goods, doctors who would not report gunshot wounds, sleazy lawyers who could manipulate the legal system, corrupt police officials and judges who could be bribed, and even tailors who could make clothes with concealed pistol pockets. In addition, there were criminals for hire who specialized in planning crimes and picking places to rob, and there were always plenty of women who were eager to become "gun molls."[3]

For criminals who needed to lay low after committing a robbery or slaying, there were "cooling-off joints," places where hoodlums could find safety—for a price. Three of the most important of these cities were Joplin, Missouri; St. Paul, Minnesota; and Hot Springs, Arkansas.

Even worse than Chicago in terms of systemic corruption was St. Paul, where lawmen and politicians ran crime operations directly. Any criminal with enough money could buy protection and sanctuary there as long as he behaved himself within the city limits. This system had existed since the turn of the twentieth century, when it was created by Police Chief John J. O'Connor, who resigned in 1920. The "O'Connor system," as it was known, continued under many of the founder's successors.

In the early thirties Harry "Dutch" Sawyer, a saloonkeeper, fence, and racketeer, was St. Paul's crime boss and O'Connor system czar. He expanded his power by becoming an underworld banker and could even protect criminals in other cities. Many outlaw gangs, including the Barker-Karpis and Dillinger mobs, used his services. Sawyer was actively involved in such crimes as the ransom kidnapping of banker Edward Bremer by the Barker-Karpis Gang, and his Green Lantern Saloon, managed by Albert "Pat" Reilly, was frequented by several notorious criminals. Reilly's wife, Helen, had sisters who were girlfriends of Dillinger associates Tommy Carroll and Alvin Karpis.[4]

Law enforcement reform was long overdue, as coordination and cooperation were very limited among the various agencies at all levels. State police were largely paper organizations, often limited to patrolling state highways; county and municipal police protected criminal activities; and police brutality was common. Scientific police work was extremely primitive in America. Although the ineffective Bertillon method of criminal identification by physical measurements, imported from France in the previous century, was being replaced by fingerprinting, there was little use of scientific methods in police work or in the courts. Ballistics was in its infancy, and only recently had the country's first scientific crime-detection laboratories been established, in Chicago (1929) and at Bureau of Investigation headquarters in Washington, D.C. (1932).

It seemed to many that only the federal government could come to the aid of ordinary citizens.[5] However, the consensus at the time was that the national government should not have anything to do with fighting crime, except in a few narrowly defined circumstances. This view, according to many legalists, was supported by the U.S. Constitution and its provisions for states' rights, which meant that only state and local governments could mount major efforts to battle crime.

The few significant federal laws pertaining to crime included the Comstock Act of 1873, enacted to combat obscenity; the Mann Act of 1910, to fight prostitution; the Harrison Narcotics Act of 1914, to deal with illegal drugs; and the National Motor Vehicle Theft Act of 1919, known as the Dyer Act, which enabled federal agents to go after criminals who had stolen cars and driven across a state line.

An important expansion of federal crime-fighting power came in 1932 with the enactment of federal kidnapping statutes, after the abduction and murder of the twenty-month-old son of aviator and national hero Charles Lindbergh. But even then, President Herbert Hoover's attorney general, William D. Mitchell, told Congress, "You are never going to correct the crime situation in this country by having Washington jump in."[6]

However, things changed when Franklin Delano Roosevelt, who believed the federal government had to become actively involved in solving the severe economic and social problems of the Depression, became president in 1933. One of his first actions was to end Prohibition, a task that was accomplished in December of that year and which put the remaining big-city bootleggers out of business. To replace the income they had previously derived from illicit alcohol, many of these criminals began to turn to bank robbery and kidnapping wealthy citizens for ransom.

With the national mood still against the creation of a powerful centralized federal law enforcement agency, which many feared could develop into a secret police force, new U.S. Attorney General Homer S. Cummings and J. Edgar Hoover, director of the Justice Department's Bureau of Investigation, the nation's top crime-fighting organization, had to convince the American people that incorruptible and professional federal crime-fighters were the only way to deal with interstate criminals. It was easy for them to show that corrupt state and local police could not or would not cope with the crime wave, and both vigorously campaigned for new federal laws and expansion of the federal government's law enforcement powers.

J. Edgar Hoover, the man who would become the nemesis of John Dillinger, joined the BOI as a lawyer in 1917. At that time, the bureau's 200 agents were poorly supervised and many were political hacks or even criminals. Hoover was active in the anticommunist Palmer Raids after World War I, initiating mass roundups of aliens across the nation, developing card files on 450,000 radicals, and organizing an effective network of informers. In 1924 he was appointed director in an effort to cleanse the bureau after several scandals. He was ruthless, firing hacks and criminals and establishing professional standards for agents. He primarily hired lawyers and accountants, instituted scientific detection methods, and in later years would set up the bureau's crime laboratory and create the FBI National Academy to train local police officers.[7]

Hoover used a dramatic tragedy known as the Kansas City Massacre to increase the importance of his then-minor federal agency. On the sunny Saturday morning of June 17, 1933, in the parking lot of Kansas City's Union Station, several federal agents and Kansas City lawmen were returning prison escapee and bank robber Frank Nash to Leavenworth Penitentiary in Kansas. While Nash and the others were getting into a pair of vehicles that would ferry them from the train station to the federal prison, they were approached by three machine-gun-toting men (believed to be Charles "Pretty Boy" Floyd, Adam Richetti, and Verne Miller, a former South Dakota sheriff who had become a gangster).

A deadly gunfight erupted, and in about a minute's time three officers, a federal agent, and Nash were killed. All three of the gunmen escaped and disappeared. Miller was soon identified as one of the killers, but the identities of the others remained a mystery.

Several months later, Hoover's agency determined that Miller, Floyd, and Richetti had been the killers, but many still believe the case against Floyd and Richetti was never proven beyond a reasonable doubt. Researchers have recently uncovered evidence that Nash and two of the officers were actually killed by a federal agent seated behind Nash in the police vehicle when the unfamiliar shotgun he was attempting to load accidentally discharged.[8]

Two major kidnappings also drew attention to federal crime-fighting efforts. The first occurred in June 1933, about the same time as the Kansas City Massacre, when St. Paul brewer William Hamm Jr. was abducted by the Barker-Karpis Gang. A month later, Oklahoma City oilman Charles Urschel was "snatched" by George "Machine Gun" Kelly and Albert Bates, who demanded a $200,000 ransom.

After these incidents, Cummings and Hoover launched a national "war on crime" and unveiled a Twelve Point Program of federal crime control. Congress was at first not interested in the program, but Roosevelt was excited by the thought of creating of a "super police force." Many new laws were passed expanding the authority of Hoover's bureau, which in July 1933 was merged with the Prohibition Bureau to form the Division of Investigation and two years later became the Federal Bureau of Investigation.

Hoover could have concentrated his efforts on powerful organized crime, but that would have been difficult. It was much easier to build up the reputations of relatively minor free-lance criminals and then catch or kill them and reap the rewards the resulting publicity would generate. A former high-ranking federal official would later say: "The whole of the FBI's main thrust was not investigation, but public relations and propaganda to glorify its director."[9]

Besides promoting the DOI as the nation's top crime-fighting organization, the war on crime would help foster acceptance of President Roosevelt's New Deal programs, for it would show that government—especially the federal government—could be effective in solving social problems.

To get results, Hoover needed a villain, but unfortunately for the DOI director, there were only a few nationally known outlaws, among them, Bonnie Parker and Clyde Barrow, Pretty Boy Floyd, and George "Machine Gun" Kelly. The Barker-Karpis Gang, although it had been very active since the twenties, was still largely unknown (the gang members would generally elude law enforcement authorities until the spring of 1934, when they would be betrayed by an associate of the Dillinger Gang[10]). Ultimately, Hoover and Cummings decided to go after Urschel's kidnapper, Machine Gun Kelly.

A minor Memphis bootlegger, Kelly (born George F. Barnes Jr.) had robbed a few banks but was not well known to the general public prior to the Urschel kidnapping. Nagged by his wife, Kathryn (who purchased the machine gun that spawned her husband's colorful nickname), to become someone important, the unambitious Kelly agreed to take part in kidnapping the oilman, who was hidden on the Texas farm of Kathryn's parents.

Federal agents claimed that after Urschel was released unharmed, he recalled vivid details of his imprisonment which helped federal agents, using scientific reasoning, determine where he had been held. Another version is that a pair of informants tipped agents to the location. Within a month, all of the kidnappers except Kelly and his wife had been captured.

Surprised by federal agents in the wee hours of September 26, 1933, Kelly, clad in pajamas, and Kathryn were captured at a Memphis residence. By this time Hoover's public relations machine was calling the innocuous outlaw the leader of a dangerous gang, "a desperate character, having served a number of terms [two, actually] for bootlegging, vagrancy, and other offenses." The agency's position was repeated by newspapers throughout the nation, including the New York Times, which proclaimed, "Kelly and his gang of Southwestern desperados are regarded as the most dangerous ever encountered." Kelly and Kathryn would be sentenced to life imprisonment after a sensational trial in Oklahoma City.

The Justice Department used the Machine Gun Kelly case to show the capability of the federal government in law enforcement. Tremendous publicity was given to the seventeen-state manhunt mounted for the outlaw and his accomplices, and arrests that took place in five states. In just ninety days federal agents had solved the case, caught the kidnappers, and recovered the ransom money. Using newspapers, the press, radio, magazines, and newsreels, the Justice Department convinced the public that the federal government was indeed an efficient crime-fighter.[11]

With Kelly behind bars, Hoover needed a new public menace to keep citizens' and legislative attention focused on his growing agency. Fortune again smiled on the director, for the Dillinger Gang was beginning to attract attention in the Midwest. Most members of the gang were homegrown American whites who had been raised in small towns or on farms. In short, they were largely "average" and, aside from committing some minor crimes in their youth, had given no indication they would be serious criminals when they became adults. An exception was "Baby Face" Nelson, who had grown up in Chicago and was sent to reform school for stealing car parts.

Congress reacted to the public's demands and in May and June 1934 passed legislation that greatly expanded the DOI's jurisdiction over interstate crimes. The Fugitive Felon Act made crossing a state line to avoid prosecution a federal crime. Other laws gave the division increased enforcement powers and protection for its agents. Severe penalties were enacted for killing or assaulting federal officers, and federal agents finally were given the authority to carry firearms and full arrest powers for offenses against the United States. The DOI was also authorized to give out up to $25,000 in rewards.

The anti-kidnapping Lindbergh Law was amended to create a presumption of interstate transportation of the victim, to cover cases in which there was no ransom demand, and to authorize the death penalty for anyone convicted of kidnapping. Also made federal offenses were: extortion of money or other valuables by telephone; robbing any national bank or member bank of the Federal Reserve System; and the interstate transportation of stolen property worth more than $5,000.[13]

But Hoover had a rival in Melvin Purvis, the special agent in charge of the agency's Chicago office, who was at the center of the war against crime during the early 1930s. In 1934 Purvis was voted eighth in a Literary Digest poll of outstanding world figures. He had been involved with more major public enemies—among them, Baby Face Nelson, kidnapper Thomas H. Robinson Jr., Pretty Boy Floyd, and John Dillinger—than any other lawman. A major reason for his fame was his involvement in the nationwide hunt for Dillinger.

After a briefly practicing law in his native South Carolina, Purvis joined the FBI in 1927. Appointed special agent in charge of the Bureau of Investigation's Chicago office in 1932, he had his share of failures and also boasted a big ego. Of all the agency's field offices, the only one that did not issue press releases beginning with "J. Edgar Hoover announces . . ." was the Chicago office. Instead, releases from the Chicago office substituted Purvis's name for Hoover's. Both Hoover and Inspector Samuel Cowley were enraged when media reports identified Cowley as an assistant to Purvis, when in fact Hoover had appointed Cowley to be in charge of all of the agency's major cases—Dillinger, the Barker-Karpis Gang, and the Kansas City Massacre.14

It was Purvis who led the cadre of federal agents who surrounded and ultimately killed Dillinger outside Chicago's Biograph Theater on July 22, 1934, ending the brief and violent career of one of America's most colorful criminals.

John Dillinger caught the public's fancy because, even in the face of death, he exhibited poise, bravery, self-confidence, and a sense of humor. He also garnered sympathy because of an excessive prison sentence he had received as a young man for a relatively innocuous crime—in the minds of many struggling Americans, the same thing could very well have happened to them.

The federal Division of Investigation did not create Dillinger's popularity among the American citizenry. In fact, it was only during a few months in 1934 that it conducted a massive nationwide manhunt for the outlaw. But once the publicity-hungry Hoover had Dillinger and the members of his notorious gang in his sights, he exploited their crimes and ultimately their demise to thrust his small agency into the limelight and ensure its development as the nation's premier instrument of law enforcement.

The Rise and Fall of the
Dillinger
Gang

"Just a Kid"

I N EARLY 1934 MOVIE AUDIENCES cheered when pictures of John Herbert Dillinger and his father appeared during newsreels. After a Justice Department official told his superiors about this happening at a Washington theater, one of them angrily wrote to the newsreel producer, accusing him of being biased in favor of Dillinger and glorifying his exploits, when Dillinger was really a mad-dog killer. According to another outraged Justice Department official, "Applause, mind you, for a coward and a killer. Applause for a man who had snuffed out the lives of husbands and fathers without the blinking of an eye. Applause for one of the most loathsome creatures in the annals of crime."

One writer thought there was a "nauseating display of mushy sentimentality" about the man considered America's Public Enemy Number One. Even his name was euphonic for an outlaw.[1] He stood five feet seven and one-eighth inches tall and weighed 153 pounds, with a medium build and complexion, chestnut hair, and gray eyes.[2]

Born June 22, 1903, in Indianapolis, Dillinger was a precocious child. His moderately well-off family operated a grocery store and owned several houses. Dillinger's mother, Mollie, died when he was three, following an operation for an apoplectic attack. His fifteen-year-old sister, Audrey, and his father, John Wilson Dillinger, took over raising him. In 1912 Dillinger's father married Elizabeth Fields of Mooresville, Indiana. The couple had two children, Hubert and Doris, half-brother and half-sister to John and Audrey.[3]

John did not give any sign that he would someday become a vicious criminal. One old acquaintance later told federal authorities that Dillinger had been well-behaved in Sunday School, and that he could not believe the boy had become a hardened gangster.[4] John was well liked, his grades were average at the Washington Elementary School in Indianapolis, and he was a superb athlete, especially in baseball. One of his classmates said of him:

> "He wasn't a bad boy, I'll tell you that. He didn't do anything any other boy wouldn't have done—play hokey [sic], steal cherries out of somebody's orchard. We were pretty fair at playing hokey, and when we did, we'd just fool around, go here and there, up and down alleys and streets. We didn't do it too often, maybe every couple of weeks. We used to scuffle with each other, but it was all in good nature—fistfights and rassling both.
>
> "[H]e used to play ball pretty good, too. We had a kind of little neighborhood team. He liked to pitch and would play the infield. In the summer we'd go up on the railroad tracks, or go swimming in Fall Creek."[5]

Nevertheless, the youngster was still a problem for his father, who would sometimes lock the unruly John in the house for punishment and often neglected and abused him. He would even chain John to the wheel of a horse-drawn delivery cart in the back of his store or beat him with a barrel stave. Once, the elder Dillinger saw his son give a pretty girl a package of Kiss Me chewing gum. After taking the gum from the girl, he vigorously pushed the boy.

Dillinger became the leader of a neighborhood youth gang called the Dirty Dozen, which engaged in petty theft, such as stealing coal from the Pennsylvania Railroad yards and selling it to neighbors. In the sixth grade a defiant John was taken to juvenile court for that crime. The magistrate told him, "Your mind is crippled!" when the grinning Dillinger placed a wad of gum on the bill of his cap when told to remove it from his mouth. No action was taken against him for his misbehavior.

Another time, Dillinger climbed abroad an untended switch engine in the railroad yards and ran it into several coal cars. He once found cases of whiskey in a boxcar and then showed up at school drunk. Another time, at a sawmill next to the Dillinger store, John and a friend tied a boy on the carrier and threw a switch that sent the terrified youth toward a large, whirring circular saw. They stopped the carrier when it was just a yard from the saw.

There is a story that in 1916 Dillinger and some of his friends met a girl with a coal cart near the railroad tracks. He told the boys to grab the girl and take her to an empty house nearby, where they raped her.[6] A few years later Dillinger was arrested in Indianapolis for speeding and had to pay an $11 fine.[7]

Apparently afraid of the bad influence that city life was having on his adolescent son, the elder Dillinger sold his store and houses in Indianapolis in March 1920, a year after John had dropped out of school, and bought a small farm some seventeen miles south of the city, near Mooresville, Indiana. For a few months Dillinger attended Mooresville High School, although he never studied and mostly received failing grades. He hated farm work and soon refused to go back to school; however, he attended Sunday School at the First Christian Church in Mooresville regularly.[8] Several years later, his father said, "My people have been farmers for generations. I liked the land. John never did. Said it was too slow. . . . I guess the city kind of got a hold on him. . . ."[9]

During World War I the young man had tried to get a job at the Link-Belt Company in Indianapolis but was rejected because he was too young. Instead, he eventually took a job as an apprentice machinist at the Reliance Specialty Company in Indianapolis, where he was rated an outstanding worker. The owner later described Dillinger as "very fast and accurate . . . sober, honest, and very industrious."[10] John also worked four months as an errand boy for the Indianapolis Board of Trade.[11]

Dillinger spent most of his spare time in the county seat of Martinsville, where he occasionally frequented "Big John" Gebhardt's poolroom. One of the regulars later recalled: "John would come in, hang up his hat and play pool at a quarter a game. He wasn't very good, and he frequently lost. When he would lose two dollars, he'd put back the cue, get his cap, and walk out without a word. Never gave anyone any trouble and never said much."[12]

He became an excellent second baseman on the local baseball team. According to his father, "When he wasn't playing baseball, he was generally out hunting. He was handy with a gun and a dead shot. We always had plenty of rabbits, squirrels, and opossums during the open season. John got his love of hunting from me."[13]

As a young man, Dillinger's major interest was pursuing girls, including prostitutes in Indianapolis. He fell in love with Frances Thornton, his uncle Everett's stepdaughter, but Everett told John he was too young and, besides, Everett wanted his stepdaughter to marry a wealthy boy from Greencastle, Indiana.[14] Dillinger also had a failed relationship with a farmer's daughter named Mary Paris because his father would not give him sufficient spending money to court her. Dillinger had a violent dispute with his father over this incident.[15]

On the evening of July 21, 1923, Dillinger stole a car belonging to Oliver P. Macy from the parking lot of the Friends Church in Mooresville and abandoned it in Indianapolis. Early the next morning an Indianapolis policeman saw him wandering around and, thinking the young man looked suspicious, grabbed his coat collar. However, Dillinger fled, leaving behind his empty coat. Believing he would soon be arrested, Dillinger left the area and enlisted in the U.S. Navy, giving his real name but a phony address in St. Louis. As it turned out, Macy refused to press charges.

Dillinger underwent basic training at the Great Lakes naval training facility near Chicago and, after attaining the rating of fireman third class, served aboard the USS *Utah* (which was fated to be sunk at Pearl Harbor on December 7, 1941). His first imprisonment was in the brig after going AWOL on October 28, 1923, for almost a full day. He spent ten days in solitary confinement on bread and water with full ration every third day, and was forced to forfeit $18 in pay. After going on AWOL again, he received five additional days in solitary confinement. Finally, on December 4, 1923, Dillinger deserted the ship in Boston; the navy offered a $50 reward for his capture.[16]

Dillinger made his way home and soon resumed his old ways, including his avid pursuit of pretty girls. On April 12, 1924, he married seventeen-year-old Beryl Ethel Hovius from Martinsville, whom he had met during a party given by one of her friends the previous December in Mooresville. She was a waitress at the Callis Restaurant in Martinsville. By most accounts, it wasn't much of a marriage, as Dillinger spent little time at home after the newlyweds moved into the home of Beryl's parents. However, this is untrue.

Actually, the couple stayed for a short time at the Dillinger farm and did move in with Beryl's parents, but after John got a job as an upholstery worker at a Mooresville furniture shop, they rented a house in Martinsville. According to Beryl, John liked to spend quiet evenings with her at home and was always very nice to her. The couple had little money, and their favorite pastime was going to the movies.[17]

Local gossip had it that Dillinger committed several minor burglaries in Martinsville during this time, which kept the town's one-man police force busy investigating the crimes. An acquaintance, Dr. R. L. Heines, and his father, Jacob, believed that Dillinger robbed Jacob's filling station in Mooresville.[18] When John and two friends were arrested for stealing forty-one chickens from Homer Zook of Lawrence Township, his father somehow managed to get the case dismissed.

Now Dillinger wanted to pull a bigger job. He was impressed with a thirty-one-year-old former convict, Edgar Singleton, the umpire for the Martinsville baseball team. The young man agreed to help Singleton with an "easy" robbery of a Mooresville grocer, Frank Morgan, who usually carried the day's receipts when he went uptown for a haircut on Saturday nights. It made no difference to the pair that Morgan had been very nice to Dillinger when he caught him stealing pennies from the store, giving the young man a lecture on honesty instead of turning him over to the police. After drinking to get their courage up, Dillinger hid near the Mooresville Christian Church and Singleton waited in a getaway car down the street as they waited for their prey.

As the grocer was passing the church at 10:30 p.m. on September 6, 1924, Dillinger brutally hit Morgan over the head with a large bolt wrapped in a rag. In his other hand he held a .32-caliber revolver. This time, however, Morgan was carrying little money, having taken the day's receipts to his home before heading uptown for his haircut. Morgan fell, and when he got up and began to fight, Dillinger hit him a second time. (Morgan's head wound would require eleven stitches to close.) The grocer screamed, and as neighbors ran to help him, he grabbed Dillinger's gun, which discharged. Thinking he had shot Morgan, Dillinger fled down the street, without any money, toward the spot where Singleton was supposed to be waiting in the getaway car, but it was gone.

Although Morgan told Deputy Sheriff John Hayworth that he didn't know who had attempted to rob him, some local youths suspected that Dillinger and Singleton were the guilty parties. One said that John had told him he wanted "an easy way to make money," and had asked him how much money Morgan might be carrying.

Hayworth and Morgan confronted John at the Dillinger farm. Morgan reminded the young man that he had bought candy at his store when he was a child.

"Why, John, you wouldn't hurt me, would you?" Morgan asked.

"No, Mr. Morgan," Dillinger answered.

After being taken to the county jail, Dillinger broke down crying and confessed that he and Singleton had committed the crime. John agreed with his father to plead guilty without a lawyer and throw himself on the mercy of the court, after the prosecutor falsely promised the elder Dillinger that his son would get a light sentence if he did so. But when John went before the very tough Judge Joseph V. Williams, he received concurrent sentences of two to fourteen years and ten to twenty years on the two charges of conspiracy to commit a felony and assault with intent to rob. In addition, he was fined $200 and disenfranchised for twelve years.

Singleton, who was arrested on September 15, insisted on being represented by a lawyer and was able to obtain a change of venue and, ultimately, a light sentence. He was paroled after serving just two years imprisonment.[19]

Dillinger wrote about the robbery while in prison:

> Saturday night of September 7 [sic], 1924, while under the influence of alcohol, me and my companion, Edgar Singleton, attacked Mr. Morgan, a grocer in Mooresville, Ind. I had a gun, a thirty two revolver, when I struck him and hit him on the head with a bat, and then ran we didn't get the money he had on him, which was three hundred and twenty five dollars. I was arrested the next day and taken to Martinsville but I denied the charge. On September 14 my Father and Sister came to see me and told me that they had arrested Singleton two days before and he was a state witness against me, having told all he knew of the crime.
>
> The prosecutor said that if I would plead guilty they would be linient [sic] with me. My Father and Sister asked me to plead guilty they were sure the county would be linient [sic] with me so I plead guilty next day Monday 15. . . . Judge Williams . . . asked me if I plead guilty and I said yes, and he sentenced me to the Indiana Reformatory 10 to 20 years for assault and battery with intent to rob and 2 to 14 for conspiracy, sentenced to run concurrently. Then Singleton plead not guilty . . . and he had two jury trials and eventually received 2 to 14 years at the Indiana State Prison. I was told that I and the three others who come [sic] with me were transferred to play ball. . . .
>
> —John Dillinger #3225.[20]

Even Morgan County, Indiana, Deputy Sheriff Russell Peterson believed Dillinger's sentence was too harsh given the circumstances. "[He] was just a kid. He got a raw deal," Peterson said. "You just can't take ten years away from a kid's life."[21]

Pendleton

THE FIRST INDIANA STATE PRISON was approved by the legislature on January 9, 1821, and built at Jeffersonville. A second state prison, located at Michigan City, was authorized by the legislature in 1859 and opened on January 1, 1861. The Michigan City facility was known as the Indiana State Prison North, and the one at Jeffersonville was known as the Indiana State Prison South until April 1, 1897, when, by act of the General Assembly, the Jeffersonville prison became the Indiana State Reformatory.

In 1909 a hospital for the criminally insane was established on the grounds of the Michigan City prison. In February 1918 fire destroyed several buildings at the state reformatory, and a new institution was approved to be built at Pendleton, thirty miles northeast of Indianapolis. On November 17, 1923, the new prison was opened and the facility at Jeffersonville was closed.[1]

The Indiana State Reformatory at Pendleton was overpopulated almost from the start, and when the twenty-one-year-old John Dillinger joined the inmate population there on September 16, 1924, the prison housed 2,340 inmates on its thirty-one-acre site. Food was poor, consisting mostly of meat and potatoes. The guards were poorly paid and

9

overworked, which provided ample opportunities for the professional criminals to pass along their skills to younger prisoners. Four factories at the reformatory were run by civilians for profit, so for eight hours a day inmates made shirts, underwear, trousers, fiber furniture, kettles, and other metalware. The most unpopular factory was the foundry, where men worked in 130-degree heat making manhole covers.

When Dillinger was processed into Pendleton and appeared before Warden A. F. Miles, the angry young convict calmly stated: "I won't cause you any trouble—except to escape." But Miles was familiar with tough men and answered, "I've heard that kind of talk before."

"Yeah, well, I'll go right over the Administration Building."

The surly Dillinger compiled a terrible prison record; however, Warden Miles did give him credit for avoiding the most vicious inmates.[2] Marshal T. H. Greeson of Mooresville wrote to prison authorities that Dillinger had plans to "rough up" the reformatory guards and had bragged that he would soon escape. Citizens of Mooresville were also threatened, Greeson noted before ending his letter by saying, "From information regarding this young man, there is very little I can say in his favor."[3]

A convict who served time with Dillinger at Pendleton later said, "You get to recognize a killer in prison. There's a lot come in that way or it makes them. First we thought he was just a hardheaded hick who got a lousy break. Then you'd see him in a fight, and it was like he didn't care whether he got killed or the other guy, just so someone got it. We learned to keep out of his way.

"Even inside, cons joke and are friendly. But year by year, Dillinger just got quieter and madder. I used to sweat every time he looked at me. He always had this expression on his face, his mouth twisted on the left side, like he was under pressure every minute. Some guys try to look tough, then they forget and it's gone. But he had that look all the time. I tell you, I knew as soon as they let his guy out, someone was gonna walk away from his hat."[4]

Dillinger was found missing from his cell on the evening of October 10, 1924. After a diligent search, guards discovered him in the foundry under a pile of excelsior. Only when the pile was set on fire did he come out. Six months were tacked onto his sentence, and he was given eight days in solitary confinement.[5] Soon afterward, the young convict saw another chance to escape when Deputy Peterson was returning Dillinger to Pendleton after he had been taken to court to appear as a witness at Singleton's trial. In the train station at Indianapolis, Dillinger kicked over a table and bolted when Peterson fell. He gave up only when the deputy fired a warning shot as he ran down a dead-end alley.[6]

Dillinger continued to make escape attempts. The next month, using a makeshift saw, he was able to break out of his cell, but guards caught him in a corridor and another half-year was added to his sentence. Just after Christmas 1924 another escape attempt earned the twenty-one-year-old Dillinger another six-month extension of his sentence. On January 31, 1925, he was accused of being "disorderly" but received only a reprimand. He made still another unsuccessful escape attempt later that year.[7]

Dillinger hated his incarceration at Pendleton, but it would not be long before he became acquainted with a group of inmates there who would change his life forever.

The Convict
Comedian

HOMER VAN METER WAS RECEIVED at the Pendleton reformatory on March 25, 1925, and before long became a friend of Dillinger.[1] Barely nineteen years old when he entered the institution, Van Meter was described as a "recluse," with a comedian's face, a scar in the middle of his forehead, and "Hope" tattooed on his right forearm. A slender young man, he stood five feet, ten inches tall and had a tapering waist, with sinews and muscles like steel.[2]

Born December 3, 1906, to Cary and Julia Van Meter in Fort Wayne, Indiana, Homer came from a family of stalwart railroad workers and grew up in that city. He was very close to his brother Harry but had a cool relationship with his sister Helen.[3] Both parents were hardworking and respectable citizens, and friends and family spoke highly of the couple. Julia was considered a fine woman, and Cary, although a heavy drinker, was said to be stern but just. He was a conductor on one of the fastest freight runs of the Nickel Plate Railroad, where Homer's uncles and nephews also worked. His associates called him "the King"—but never to his face. He died at the age of forty-seven of a "general nervous collapse" on March 15, 1918, when Homer was eleven. An uncle of Homer died in an insane asylum.

Overly strict home conditions did not force the young Van Meter into a life of crime. Many who knew the family believed that some strange ailment or condition in his brain caused Homer to pursue that dubious calling. One family member would later say, "Homer never wanted to walk the straight path, and it is not surprising that he ended his life as he did." His desire was "to beat the law." His father tried to cure Homer of such bad habits as joining a juvenile gang and skipping school, but the youngster could not stand his home life. Before he finished the sixth grade, he ran away to Chicago, where he worked as a waiter and bellboy. He also contracted syphilis.[4]

At the age of sixteen, Van Meter was arrested by two policemen in Aurora, Illinois, on June 23, 1923, for shoplifting and was charged with larceny under the name Kenneth R. Jackson. The charge was changed to "disorderly conduct and intoxication" on June 29, and he was sentenced to forty-one days in jail and fined $200. That same year he stole a car and was caught, convicted, and sentenced on January 11, 1924, as Kenneth Jackson to a one- to ten-year term at the Southern State Prison in Menard, Illinois.[5] He was allowed to attend the funeral of his fifty-two-year-old mother, who died on March 30, 1924. At that time he laid claim to his portion of his parents' estate. Van Meter was paroled in December 1924.[6]

Shortly thereafter, on the night of February 26, 1925, Van Meter and Con Livingston (alias Carl Hern), a twenty-two-year-old fellow ex-convict, staged a daring but only modestly lucrative train robbery. At 7:20 p.m. in Toledo, Ohio, Van Meter, wearing a light cap and a dark-brown overcoat, and the five-foot-seven Livingston, wearing a light overcoat and a soft fedora hat, boarded the New York Central Railroad's *Western Express* bound for Chicago. Fourteen miles east of Gary, Indiana, as the train passed the town of Chesterton, the two men left the day coach and headed toward the train's single sleeping car. Arriving there, they forced Paul Fornier, a flagman, and T. D. Robertson, a porter, to precede them into the sleeper.

After locking the door to the sleeping car, Van Meter and Livingston, making no effort to search the nine passengers inside, proceeded to rob them and the two crewman of $50 in cash and $500 in jewelry. While Livingston, pistol in hand, passed along the aisle with a hat in his hand, collecting money and jewelry from the passengers, Van Meter, armed with a shotgun, sat on a seat and made threats. One woman became hysterical, but her screams could not be heard beyond the sleeper. The two bandits jumped from the train as it slowed while approaching the Gary rail yard. Railroad officials contacted the police in Gary and Chicago as well as other Indiana lawmen about the robbery.

Van Meter and Livingston rode to Chicago aboard an electric train, where they met Frank Zelinski, another former convict on parole, and twenty-two-year-old criminal Michael Spicuzza, both of Chicago. Over the next few days, the thugs spent the loot from the sleeper caper and other holdups. After relieving E. J. Guttman of his car and money on March 5, the four men drove to South Bend, Indiana, where they planned to rob a bank.[7]

At 2:30 a.m. on March 6, 1925, the quartet sat in their auto at the New York Central Railroad station in South Bend, Van Meter armed with a sawed-off shotgun and the others with an automatic pistol and two revolvers. Policeman Homer Ames passed by the group and went into a restaurant to call the police station and report any stolen cars he had seen. One of the criminals followed Ames into the restaurant and eavesdropped on his conversation, then went back outside and told the others.

Exiting the restaurant, Ames approached the vehicle and asked to talk to the occupants. When one of the outlaws shouted, "Stick 'em up!" the group opened fire on the lawman, who returned the gunfire. During the exchange, Livingston was shot over the heart. After a cab driver and a night mail truck driver also joined the gunfight, Van Meter, Zelinski, and Spicuzza fled down the railroad tracks. Spicuzza was captured after being hit in the right leg by a volley from two railroad detectives who had heard the gunshots. Van Meter and Zelinski escaped, but the next day Livingston died and Ames was commended for his bravery by the South Bend Board of Safety.[8]

On the morning of March 10, Van Meter and Zelinski were arrested by railroad police at the Chicago train station while they were waiting to board a train heading west. Van Meter confessed to Chicago Chief of Detectives William Schoemaker late in the day that he and "Carl Hern," who had been killed at South Bend, had held up a train.[9] The next day Van Meter was brought before federal Judge James H. Wilkerson in Chicago under the National Motor Vehicle Theft Act for attempted car theft in South Bend.[10] Arrested again under his own name in Chicago by lawmen from Crown Point, Indiana, who took him to that city on March 12, 1925, Van Meter was charged with two counts of train robbery. He was sentenced to ten to twenty-one years on each charge and sent to the Pendleton reformatory.[11] A Gary, Indiana, police officer wrote, "This fellow is a hardened criminal and would not hesitate to shoot and kill in order to accomplish his purpose."[12]

The following January, Van Meter was taken to Chicago to testify against an accomplice in federal court. The handcuffed prisoner managed to escape from guard William Taylor at Chicago's Union Station on the night of January 5, 1926, as Taylor was asking for directions to the Des Plaines Police Station. Evading police on the streets for more than an hour, Van Meter, who had absolutely no money, concealed his handcuffs in his coat sleeves and panhandled thirty-five cents from a passerby. He was finally arrested near the intersection of Van Buren Street and Wabash Avenue, and a *Chicago Tribune* photographer took two photos of him.[13]

A few weeks later Van Meter and a cellmate tried to escape from Pendleton by using a saw to cut their way to freedom. After making it out of their cell, Van Meter was observed by respected guard Charles Stewart, whom the convict hit several times with a lead pipe. Van Meter was captured in the yard near the flagpole and was was beaten so badly by guards that he had to be taken to the hospital. He was consigned to solitary confinement, or the "hole," for the next two months.

Van Meter often would provoke the guards into beating him, and they knocked out several of his teeth. On his release from the hole, he frequently would do comic imitations of the guards to entertain his fellow prisoners. He also would amuse the convicts by throwing himself out of joint and acting like a paralytic. At times, Van Meter entertained the other prisoners so much that he did not complete the work to which he had been assigned. As punishment, he would be forced to stand on a small mat facing a brick wall. Homer would sometimes catch flies and attach threads to them, which often surprised guards who looked up to see gaily colored tendrils buzzing through the air.

Dillinger became fond of Van Meter and found his actions amusing, but Harry Pierpont, another inmate at Pendleton whom Dillinger both liked and admired, detested Homer's clown-like behavior.[14]

The prison's director of research wrote of Van Meter:

> This fellow is a criminal of the most dangerous type. Moral sense is perverted and he has no intention of following anything but a life of crime. . . . He is a murderer at heart, and if society is to be safeguarded, his type must be confined throughout their natural life.[15]

On July 28, 1926, Homer Van Meter was transferred from the state reformatory at Pendleton to the prison at Michigan City, where he would join a prison clique, or gang, headed by Harry Pierpont.[16]

"Wild as a March Hare"

W HEN HARRY "PETE" PIERPONT ENTERED the Pendleton reformatory on July 3, 1925, he was guarded by a sheriff and a dozen heavily armed deputies. An angry man when he arrived at the facility, Pierpont gave officials a phony name, ignored Superintendent Miles, was loath to have his picture taken or provide a statement, and spit at a guard. Soon he also became a friend of John Dillinger.[1]

"There never was a boy in the world who thought so much of his mother as Harry," Pierpont's mother, Lena, once said. "When Harry was a little fellow he would never tell me his troubles. One time, when I saw him limping, I asked him why he didn't tell me he'd hurt himself. 'Mother' he says, 'I didn't want to worry you.' Harry was always like that. He wasn't over seven years old then."[2]

His father, Joseph, a moderately successful farmer, drank a lot of beer and sometimes became drunk.[3] Harry had a younger brother, Fred, and was very fond of his sister Fern, born in 1900, who died of pulmonary tuberculosis on August 7, 1919.[4]

Born on October 13, 1902, in Muncie, Indiana, Harry enjoyed a healthy and largely uneventful childhood. When he was three, his family moved to a farm in Marion County, Indiana, near Indianapolis. At the age of nine, he fell and injured the back of his head, but it was not serious. Harry never used alcohol in any form and did not smoke.[5]

Raised a Catholic, Harry graduated from the eighth grade at Assumption School, a parochial institution in Indianapolis. He boasted above-average intelligence and did well in school.[6] But as he became older, Pierpont became more stubborn and irritable. He was not a good mixer and avoided the company of girls.[7] He secured employment as a host engineer for auto repair shops.[8]

As a young man, Pierpont was slender and good-looking, standing six foot one and weighing 162 pounds. He had a light complexion, a scar on the back of his hand, and chestnut hair. Known as "Handsome Harry," he had a soft and pleasant voice and very blue eyes that seemed to darken when he became angry. However, Pierpont had a physical deformity: the second and third toes of his feet were grown together.[9]

Supposedly accidentally hit on the head with a baseball bat and rendered unconscious for five minutes on June 1, 1921, Harry was laid up for about three weeks. He "has not been right since then" a relative once said. After that incident, Pierpont complained of eye problems, with dizziness and headache, and stomach and bowel trouble. Signs of insanity first appeared in early July 1921. The melancholy Pierpont was quiet, reclusive, restless, suffered bouts of sleeplessness, and had a poor memory. He also had a mania for firearms. The young man imagined he had money he did not have and was known to write checks for sums he had never deposited, yet he somehow managed to own a car. Pierpont claimed there was nothing wrong with his moral condition.

Father Webber, an acquaintance, once wrote:

> Known him 10 to 12 years. Noticed acting different from other people. He would ask immense sums of money from me, which was impossible. He never acted like other boys. Would carry a gun at times, and I would consider him dangerous and that he should be confined to an Institution."[10]

Pierpont's mother, Lena, told doctors:

> He has been melancholy, nervous, walks the floor, and wants to carry a gun. He imagines he has money, wrote a check for $1,401 when he had no money in the bank. He insists he has sums of money, which is untrue. This check was given to the Cleveland

Auto Co. He refused to talk to me in past two weeks. Harry was hurt in past year with a ball bat. He since said he did not feel good. He is dangerous to be at large and should be in a hospital.[11]

In 1921 Pierpont was arrested in Indianapolis for carrying concealed weapons and held for ten days.[12] At the request of his mother, he was sent to the Central Indiana Hospital for the Insane (later Central State Hospital) on September 21 of that year, and he was furloughed on October 20. To doctors, who thought his "conduct is that of one who thinks he knows it all," Pierpont talked incoherently and was giddy at times. Moody, cross, and contrary, as well as very nervous and excitable, he appeared extremely melancholy. The "explosive, volatile" Pierpont was finally discharged from the hospital on March 14, 1922, in an "improved condition."[13]

On January 2, 1922, at the age of nineteen and while still undergoing periodic treatment at the asylum, Pierpont stole a car in Indianapolis and drove to Greencastle, Indiana, where he broke into the Cook Hardware Store and stole nine handguns. Two nights later, in Terre Haute, he tried to drive off in Edward Devine's car but was confronted by the owner. Pierpont fired four shots from a handgun at him, but fortunately Devine was only wounded slightly. The melee ended when Devine's wife hit Pierpont over the head with a package of meat.

Pierpont was arrested, tried, and convicted of attempted car theft and assault and battery with intent to murder. While awaiting trial Pierpont tried to saw through the bars of his cell and almost accomplished the task before being discovered. His younger brother Fred was put on trial for helping Pierpont try to escape, but he was later acquitted.[14]

Pierpont entered the Indiana State Reformatory at Jeffersonville on March 12, 1922, and on November 17 of the following year, he was transferred to the new reformatory at Pendleton.[15] Describing the convict in a letter to an Indianapolis attorney, the prison's superintendent wrote, "He is in measure, mustang and must be curbed. I think it can be done with kindness and time better than with force and an early release."

Although Lena Pierpont complained about Harry's incarceration, the superintendent replied, "This young fellow has been as wild as a March hare. . . . I only wish I could write a different letter to you, but this boy has put a ten-rail fence up for me and it is hard to climb."[16]

But Lena, a big, determined woman who thought her son deserved to be free and had meant no harm, visited the superintendent and told him about Pierpont's mental illness. At first parole was rejected, but Pierpont was released from Pendleton on March 6, 1924.[17]

After his release Harry worked in his father's Brazil, Indiana, sand and gravel business for several months. He became involved with several bank robbers, including Earl Northern, and may have robbed the Sourwine Theater in Brazil. Pierpont was good friends with Earl's thirteen-year-old sister, Mary. A slender, four-foot-eleven redhead, Mary was one of thirteen children and had helped support her family after her father died. A few years later she would be close to four inmates at the Michigan City prison: two brothers, including Earl; Pierpont; and an ex-husband named Kinder, the son of an Indianapolis police sergeant, imprisoned for robbing a grocer.[18]

Pierpont and his outlaw associates committed a series of robberies in Indiana, including bank heists at Marion, New Harmony, and Kokomo. Harry was also suspected of helping to rob banks at Converse, Noblesville, Upland, and New Albany, Indiana. During the robberies Pierpont pistol-whipped victims at least twice.[19] On November 26, 1924, Pierpont and his gang, including James Robbins and William Behrens, raided the South Marion State Bank and made off with some $4,000.[20] A week later, on December 23, robbers took about $2,500 from the Upland State Bank. The six bandits who took part in the latter heist were described as "not clean and shabbily dressed," while the Marion robbers were reported to be "well-dressed."[21]

On March 11, 1925, Pierpont and associates robbed the New Harmony Bank and stole $4,828 in cash, $4,300 in Liberty bonds, and $2,000 in nonnegotiable securities. On March 27, seven robbers—including Pierpont, Roy Bridgewater, George Frazier, Thaddeus R. Skeer and Earl Northern—entered the South Side Bank at Kokomo and stole $3,000 in cash and $7,000 in Liberty bonds. Three emergency squads of Indianapolis police armed with riot guns fruitlessly searched the roads between Kokomo and Indiana's capital city. However, a girlfriend of Skeer, Louise Brunner of Fort Wayne, Indiana, was trailed to Detroit by detectives, and the couple was arrested at a prearranged meeting place on April 2. Pierpont, using the aliases Frank Mason and A. L. Pierpont, was arrested later that day, also in Detroit. The next day the three were taken to Kokomo. All of the bonds were recovered, as was part of the cash.[22]

Pierpont was sentenced to ten to twenty-one years on May 6, 1925. Since he was still a young man, he was returned to the Pendleton reformatory on July 3. Two months after arriving there, Pierpont tried to escape by drilling through the bars of his cell. He was caught and subsequently transferred to the state penitentiary at Michigan City, where he would become the leader of a prison clique.[23]

Turnabout

NOT TAKING THE LOSS OF his pals Van Meter and Pierpont very well, Dillinger responded by committing such juvenile acts as "braying like a jackass." Then he avoided trouble for several months. On February 25, 1926, he was found gambling and sentenced to another thirty days. In August he was again disorderly and got another thirty days added to his term. He was put in solitary confinement on December 27, 1926, and as soon as he was released got into a fistfight and landed in solitary again, on New Year's Eve. On October 17, 1928, he was charged with destroying prison property.[1]

To get out of his horrible job of making manhole covers, Dillinger poured hot iron into one of his foundry shoes to injure his heel. Nevertheless, he still had to continue working. The determined convict finally was transferred to yard duty after he poured acid on his injured heel. Later, Dillinger worked with Van Meter when he was transferred from yard duty to the prison's shirt factory. Demonstrating a great affinity for the job, Dillinger easily did double or even triple the required work. Although it was forbidden, Dillinger often helped slower workers make their quota. Sometimes he was caught at it.[2]

Dillinger got a good deal of bad news. His wife, who had visited often, divorced him in 1929. On August 18, 1928, he had written to her:

> My dearest wife:
> Received your sweet letter Tuesday eve, the only one this week, and I'm still waiting for that interview. Gee honey I would like to see you. Hubert wrote to me last week I would sure like to see him if he wants to come see me let me know and I will send him the car fare.[3]

After defending himself for not writing to her ("You ought to have known that I would have wrote if I could"), he continued:

> Dearest we will be so happy when I can come home to you and chase your sorrows away. . . . I wonder if I will get an interview Monday. I sure hope so for I am dying to see you. Darling have some pictures taken. Every time I see you you look dearer and sweeter to me so I want late pictures. Now say rassberries, but honey it's the truth. . . .You can imagine what a disappointment it was to me when you didn't come on your birthday. I've been cross as a bear ever since. . . . Lots of love and kisses to the sweetest little wife in the world.[4]

Dillinger finally got smart and decided the best way to get out of prison was to be a model prisoner. He even joined the eighth-grade class at the reformatory school, where he was an excellent student and was active in student discussions. His teacher believed he had a very strong desire for knowledge.

In 1929 he came up before the parole board. Members of the board had seen Dillinger play an excellent game of baseball that afternoon, and for the previous two years he had been a model prisoner. But since his overall record was bad, the board chairman told him, "Maybe you's better go back a few years."

One of the parole board members attending the meeting, Indiana Governor Harry Leslie, who had seen the convict's performance on the reformatory's baseball field, remarked, "That kid ought to be playing major-league baseball." Dillinger had asked to be sent to Michigan City "because they have a real team up there." Since Leslie believed that a transfer to that institution could lead to "an occupation for him later," the move was approved by the board and Dillinger was sent to the facility on July 15, 1929.[5]

Turnabout

Ironically, he did not join the prison baseball team. In the spring of 1930 he wrote home:

> Well, baseball season is nearly here but I don't care to try for the team here although I love to play. If I hadn't played on the team at the reformatory I don't think I would have been sent up here; and I'm sure I would have made a parole there this winter, so you can see why I am not so enthusiastic about making this team.[6]

Reunited at Michigan City

THE INDIANA STATE PRISON AT Michigan City had a silent system—men ate, marched, and worked in silence. Like children, prisoners had to raise their hands if they wanted to go to the toilet. Inmates learned to talk without moving their lips.

A typical cell measured just six by nine by seven feet and had an unshaded fifteen-watt lightbulb. On the wall was a card listing twenty-two rules—no books, magazines, or newspapers were allowed. Each prisoner was allotted one piece of soap, a corncob pipe, tobacco, and a towel. An inmate could smoke three times an evening in his cell, and the pipe or cigarette had to be lighted by a trusty. However, there was a lot of illegal smoking. With some 2,800 prisoners packed into the institution, there were too few guards and many escape attempts. In response, prison authorities increased restrictions on the inmates, leading to a strike by prisoners in late 1929 that was quickly suppressed.

While conditions at Michigan City were harsher than at Pendleton, there were some advantages to being incarcerated there. There were few professional criminals in the inmate population at Pendleton, but at Michigan City a convict could learn much from men who were virtual experts in forgery, bank robbery, and confidence games. The toughest of these were known as "red shirts." Deputy Warden H. D. Claudy, in charge of security, was hated by the convicts.

It was here that Dillinger rejoined his old friends Pierpont, now the leader of a prison clique, and Van Meter. They introduced him to three other inmates who one day would become members of what would be known as the Dillinger Gang: John "Red" Hamilton, Charles "Fat Charley" Makley, and Russell Lee "Boobie" Clark.

Although Dillinger, not a vicious character and considered to be just another young punk, was young and had little experience as a criminal, he was accepted into the group because of his trustworthiness and willingness to help other prisoners. While he often tested authority, he committed only relatively minor offenses and was very likable, possessing a good sense of humor, which won him many friends. He often loaned money to his fellow convicts and did not insist on repayment. Pierpont, although he hated homosexuals, even overlooked the fact that Dillinger had an "old lady," or prison lover. Dillinger was said to be so oversexed that he would do anything to satisfy his carnal urges.[1]

Considered to be incorrigible, Harry Pierpont compiled a dismal record at Michigan City. Known for his ability to withstand hunger and beatings, he planned four escapes and assaulted and bound a guard during one attempt at a breakout. Furthermore, he wrote to acquaintances on the outside, requesting that they try to smuggle guns and saws into the institution. He was cited for possessing a handcuff key, making a key for his cell door, and talking in the dining room and in chapel, both minor offenses.

On the evening of December 29, 1929, he used a homemade key to get out of his cell and then release eleven other convicts. They made a ladder out of iron beds, but while sawing the bars of a window, the convicts were caught by prison guards.[2]

Van Meter gave prison officials almost as much trouble as did Pierpont. He smuggled saws into his cell, illegally mailed or kited notes to friends on the outside, and made two escape attempts. Then Van Meter decided to try for parole by becoming a model prisoner. Although he had very little formal schooling, he somehow became an educated, skilled, and polished man in prison, and could even speak a little German. The convict was able to convince the prison officials that he was sincere in mending his ways. Van Meter wrote to a friend, "I am sure I have not lost my formula of salesmanship." He was rated "an industrious, quiet and peaceful" worker in the prison's hospital tubercular ward.[3]

Chaplain Robert Hall wrote the parole board:

> I verily believe that Van Meter #11561 is ready to prove that he is no longer the man who got off on such a bad start. He has put off the old man. Judge him by the new man. [4]

Van Meter sent a flowery plea to the board in a meticulously hand-written letter:

> Through self education, I have become aware of life as a social minded man sees it. The more I read, the more I become convinced that a man has a purpose in life with his duty towards society. That a life dedicated to humanity is far more important than to be a Croesus. I began to age and mellow like a fine old wine. I rebuilt a new philosophy and ethics; and when I felt sure I could give a promise and honorably keep it—I went to see Mr. H. D. Claudy, Deputy Warden. I respected him as a square-shooting man and I told him I was ready to be trusted. He did not hesitate. He was shrewd enough and big enough to stake his judgement on men, and transferred me to a position of trust . . .
>
> All I ask of you, is to get in touch with Mr. Claudy and feel sure he will substanuate [sic] this. I want you to judge the—reformed man of today—who has developed into a self-educated, honest, mature man; from the ignorant, wild boy of yesterday.[5]

In a second letter to the board he wrote:

> My plea is—be big enough to cast aside the musty archives dealing with the follies of an unthinking boy before the needs of a clean matured man. If reformation is the theme of penology, then I am ready to become a useful citizen. If it be not, then society defeats itself along with the reformed felon, and adds an extra tax burden upon a tax ridden public. This is the age of the new deal. I place my destiny in your hands. You can restore a sterling citizen and a sound matured man to freedom.[6]

His material uncle W. E. Dowd and his brother Harry worked hard to secure his parole and appeared before the state board of pardons. Van Meter made plans to meet Dillinger in Indianapolis after his release and show him how to get rich quick. Van Meter was paroled from the Michigan City prison on May 20, 1933.[7]

Redheaded Robber

J OHN HAMILTON, WHO APPEARED LEVEL-HEADED and stable, entered the state prison at Michigan City in March 1927. Never one to refuse a challenge, as a boy he had once climbed a 175-foot factory chimney for ten cents. Another time, trying to show how fast he could move his hands through a train's speeding wheels, he steered his sled so close to a passing freight that the index and middle fingers on his right hand were sliced off. As a result, Hamilton acquired the nickname "Three-Fingered Jack."[1]

Born in Binginlet, Ontario, Canada, on August 27, 1898, to John B. and Sarah Hamilton, both Irish-German Methodists, John had eight brothers and sisters.[2] His brother Foye also became a criminal.[3] When he was three years old, Hamilton's family moved to Sault Ste. Marie, Michigan, although John later returned to Canada for brief visits.[4] He spent his boyhood in the Soo region of Michigan and attended McKinley Public School in Sault Ste. Marie. His father, a train engineer, died when Hamilton was still a schoolboy. A model Sunday School student, Hamilton's deportment in school was better than average. "There was a certain wildness about him," one of his teachers later said, but Hamilton was still considered a typical American boy who liked to go hunting and trapping. He frequently practiced shooting and was a good marksman who often won contests.[5]

After leaving school in the tenth grade, Hamilton, whose hair color spawned the somewhat less colorful nickname "Red," worked as a lumberjack and as a deckhand on the *Val Cartier*, a Canadian grain hauler plying the Great Lakes, in June and July 1917.[6] About 1919 the young man and two friends left town and went to Pontiac, Michigan, where all three worked as freight hustlers for the Oakland Motor Company. A year later Hamilton returned to Sault Ste. Marie.[7]

On August 22, 1921, Hamilton married Mary Stephenson, a Pickford, Michigan, girl, in Sault Ste. Marie. Mary, whose desire for high living was thought by many to be the cause of Hamilton's criminal behavior, was a member of a lawless family led by her brother Alvia.[8] During their marriage the couple lived in the Gogomain Swamp, between the Soo and DeTour, Michigan. While his wife made a garden and kept chickens, Hamilton worked in the lumber camps of Jerry Lynch and trapped and hunted.[9] Their son Howard was born in Sault Ste. Marie on November 8, 1922, and their son Orville was born at Muskegon Heights, Michigan, on October 8, 1923.

About 1923 Hamilton was driven out of town for bootlegging after he was caught with a small still in his chicken coop. He left home for the "life of an outlaw" when he jumped a $500 bail in 1924 and traveled with the Stephenson Gang. There were false rumors that he had deserted his wife and children.[10] Alvia was closest to Hamilton, who the gang thought "was a very close-mouthed individual."[11] The first big robbery in which Hamilton was known to have participated was a $33,000 payroll heist at the Lakey Foundry Company in Muskegon Heights on July 20, 1925, with the Stephensons.[12]

By 1926 Hamilton was working as a carpenter, and his family was living in Detroit. Red became a rumrunner in Ecorse, Michigan, near Detroit, and was arrested there that year, but it is unknown if he received any punishment for this.[13] Hamilton was also employed for two weeks that year by Freddie White in a liquor warehouse in Port Lampton, Ontario.[14]

With Raymond Lawrence, a rumrunner and former police officer, he tried to burglarize the safe of the Walter E. Miles Coal Company in Grand

Rapids, Michigan, early on the morning of December 23, 1926. Two police officers drove up to check the office's outside door, and finding it locked, they looked through a window to check the premises. Seeing a set of burglar tools on the floor and thinking they may have surprised the thieves, the policemen attempted to surround the office, but their entry was delayed by a high board fence surrounding the property. Meanwhile, the robbers fled out a rear door they forced open, leaving behind the burglar tools, a pinch bar, and a punch. Hamilton and Lawrence got away with less than $200.[15]

On January 3, 1927, the Stephenson Gang—Hamilton, Lawrence, Clayton Powers (married to a sister of Mary Hamilton), Curtis Turner, and the Stephenson brothers Alvia, John, George, and Joseph—stole $25,000 from the Fulton Street Branch of the Kent State Bank in Grand Rapids.[16]

A woman's tip on Sunday, March 13, led to Turner's arrest in Detroit that same day. He admitted his role in the Grand Rapids heist, implicated Hamilton, and then told Detroit detectives that his partner in crime would soon rob a bank in South Bend, Indiana. Meanwhile, Hamilton and Lawrence went to South Bend, planning to hit the South Bend State Bank two days later, on March 15. It would be the first bank robbery in that city in seven years.

Early on the morning of March 15 the two bandits slipped into the bank before it opened, took employees captive as they came to work, and waited for the 8 a.m. opening of the time lock on the vault. Ten minutes before the vault was to open, a bank official managed to slip past the bandit covering the door. A minute later the robbers counted their prisoners and realized one was missing. They immediately fled, leaving behind $48,500 in cash and $85,000 in securities. A squad of police officers soon arrived, but the robbers were nowhere to be seen.

Late that afternoon Chief of Police James J. Hatt, dining at home, received a mysterious phone call from a man who claimed to have seen a Chevrolet coupe parked in his neighborhood shortly after 8 a.m., and that several hours later he had observed a young man changing the car's license plates from Michigan to Wisconsin tags. "It looked rather funny to me," the caller said.

Hatt investigated, found the car, and discovered that it contained a sawed-off shotgun and a box of shells. He ordered six policemen from the local station to help him raid the house where the car was parked. The police entered the house, which was owned by Hamilton's brother William, and arrested Red, Lawrence, and three unnamed men. Early the next morning Lawrence confessed that he and Hamilton had tried to rob the South Bend bank and had in fact robbed the Grand Rapids bank. Hamilton, upset that his companion had confessed, refused to say anything.

Less than thirty-six hours after they had attempted to rob the South Bend bank, the two bandits were each sentenced to twenty-five years in the Indiana State Prison after pleading guilty to the charges in order to avoid possible life sentences in Michigan. As the court pronounced sentence, Hamilton's wife and their four-year-old son, Howard, wept.[17]

Hamilton's only reported offenses at Michigan City were making too much noise in 1927 and skipping rope in the shirt factory in 1932. He was more stable and mature than the other convicts, but his pleas for clemency were rejected because the parole board considered him to be a dangerous man.[18]

While Red was in prison, his wife, Mary, obtained a divorce and then married a man in Toledo. She died in childbirth about 1930, and Hamilton's two sons were sent to live with his mother-in-law in Toledo.[19] Several boyhood friends visited Hamilton at the prison, including one who called the bandit a "most likable person."[20] Hamilton was very embittered when the governor refused to grant him a furlough to attend the funeral of his mother, Sarah, in April 1933.[21]

The Fat Man

CHARLES "FAT CHARLEY" MAKLEY WAS sentenced on June 23, 1928, to serve ten to twenty years in the Michigan City penitentiary. He was remembered by residents of his hometown of St. Marys, Ohio, as a "likable fellow." According to a newspaper report, "Some of them cannot picture him as the vicious type which the law has decided he was during his latter years."[1]

Makley was one of six children born into the poor Catholic family of Edward and Martha Sunderland Makley on November 24, 1888, in St. Marys. His father, a German-born stonemason, and his mother separated when he was young.[2] A childhood friend, Jim Tully, labored with Makley for only fifty cents a day in a mill when both were about twelve. He recalled Charles as a quiet, hard-working boy, "the gentlest one among us."[3] In later years, as Makley reflected on his youth and his subsequent foray into a life of crime, he would say, "Look at my dad. He worked like the devil all his life, and what did he get out of it? I have lived as long in forty minutes at times as my dad did in forty years."[4]

Makley, who left school after finishing the seventh grade, left home at the age of seventeen and engaged in various ventures, including mining and selling cars, in Boise, Idaho; Detroit; and other places.[5] Standing five feet seven and a half inches tall and weighing 180 pounds, he had a heavy build, slate-gray eyes, and medium-dark hair. The tip of his left index finger was missing, and his right leg was shorter than the left, resulting in a slight limp.[6]

Makley embarked on his criminal career during his teens, beginning with petty theft. With the advent of Prohibition in 1920, he turned to bootlegging and became a con man. Within a few months he stole a furnace salesman's car, traded it in on a new Terraplane, and, using a pamphlet left in the stolen vehicle by its owner, sold the car dealer a furnace for cash.[7] Makley was first arrested in 1921, while working as a railroad switchman in Detroit, on a charge of receiving stolen property.[8]

On January 2, 1923, he and another man were arrested in St. Louis in connection with the $97,000 robbery of messengers from the Drovers National Bank in Kansas City, Missouri, which had occurred nearly two years earlier, on January 26, 1921, and was the biggest robbery in the city's history. The Missouri Supreme Court reduced bond for Makley (using the alias Charles McGray) from $125,000 to $14,000 on July 12, 1923, when two Kansas City physicians testified that the hefty "McGray" was physically unable to run away because of a knee injury. Apparently, Makley was able to pay the bond and was released.

On July 28, 1924, Makley and two other men robbed a couple in Kansas City of $571 in cash and jewelry and took their car, which was valued at $900. He was arrested in late August in Wichita, Kansas, for the August 20 holdup of the Corn Exchange Bank in Kansas City, which netted $13,000. The outlaw was charged with two bank heists and the July 28 robbery, and was sentenced to fifteen years in prison on September 23. He confessed to stealing the car but strongly denied committing the two bank jobs.[9] Makley, under the name Charles McGray, was received at the Missouri State Penitentiary in Jefferson City on October 15, 1924, and was freed on parole on June 5, 1925.[10]

Back on the outside, Makley became the leader of a gang that robbed banks throughout Ohio, Indiana, and Missouri. The outlaws had headquarters in Hammond and Lafayette, Indiana, as well as Kansas City, Missouri, until it became "too hot" to remain there. The portly Makley looked like a bank president or other prosperous businessman and frequently was able to bluff his way out of trouble. He bragged that he often addressed civic luncheons just before robbing the town's bank.[11] From 1925 to 1928 he lived at his half-brother Fred's home in St. Marys.[12]

The Makley mob garnered about $3,500 from the Bank of Ferguson in Ferguson, Missouri, on January 5, 1926.[13] But disaster struck after the gang grabbed $26,320.85 in cash and bonds from the Citizens Bank of Festus, Missouri, on September 25 of that year, when a posse captured most of the bandits at a clubhouse near Eureka, Missouri. Another of the outlaws was arrested in St. Louis. Makley was the only member of the gang to escape, and he returned to St. Marys to recruit a new crew.[14]

Shortly before noon on September 30, 1926, four members of Makley's new gang, wearing goggles and false mustaches, pulled off the first bank robbery in the history of Portland, Indiana, making off with about $25,000 in currency and gold.[15] Six days later, Makley and his associates robbed the Chickasaw Farmers Bank in Chickasaw, Ohio, of about $5,000 in cash and securities.[16] Two and a half months later, on December 17, the bandits held up a bank messenger and guard who were taking $79,000 to the Fidelity National Bank and Trust Company in Kansas City, Missouri. Five men, including Makley, were convicted of the robbery and sent to prison. Makley was released on an appeal bond and fled the state.[17]

Fat Charley recruited more new gang members, and the bank robberies continued. Shortly after noon on March 24, 1927, the gang hit the Indiana State Bank at Linn Grove and escaped with about $2,500. On June 8, the outlaws stole $4,500 in cash and $45,000 worth of government securities from the First National Bank of Ansonia, Ohio.

The Makley outfit also may have taken about a thousand dollars on November 1, 1927, from the Tippecanoe Loan and Trust Company, located across the street from the police station in Lafayette, Indiana. During the heist seven heavily armed gangsters killed police Captain Charles Arman when he tried to prevent the daring daylight robbery. On March 27, 1928, the gang again hit the bank at Linn Grove, this time making off with $1,900. Just over a week later, on April 4, Makley and another bandit stole about $6,000 from the Bank of St. Henry in St. Henry, Ohio.[18]

Over the previous two years, the gang had stolen about $500,000 from banks in Indiana, Ohio, and Missouri, and its members were suspects in all of the recent Indiana bank robberies. Six confederates were also being sought by the authorities.

Gang member Eddie Meadows was arrested by a Hammond, Indiana, police detective on June 5, 1928, for the Kansas City bank job after he was overheard boasting about the robbery. Makley, the "brains" of the gang, using the aliases Albert Owen and Charles McGray, and his sister-in-law, Edith Makley, were also arrested later that day by five policemen at his hideout. He was just about to lay his hands on a small arsenal, but Makley surrendered without a struggle, although he had said he would not be taken alive. Three other gangsters were also arrested later that day in Hammond.

Makley broke down and told all when confronted by a tearful Edith, who begged him to clear her name. Edith, who had an eight-year-old daughter, was not charged with any crime but instead appeared as a state's witness during the trial. Makley confessed to the bank robberies at Linn Grove, Ansonia, St. Henry, Chickasaw, Festus, and Ferguson, but he denied taking part in robberies at Portland, Howe, and Angola, Indiana. Other members of his band told police it was they who had robbed banks in Kansas City and Portland.[19]

Sentenced to ten to twenty years in the Michigan City penitentiary, Fat Charley compiled an almost perfect prison record, with only a few minor offenses, such as possession of contraband cigarette papers, possession of a five-dollar bill, having an electric stove in his cell, and changing his clothes from "second grade" to "first grade" to attend a prison baseball game.[20]

Bad Boy Boobie

R USSELL LEE CLARK ENTERED THE Indiana State Prison at Michigan City on December 16, 1927. Known as a smooth talker, "Boobie" could, according to his wife, "talk anybody's language and make them think he was one of them, and that helped him out of many a tight spot."[1] One of seven children, Clark was born August 8, 1896, in Terre Haute, Indiana, to Dan and Minnie "May" Clark, a poor farming couple.[2]

He graduated from the eighth grade and left home at the age of sixteen. Standing just a quarter-inch over six feet tall and weighing 167 pounds, Clark had gray eyes, dark-chestnut hair, and a medium build. His body was covered with moles, and he had a scar in the middle of his back.[3]

Clark enlisted in the army in 1919, just after World War I, at Camp Zachary Taylor in Louisville, Kentucky, but after just four months received a dishonorable discharge for some unknown offense.[4] Drummed out of the service, he became a tailor, a truck driver, and a coal miner, and later worked in a Terre Haute glass factory, a commercial distillery, and a tie plant.[5]

On June 22, 1922, Clark married Frances M. Wilson (also known as Bernice Clark and more popularly as Opal Long) in Edgar County, Illinois. She was the sister of Pat Cherrington, the girlfriend of John Hamilton.[6] An unattractive, heavyset, red-haired woman with freckles, Opal had a big bust and large buttocks, which led to her being saddled with the unflattering nickname "Mack Truck." But she had an intense interest in Clark.

Opal lived with her grandmother until she was eight and then went to live with her mother and the latter's new husband. She came from a very deprived background, had little education, and often went hungry. To survive, Opal worked anywhere she could, such as in five-and-dime stores and restaurants.[7]

In 1921 Boobie Clark was arrested by the Terre Haute police on suspicion of robbery but was soon released. He became associated with Ralston "Blackie" Linton, a Terre Haute criminal known for robbing roadhouses during Prohibition. On November 6, 1923, Linton's gang blew the safes in two Spencer, Indiana, banks. Linton went to prison for the robberies, but he refused to tell who else was involved. Clark was arrested again by the Terre Haute police on suspicion of robbery, but again he was released.

With Jack Morrison, Clark may have kidnapped West Terre Haute bootleggers Oscar Moore and A. L. LeClerq in 1926. He was also a suspect in the murder of Joe Popolardo in Danville, Illinois, on June 1 of that year. Clark was caught transporting illicit liquor with John Considene of Chicago, but the charge was dropped.

On August 22, 1926, Clark, Morrison and C. T. Holmes of Detroit robbed the Bellevue Club in Evansville, Indiana. Unmasked and waving around revolvers, the trio took $3,000 in cash and jewelry from the club's co-owner, Charles "Cotton" Jones. Clark was arrested by the Terre Haute police on a fugitive warrant on August 30 and the next day was picked up by Evansville police and charged with the Bellevue Club robbery. His case was continued to September 15, but the charges were dropped when Jones decided not to prosecute.

In July 1927 Clark, living in Detroit with his wife, Opal, joined Frank Badgley and his band of bank robbers after meeting Badgley at a poker game in Indianapolis. Clark and Badgley's brother-in-law Charles Hovious were introduced in a Detroit rooming house by Badgley. Clark's brother Edward was also a member of Badgley's gang, who used Edward's Indiana farm as a hideout.[8]

On July 21 Clark, Badgley, and another man robbed the Paragon State Bank in Paragon, Indiana, of $2,238.15. The same three men stole $4,855.13 from the New Augusta State Bank in New Augusta, Indiana, on

August 8. Late in September the Badgley gang traveled from Detroit to Whiteland, Indiana, where they held up a drugstore, and then to Straughn, Indiana, where on September 26, Badgley, Clark, and Hovious raided the Peoples Bank and escaped with $1,002.85.[9] Badgley, operating alone, unsuccessfully tried to rob the Huntertown State Bank in Huntertown, Indiana. Three days later he was caught after a robbery in Amboy, Indiana, and was imprisoned for life as a habitual criminal.

Early in December 1927 Clark and Hovious stole an automobile in Detroit and drove by way of South Bend to Indianapolis, where they visited friends. Then they traveled through Anderson and Fort Wayne, Indiana, and decided to rob the Huntertown bank themselves. Early in the afternoon of December 8, the two made their attempt, and while one of the bandits aimed a pistol at cashier Horace Tucker, the other scooped up $1,313. As the two robbers were making their escape, Tucker fired at them with a brand-new revolver. The robbers returned fire, and a bullet grazed the cashier's arm.

Near Pioneer, Ohio, at the Michigan state line, Clark and Hovious abandoned their car when it punctured a tire. They seized two other vehicles from passing motorists, but those also suffered tire punctures after a short distance. Sheriff Lloyd Bly was notified that the two criminals were headed toward Pioneer and set a trap to catch them. After seeing the robbers run across a farm field, lawmen fired at them. Clark, armed with two guns, and Hovious, with one gun, shot back several times. Hovious ultimately was captured, but Clark ran into the woods. A posse of 150 officers and farmers continued the chase for about six miles, with Clark and his pursuers exchanging more than thirty shots. Several times the posse almost captured the outlaw as he ran from Pioneer toward the nearby town of Frontier, Michigan.

On the morning of December 9 a farmer near Hillsdale, Michigan, saw Clark on his property, acting suspiciously, and ordered him to go away. Instead, Clark hid in the man's barn and nearly froze to death. When the posse approached, looking for the bandit, the farmer told them about the mysterious stranger. During a search of the farm, Clark was discovered and taken to the county jail, where he and Hovious confessed to the Huntertown robbery.

The two men waived extradition and were turned over to Indiana authorities on December 10.[10] After being tried and convicted for the Huntertown bank robbery, Clark was sentenced on December 12 to twenty years, a term he felt was excessive. His brother-in-law Andrew Stracham felt sympathy for Clark because the legal proceedings took place so quickly that he was shipped off to prison before his family was notified or he had time to hire a lawyer.[11]

Nearly three years later, on November 5, 1930, he was taken to New Castle, Indiana, as a witness in a trial. Two days later, at about 6 a.m. on the return trip, he and other prisoners made a determined effort to escape from an automobile. Other officers saw the fracas and forcefully subdued the convicts, then returned them to the penitentiary. When the badly beaten prisoners arrived at Michigan City on November 8, Clark was in such a poor state that he remained in the prison hospital until November 12.

Undeterred, he attempted to escape three times during his incarceration and was one of five leaders of a late-1929 prison strike. Although several convicts stopped working, the strike ended quickly after prison officials punished the ringleaders. Clark talked of spending "stretches" in the hole for the following offenses:

> Not making tasks, striking—solitary 6 days.
> Attempting to escape—solitary 4 days
> Talking—solitary 5 days
> Talking in line—reprimand
> Passing stuff in 4A shop—solitary 2.5 days
> Attempting to escape—15 days solitary
> Escaped enclosure—9 days solitary.[12]

Late in 1932 the members of Harry Pierpont's prison clique received a valuable education in the art of bank robbery from Walter Dietrich (Detrick, in some accounts), a member of the "Baron" Herman K. Lamm gang, who shared with them the methods Lamm and his minions had employed to good advantage. Lamm, a young Prussian officer, had been forced to leave the German Army just before World War I for cheating at cards. He emigrated to the United States and traveled to Utah, where he was arrested on robbery charges and spent 1917 in the Utah State Prison at Salt Lake City. While doing time, he developed a system for robbing banks that would prove very successful.

Planning, precision, and timing were the keys to Lamm's method. Before robbing a bank, Lamm would case it for days to determine the floor plan, the locations of the safes, how the safes operated, and who was supposed to open them. Then he would rehearse the robbery plan—sometimes even using a mock-up of the bank—with the best professional criminals he could find. Each member of the crew would have his own job and was required to do it within a certain amount of time.

Lamm had a rule that the gang would leave the bank at the scheduled time regardless of the amount of money they had obtained. The escape route was planned in advance, and several dry runs usually were made before the robbery actually took place. For the getaway, Lamm always used a high-powered and nondescript car, and he employed a highly skilled driver, often a racing driver, as his wheelman.

Everything went smoothly until December 16, 1930. That day Lamm, G. W. "Dad" Landy, Walter Dietrich, and James "Oklahoma Jack" Clark (no relation to Russell) robbed the Citizens State Bank in Clinton, Indiana, of $15,567. While things went smoothly inside the bank, the getaway proved a disaster when, in the midst of making a fast U-turn, the getaway car jumped a curb and blew a tire. The robbers seized another car, but it would only go thirty-five miles an hour. Abandoning that vehicle, they took a truck which had almost no water in its radiator and soon overheated. The bandits stole yet another car, but it had very little gas in its tank.

When the huge posse chasing the bandits caught up with them in Illinois, a furious gun battle ensued between the almost 200 police and vigilantes and the outlaws. Lamm and the driver of the getaway car were killed during the shootout, and Landy killed himself. Clark and Dietrich were captured and ultimately sent to Michigan City for life.[13]

Back on the Outside

I T DIDN'T TAKE LONG FOR John Dillinger to realize that he had made a mistake coming to Michigan City, and he responded by committing several offenses. He was found toasting sausage and bread over a high fire in his cell, and in the spring of 1930, he was discovered gambling. A few weeks later Dillinger was cited for being "in bed with George 13529 on E Range." Other offenses were that he "broke into the garden house and stole all the melons and tomatoes"; "having [a] razor in his cell and shaving with it"; and being in possession of books of cigarette papers and a lighter. Twice he was placed in solitary confinement.[1]

Dillinger wrote his half-brother, Hubert, "I can't keep out of trouble here." However, it should be noted that he did not join an inmate strike in late 1929 nor did he make any attempts to escape. After almost seven years of imprisonment he finally matured and became a model prisoner, which hastened his release.

Since he would be paroled before any of the other members of Harry Pierpont's clique, Dillinger was appointed the gang's contact man on the

outside. His job would be to rob several small-town banks on a list prepared by Pierpont and Red Hamilton to get enough money to finance a
big breakout from Michigan City.

Late in April 1933, with his stepmother seriously ill, Dillinger's family started a petition they hoped would convince the state parole board
to pardon the now twenty–nine-year-old convict. They wrote that his
father needed John to help him on the farm and his ailing stepmother
wanted to see him. The petition was signed by 184 residents of
Mooresville, including the town clerk, auditor, treasurer, recorder,
assessor, the sheriff of Morgan County, former Judge Joseph Williams,
and even Frank Morgan, the victim of the robbery for which Dillinger
was sentenced to prison.[2]

In a letter to the parole board, Judge Williams wrote:

> I have read the petition . . . in behalf of J. H. Dillinger for clemency.
> I see that B. F. Morgan signs the petition. He was the party that was
> assaulted. I join in the recommendation for clemency petitioned
> for. Mr. Singleton, his partner, only received a sentence of from 2
> to 14 years and has been out of prison for about six years. As the
> trial judge I am entirely free to say that I think he should receive
> clemency as you in your judgment may see fit to grant, and trust
> that he may without delay be paroled to his father who will act, if
> appointed, as his parole officer. . . . The father of this prisoner is
> getting up in years and needs the assistance of his son on the farm.
> . . . I believe the prisoner has learned his lesson and that he will go
> straight in the future and make a useful and honorable citizen.[3]

Dillinger was ordered released on May 10, 1933; however, because of
delays in processing the paperwork, he was not actually released until
May 22. Meanwhile, his stepmother had suffered a stroke, and the elder
Dillinger sent a telegram to the state prison on May 20 asking about the
delay in releasing his son. Two days later Hubert drove from
Mooresville to Michigan City to pick up his brother. They arrived at the
farm less than an hour after Lizzie Dillinger had died, and soon the
undertaker came.[4]

Sometimes Dillinger, when depressed and more reserved than usual,
had "a twisted smile." The Sunday after his release from Michigan City,
he and his father heard Gertrude M. Reinier, pastor of the Friends

Church in Mooresville, give a sermon on the prodigal son. Dillinger appeared to be moved by the oratory and even cried. After the service, he told the minister, "You will never know how much good that sermon has done me." But what he was actually doing during church was working on the list of criminals to contact and places to rob that he had been given in prison. He found that the list was now outdated, as some of the criminals were no longer available and some of the banks had failed during the Depression. Dillinger was able to locate Homer Van Meter, who had gone to St. Paul after his May 1933 parole from Michigan City.

In an effort to raise the cash he needed to free his friends, Dillinger joined an Indianapolis gang led by William Shaw that specialized in minor local robberies such as drugstores and supermarkets. Known as the White Cap Gang because of the headgear Shaw insisted his associates wear, its members included Paul "Lefty" Parker and Harry Copeland, a Muncie, Indiana, burglar who had served a term in Michigan City.[5] Copeland, a swarthy, heavy-eyed man, had been arrested on December 20, 1926, for burglarizing the Boniface, Weber, and Allen Wholesale Grocery Company in Muncie and stealing $2,000 worth of cigarettes. On November 19, 1927, he was sentenced to two to fourteen years for burglary in Delaware County, Indiana.[6]

Dillinger, who said his name was Dan, told Shaw, "I like you, kid. You're smart to check on a guy like me."

On June 4, 1933, Dillinger, Noble Claycomb, and Shaw, a handsome and slender nineteen-year-old who came from a law-abiding middle-class family, met and decided to rob an Indianapolis supermarket that evening. But first they had to steal a car. After stealing an appropriate vehicle, the three men soon attracted the attention of a policeman in a patrol car, who thought they looked suspicious and gave chase. They were able to elude him, but the trio's troubles were not over. As they were changing license plates in an alley, another police car came by and the criminals quickly sped away, smashing an unclosed rear door into a telephone pole.

The three managed to elude their pursuer and headed for the supermarket. Shaw and Dillinger entered the building, while Claycomb double-parked the getaway vehicle near the front entrance. When a girl saw the men come through the door, she told the store manager, "Here comes the White Cap Gang."

After drawing an automatic pistol, Shaw rifled about a hundred dollars from the cash register in the office. Meanwhile, Dillinger ordered the customers and employees to go to the rear of the store. An elderly man refused to do so, and Dillinger, who could be brutal at times, hit him in the mouth with his gun. When Shaw saw the old fellow spitting blood, he gave Dillinger a dirty look. Later, Dillinger defended his outburst, telling Shaw, "I'll never go back to the pen. They're not going to catch me—not if I have to kill someone."[7]

11

A Taste for Bank Jobs

NEEDING TO MAKE BIGGER SCORES to raise the cash he needed for the Michigan City breakout, Dillinger decided to put the knowledge he had acquired in prison to good use and rob a bank. With two, or possibly three other men whose identities are uncertain, Dillinger embarked on his first bank job—the New Carlisle National Bank in New Carlisle, Ohio, on June 10, 1933. A minor member of Dillinger's mob would later claim that the robbers were Dillinger, Harry Copeland, Sam Goldstein and Homer Van Meter.

What is known is that early on the morning of June 10, three armed men, their faces covered with handkerchiefs, entered the New Carlisle bank through an unlocked window. At 8 a.m., the bank's bookkeeper, Horace Grisso, unlocked the front door and was confronted by the bandits as he was entering the teller's cage.

"All right, buddy," Dillinger said, "open up the safe."

When Grisso failed twice to open the safe, one of the robbers told him, "Let me drill him, he's stalling."

But Dillinger told Grisso, "Take your time and open it."

A female clerk entered the bank, and Dillinger gallantly put a banker's smock on the floor and told her to lie down on it. Finally, Grisso opened the safe and handed over $10,600 in cash. When two men—the bank's cashier and a customer—came in the front door, Dillinger waved a handgun at them and then bound all the prisoners with wire. He told the frightened customer, "You hadn't ought to come in the bank so early."

Not a lazy criminal, Dillinger, along with Shaw and Paul "Lefty" Parker, a new man who served as the White Caps' wheelman, decided to rob two more establishments in Indianapolis that evening. First, Dillinger and Shaw grabbed money from the main cash register and the soda fountain cash register at Haag's Drugstore. As the robbers were leaving, they discovered that their getaway car, a Ford, was wedged too closely between two cars and became very nervous when it took a few minutes to maneuver the vehicle out of the parking space.

Next, the gang headed for a supermarket that Shaw had robbed before. When Dillinger and Shaw entered the building, the manager said, "Uh-oh, here they are again," and told Shaw there was no money in the cash drawers. "You guys have started the company collecting and the collector just left," he said.

Shaw grabbed several tin cigarette boxes, and he and Dillinger left the store. Dillinger jumped into the Ford, but before Shaw could enter, Lefty screeched away without him. After he had driven a block, Lefty backed up and retrieved Shaw. Next, Lefty ran a stop sign, at which point Dillinger growled: "If you can't drive, let the kid take over."

On June 24 Dillinger and Shaw attempted to rob Marshall Field's Thread Mill at Monticello, Indiana, but did not get any money. As Shaw wrestled with manager Fred Fisher, he lost his .45 pistol. When Fisher chased after Shaw, Dillinger, arriving at the getaway car, fired a shot into the ground to scare Fisher, but the bullet ricocheted and hit the manager in the leg. "I either got him or scared him half to death," Dillinger said as the bandits piled into their car. Fleeing down a dirt road, the two became lost. After driving about fifty miles they turned onto a paved highway just twelve miles from Monticello. As they drew close to an ambulance, Dillinger saw Fisher inside.

While driving back to Indianapolis, the two robbers argued about what place to rob next. They finally decided on a fruit market in the city. As they entered the market, Shaw saw a boy who lived in his neighborhood and told Dillinger they should leave quickly. After grabbing $175 from the register, the outlaws ran for their car. Someone threw a milk bottle at them, and Dillinger fired a shot in the air.

As they drove toward home, Dillinger sarcastically told his partner, "You're didn't even make expenses today. You've got to pay for a forty-five."

After leaving town for a few days, Dillinger returned on June 29, and he and Shaw robbed a sandwich shop in Indianapolis.[1] Afterward, according to author John Toland, Dillinger "went to Muncie, Fort Wayne, the East Chicago area, and even Kentucky, arranging bank robberies with at least three different gangs, including Homer Van Meter's. Probably no other robber in history was more industrious. In the next three weeks he helped loot some ten banks in five states."[2]

During the next few days Dillinger drove south to see ex-convict Frank Whitehouse, whom he had known at Michigan City. "I told Johnnie that I'd married and was trying to go straight," Whitehouse said. Dillinger offered to take him and his wife to visit the World's Fair in Chicago, after flashing a large amount of cash and saying he would pay for the trip. The three left Lebanon, Kentucky, on July 3, stopping in Fort Wayne and East Chicago to see other ex-cons Dillinger knew.

The outlaw was a big spender at the World's Fair. Afterward, while taking his guests home by way of southern Illinois, he stopped to see yet another ex-convict. Dillinger returned to Indianapolis on July 7 and indicated to Shaw that he had been in Kentucky and had gone to the exposition in Chicago. Dillinger showed Shaw, who had recently married, a suitcase containing a considerable amount of money, leading his partner to believe that he must have robbed a bank in Kentucky while on his road trip.

Dillinger decided to rob a bank in Daleville, Indiana, but first Shaw, Parker, Claycomb, and Dillinger held up the Bide-A-Wee tavern in Muncie just after midnight on July 15. While Parker remained at the wheel of the getaway car and Shaw stood guard outside, Dillinger and Claycomb entered the tavern and took about $70 from proprietor A. C. Skiff, who was there with his wife and three male customers.

As the bandits left they met a couple coming in. Dillinger pinched the woman's bottom and then slugged her male friend when he protested.

The next day Shaw, Claycomb, and Parker were arrested at Shaw's home in Muncie. Shaw attempted to escape and hid in the cellar until police ordered him to "come out or shoot it out." None of the gang members was armed, although police found revolvers in the apartment. Dillinger and Copeland barely missed being captured. As they were driving a stolen Chevrolet down an alley near Shaw's apartment, they saw

their cohorts standing outside with their hands in the air and surrounded by policemen. Dillinger immediately slammed on the brakes,
threw the transmission into reverse, and raced back down the alley,
making a clean escape.

Later, Shaw would marvel, "He drove faster [backward] than some
people drive forwards." Recalling that Dillinger had recently run into a
fence with a late-model car, he added, "I thought that he couldn't drive.
He did better than I could have."

Under interrogation, Shaw confessed to more than twenty robberies.[3]

On July 17, Dillinger and Copeland robbed the small Commercial
Bank of Daleville. After parking their car in front of the bank, Dillinger
entered it first, pulled his gun, and told cashier Margaret Good, "This is
a stickup, honey." Leaping over a five-foot railing with ease, Dillinger
went into the vault and took $3,500 in cash and two diamond rings
belonging to the daughter of the bank's owner. Meanwhile, Copeland
herded customers against a wall. Just as customer Frank Mowrey
entered the front door, he noticed Good holding her hands high above
her head, but before Mowrey could leave, Copeland waved his gun at
the man and told him to go to the back.

"If I'd had a thimbleful of brains," Mowrey said later, "I'd have known
something was going on."

His work done, Dillinger ordered everyone to get inside the vault,
locked its door, and then he and Copeland exited the building without
incident, got into their car, and drove away. Margaret Good eventually
was able to open the vault door from the inside. When local lawmen
arrived, she told them that Dillinger had been very courteous. The
police determined who the robbers were from witness reports, and an
intense manhunt was launched.

The press had a field day, presenting Dillinger as a daring yet courteous bank robber who showed a theatrical flair with his impressive
leaping ability. The townspeople put a sign over the vault that read:

DILLENGER [sic] WAS HERE.[4]

Bandit with a Baby Face

I N THE EARLY 1930S THE name George "Baby Face" Nelson began appearing in the press with increasing regularity in connection with holdups and robberies that were often punctuated by senseless violence. Small, standing just a quarter-inch under five feet five, but extremely agile and powerful, the young man in a few short years would become the nation's most-wanted criminal. Much of his dubious celebrity would stem from his association with John Dillinger.

Born Lester Joseph Gillis on December 6, 1908, in a three-story townhouse at 9422 North California Street on Chicago's Near West Side, the child who would one day become Baby Face Nelson was the youngest of seven children, one of whom died in infancy. His Belgian immigrant parents, who married in the United States, came from respected families. His mother, Mary, had been a teacher of French in the old country and believed in the importance of a good education. His father, Joseph, was a skilled and hardworking tanner, who eventually became assistant superintendent of a local leather company. In 1925 he committed suicide by natural gas while drunk.

Lester was a well-groomed, bright boy who made good grades during his first three years at the Lafayette public school, but when his parents transferred him to St. Mark's parochial school at the age of nine, problems with bad behavior and truancy began to surface. He was put into a respected Catholic boarding school attended by one of his sisters, but his attendance was still poor.[1]

His mother, Mary, could never bring herself to believe that her son was bad, and she always supported and said nice things about him. When Lester began to become involved in crime, she would call car theft "borrowing" and shooting "an accident with a revolver." Later, she would say, ". . . he met issues squarely, never ran from them. And he never shot a man in the back."

According to Mary, her husband was partly responsible for Lester's penchant for "misbehavior." She believed that if only Joseph had let Lester play with toy guns and drive the family car, he would have turned out to be a good boy. Once, on the Fourth of July, Lester found a gun in a neighbor's car and fired it at a fencepost in an alley. The bullet ricocheted and struck the jaw of a small boy, who was taken to a hospital. Afterward, Joseph would never let Lester play with toy guns, and he even criticized one of Lester's uncles who let his children play Cowboys-and-Indians with theirs.

Although Lester liked cars while growing up, his father would never let him drive the family automobile, so the youngster would occasionally "borrow" neighbors' vehicles to go on joyrides. Punishment for such peccadilloes was not effective. Spanking had no effect on him, and he would not even cry. Mary would recall, "Sometimes, if I asked him about some wrongdoing, he'd say, 'Mother, I didn't do this.'" And for her part, Mary "believed him every time, for I know that one thing he couldn't stand was a lie."[2]

Lester grew up in the Patch, a jumble of ethnic European enclaves on Chicago's Near West Side. Although the young Gillis lived in the same neighborhood as the infamous Alvin Karpis for a short time, the two did not know each other. Both were very familiar with West Division Street and Sacramento Boulevard and even knew some of the same kids.[3] According to his mother, Lester came under the influence of an adult criminal who "organized young boys into theft gangs."

In 1922 Lester was arrested for auto theft while attempting to sell some car accessories he had stolen. Because of his bad attitude and lack of cooperation, he was sentenced to an indefinite term at St. Charles Reform School. His behavior there was exemplary, and in April 1924 he was paroled for "good behavior." Five months later Lester was sent back for parole violations. Released on parole in July 1925, he remained free for only a few months before being returned to the institution in October. Some nine months later, in July 1926, he received his final release from St. Charles and was now too old for reform school. While there, however, the youngster had received a good education for a criminal, learning how to steal cars and blow safes.[4]

Now seventeen, Lester returned home to Marshfield Avenue and initially appeared to be interested in honest work. He was a natty dresser who was very fond of brown clothing, and he did not drink, smoke, or gamble.

Legend has it that the young Gillis was one of the robbers of a Spring Grove, Illinois, bank in November 1926, a heist that netted $2,028.[5] By 1927 the young man was hungering for good times with lots of money, girls, cars, and excitement. Bored with dirty, low-paying jobs, he became active in a Chicago tire-theft gang that included George Ackerman, Jack Perkins, and Albert Van de Houten, who owned a tire shop. Lester's mother would later say that she believed the police had "pushed him over the line into a definitely antisocial life."[6]

Ackerman was "a well-known police character," but the authorities had been unable to convict him of any major crime. Perkins was Lester's best friend, and another friend, Arthur N. Johnston, ran a racetrack book. Garage owner Howard Davis also was an associate, as was mob figure Rocco de Grazia.[7, 8] Gillis and Perkins frequently saw a member of the mob, bootlegger Anthony "Tough Tony" Capezio, in their neighborhood. After Prohibition, Capezio turned to gambling, especially horseracing.

Arrested for smashing store windows and grabbing merchandise in early 1927 by the Chicago police, Gillis was sentenced on March 17 of that year to a year's probation.[9] He also shot and wounded a tire thief named Ray Miller, who had been "put on the spot" to prevent him from demanding repayment of a debt. Soon after that, Miller was arrested and sent to the Illinois State Penitentiary at Joliet.[10] Van de Houten and Gillis operated an illegal still, but they were inexperienced in bootlegging and it failed.[11] According to one writer, Gillis could not enter the Chicago underworld because "his tough talk and egotistical boasting sounded like the crow of a bantam rooster . . ." to the city's gangsters.[12]

In June 1928 Lester married Helen Wawrzyniak, shortened to Warwick, in Indiana. Not beautiful "but with large dark eyes that lighted up a pleasing countenance," Helen was a sixteen-year-old petite brunette.

She was just five feet, two inches tall and weighed about ninety-four pounds. Lester, who had met her in a Chicago store, called her his "million-dollar baby from the five-and-ten-cent store."

The daughter of poor Polish parents who had settled in Chicago, Helen was a graduate of Chicago's Harrison High School. Although Lester did not want children, ten months after their marriage Helen gave birth to a son, Ronald, on April 27, 1929, and a daughter, Darlene, on May 11, 1930. The children ultimately proved a nuisance to the Gillises, and they soon sent them to live with relatives. Both initially went to live with Lester's mother in Chicago, but Ronald was later sent to Bremerton, Washington, to live with a married sister of Helen. Darlene came to know her mother as "Aunt Helen." Neither Ronald nor Darlene knew much about their father.[13]

Lester was employed as an auto repairman's helper and driver in the transportation department of the Commonwealth Edison Company in Chicago from March 19, 1927, until he resigned on August 14, 1928.[14] He was also employed at a gas station operated by Cliff Johnson at Sacramento and Grand Avenue, a garage on the West Side owned by bootlegger Tony Romano, and a garage which sold Chrysler automobiles.[15]

It was during this period that Lester began using the name George Nelson, one of several aliases he would eventually employ. Others included Alex Gillis, Lester Giles, Jimmie Nelson, and Jimmie Burnett, among others. The Chicago underworld generally held Nelson—the only major Depression-era outlaw to hail from the Windy City[16]—in low esteem, and many of its denizens referred to him as a "bedbug," "crazy cockroach," or "poisonous toad." Several cautioned their pals, "Don't prod that squirt—he's poison."

Many on both sides of the law feared him, for while his cherubic face—which would soon spawn his famous nickname—and small stature might lead some to try to bully him, Nelson was a vicious fighter who carried a switchblade. He got a thrill from killing, and it was often said that he killed for the sheer hell of it.

One longtime friend was Clarence "Clary" Lieder, a naturalized Polish immigrant who ran the Oakley Auto Construction Company at 2300 West Division in Chicago, where he fenced stolen auto parts.[17] Clary always kept Nelson's Chrysler coupe, which could go about ninety miles an hour, in good condition and sometimes repaired racing cars for Nelson, who was an exceptional driver and drove in a few dirt-track races at Chicago's Robey Speedway around 1930.[18]

Unhappy with the low wages he was earning, Nelson decided to become a jewel thief. On January 6, 1930, he and four accomplices took $25,000 worth of jewelry from the mansion of Mr. and Mrs. Charles

Richter at 1418 Lake Shore Drive in Chicago. On January 22, Nelson and three accomplices stole $5,000 in jewelry from the Lake Forest, Illinois, home of attorney Stanley J. Templeton. Two months later, on March 31, the diminutive criminal, along with Stanton Randall and Harry Lewis, alias Harry Powell, robbed "Count Enrique Von Buelow" (actually German gigolo Henry Dechow) and his wife in their Chicago home, making off with $95 in cash and more than $50,000 worth of jewels.[19]

Later that year Nelson, Lewis, and Randall concentrated on robbing banks. On October 3, two smartly dressed young men entered the First National Bank of Itasca, Illinois, just as it opened. Both drew their revolvers and ordered the only other people in the building—assistant cashier Ray A. Frantzen, son of the bank's owner, and clerk Emma Droegemueller—to raise their hands and "make it snappy." After forcing the employees to lie facedown on the vault floor, the bandits stuffed $4,678.75 into a small cloth bag and drove toward Chicago. Although Frantzen notified the sheriff and police in a half-dozen nearby towns, the bandits vanished. Later, Nelson threatened Frantzen with death if he testified against him.[20]

On October 6, 1930, Nelson and two others may have dared to rob the wife of Chicago Mayor William Hale "Big Bill" Thompson, even though she had a bodyguard. Accosting her in front of her apartment building, the trio forced Mary Walker Thompson to hand over a six-carat blue-diamond ring, a forty-diamond bracelet, and a brooch set with fourteen small stones, the pieces having a total value of $18,000. She told police and reporters that one of the robbers "had a baby face. He was good looking, hardly more than a boy, had dark hair, and was wearing a gray topcoat and a brown felt hat, turned-down brim."

A month later, on November 7, Nelson and an accomplice tried to rob the State Bank of Plainfield, Illinois, but bulletproof glass in the cashier cages prevented the outlaws from reaching the bank employees or the loot.[21]

The brash young gangster's third bank job was the Hillside State Bank in Hillside, Illinois, near Chicago, on November 22. Shortly after the bank opened, three men came through the front door, one of them firing a couple of shots into the ceiling to get everyone's attention. Two of the robbers forced the three employees and a seventeen-year-old boy to line up against a wall in the lobby, while the third outlaw rifled the cashier's cage and vault. When a cashier attempted to set off the alarm, one of the bandits yelled at him to stay away from the device. No customers entered the bank during the robbery, and after Nelson and his partners escaped to Chicago, they split the $4,155 take and separated.

A bank employee told investigators that one of the hoodlums was "a young man with a baby face." As law enforcement officials scrambled to solve the string of robberies, this statement, and a tip from an under-world informant that a young punk known as "Baby Face" or "Big George" had been pulling heists in the area, would lead police to Nelson. The press picked up on the "Baby Face" nickname, which Nelson hated, but which Helen thought was "kind of cute."[22]

According to Randall, the morning after the Hillside robbery Nelson was involved in the deaths of two female entertainers and a woman customer at a roadhouse owned by Harry Goetz in Summit, Illinois, near Chicago. Fifteen persons, most of whom were dining, were at the roadhouse when Nelson and seven other masked gangsters armed with shotguns and pistols raided it just before 1 a.m. They marched the bartender and two patrons into the rear room, where several people were dining, a male pianist was playing a jazz tune, and a woman was singing.

"This is a stickup!" one of the robbers yelled. "All hands up! Everyone get over and face the wall."

As the crowd rushed to the wall, James Micus, a police lieutenant with the Indiana Harbor Belt Railroad, walked out of a washroom. He too was forced to stand in line with the others, who were being relieved of their valuables by three of the gunmen. As Micus reached the wall, he pulled a pistol and fired two shots at the gang's leader. Pandemonium ensued, and soon all of the lights went out except for a few dim bulbs at the rear of the room. The gang leader told one of his men to turn the ceiling lights back on, but he turned off all of the lights by mistake. The hoodlums returned fire at Micus and in the confusion made a successful escape, leaving behind a ghastly scene: two wounded men, one mortally wounded woman, and two dead women lay on the floor, while terrified guests screamed for help. The bandits' haul amounted to just $300, including $30 from Goetz.[23]

Three days later Nelson and other criminals raided a tavern north of Chicago and stole $125. The baby-faced bandit became angry when a customer, Edwin R. Thompson, nervously smiled at him, and he killed him with a shotgun blast.

After the Hillside robbery Nelson and Helen, who were living in Cicero, Illinois, went on a spending spree. Helen liked the lavish way her husband spent money and his bragging about his success. Unfortunately for them, informers passed along rumors about the couple to the police, and on February 14, 1931, officers arrested Nelson and took him to the downtown station, where he was charged with armed robbery. Someone recognized him as one of the men who had robbed the Hillside bank, but Nelson refused to name his cohorts. Meanwhile, police picked up Powell and Randall.

Nelson, Powell, and Randall were each indicted on a single count of robbery on February 20. Howard Davis testified on Nelson's behalf and provided an alibi, but the jury convicted Nelson on June 25, and on July 9 he received a maximum sentence of one year to life at Joliet. He entered the facility on July 17. Davis was later found guilty of perjury.

Nelson's rebellious nature worked against him in prison, as he antagonized both guards and inmates.[24] Convict Ray Miller assaulted Nelson,[25] and on December 6, 1930, Nelson was placed in solitary for calling a guard "obscene names."[26]

Meanwhile, investigators decided that Nelson fit the description of one of the robbers in the Itasca bank robbery, and on January 6 he was taken to Wheaton to be formally charged. In February, after a three-day trial at Wheaton, during which Nelson stayed at the DuPage County Jail, he was found guilty of the Itasca holdup and was sentenced to another one to twenty years in Joliet.

Nelson knew that he would likely spend his remaining years behind bars unless he was somehow able to escape from custody while still outside Joliet's forbidding walls. On February 17, 1932, handcuffed to his guard and in leg irons, he boarded the *Rock Island Special* at the Wheaton train depot for the ride back to the penitentiary. Arriving at the train station in downtown Joliet, the guard hailed a cab to take them to the prison, which was the policy since no prison car was available.

As the cab drew within sight of the institution's main gate, Nelson suddenly pulled a pistol and forced the guard to remove his handcuffs while telling the cabbie to drive on. When the cab passed a secluded cemetery in the suburbs, the gangster yelled for the driver to stop and then forced both men to get out. He cracked the cabbie and the guard over their heads with his gun, and they fell to the ground, unconscious. Nelson got back into the cab drove toward Chicago, making a clean escape.

It is a mystery how Nelson got the weapon. Someone could have slipped the gun to him on the crowded train or on the station platform. The guard and cab driver were not considered suspects. Since Nelson had no gang or money to bribe someone to help him, it is probable that the pistol was provided by a relative at the Wheaton depot. Most likely it was his wife, Helen, or sister Leona.[27]

To pick up quick money after his escape from custody, Nelson and a criminal named Mike Jeska staged a series of movie theater holdups.[28] Then, fleeing to Reno, Nevada, he worked for a few days as a chauffeur for gambler William J. Graham. Graham and another gambler, James C. "Red" McKay, sent Nelson to see San Francisco rumrunning king Joe

Parente, who controlled criminal activities, especially bootlegging, in most of the Bay Area and as far south as the San Joaquin Valley.

San Francisco was wide open, and Prohibition was generally ignored. With little interference from the authorities, fancy speakeasies did big business on Market Street and in Chinatown and the Embarcadero.

Nelson, going under the name Jimmie Burnett, took up residence in the small village of Sausalito and was invited to join Parente's mob as a liquor truck driver and guard. As soon as he had made enough money, Helen joined him with their daughter, Darlene, in the spring of 1932. Helen thought the appearance of family life would lessen neighbors' suspicions, but Nelson did not like it. Even during the worst of times, however, Helen stayed by his side, as both were deeply devoted to one another.

Through his association with the Parente gang, Nelson met two men whose fates would ultimately become entwined with his: John Paul Chase, a tall bootlegger with a small, trim mustache and patriotic name who would soon become his lieutenant, and Joseph Raymond "Fatso" Negri, a minor hoodlum with little intelligence who was useful mainly because he would gladly run any errand for money.

Chase was born in 1901 in California to parents who had come from Omaha. After quitting grade school he worked on ranches and farms, as well as driving for a Reno gambler. But since 1926, when he was fired from his job as a machinist's helper in a railroad shop, he had earned his living as a bootlegger. Although he was suave, popular with women, industrious, and ambitious, he lacked the innate intelligence to be a success.

In the brash braggart Nelson, Chase found a leader who could help him become someone important. Impressed when the bantam gangster revealed his real name and told him about his prison escape and bank robberies, Chase was excited by Nelson's grandiose plans. He even called the outlaw "Big George," in his case meaning it as a sign of respect.

Like Nelson, the chunky Negri, who had been involved in crime since his teenage years and served a four-year stretch in San Quentin for armed robbery, was also a newcomer to Parente's operation. Nelson did not reveal his true identity to Negri, but he did gain a measure of respect for the hoodlum when he showed strong nerve during their first job together, which also included Chase. The way in which the trio accomplished their assignment impressed Parente, who quickly began using them as security for liquor shipments.

Helen fell ill at the end of the summer, and as her stomach pain worsened, a friend of Nelson recommended that he take her to a private hospital in Vallejo, California, operated by Thomas C. "Tobe"

Williams. Williams, whose real name was Thomas C. Cohen and was well known among the West Coast underworld as "the Goniff from Galway," was a former bank robber, burglar, and safe blower. For very high fees, his hospital discreetly provided such medical services to criminals as bullet removal, plastic surgery, and fingerprint eradication. Nelson himself spent a fortune to get rid of his fingerprints by having his fingers burned with acid, but it was a total failure.[29]

Helen was admitted to the hospital on September 12 and quickly underwent an appendectomy. Nelson visited her frequently over the next five days and was sometimes joined by Negri and Chase. With Helen recovering nicely, the couple returned to Sausalito on September 17.

In October, Negri received a shock when one of Parente's men showed him a detective magazine that included a mug shot of escaped bank robber Lester Gillis, alias Baby Face Nelson, who looked exactly like his pal Jimmie. As others became aware of the resemblance between the photo and Parente's stocky security guard, Nelson was alerted that his ruse had been exposed, and he, Helen, and the children soon headed to Reno, where Nelson became William Graham's driver and bodyguard.[30]

Nelson's
New Gang

AFTER NEW YEAR'S, NELSON BOUGHT a new car, and in mid-April he, Helen, and Chase drove to St. Paul, where the Nelsons rented an apartment. In mid-May the couple rented a summer cottage near the shore of Lake Michigan in the underworld haven of Long Beach, Indiana. With the repeal of Prohibition slated for December 5, 1933, Nelson knew he would need to find other sources of income than bootlegging. He began recruiting members for a new gang that would target well-off banks in the Midwest during the coming summer and fall.

Among those Nelson chose were Homer Van Meter, recently paroled from Michigan City; Thomas Carroll, a top machine-gunner and light-hearted character who had once been a promising boxer; and "jug marker" Eddie Green, a specialist in selecting the best banks to rob. Father Phillip W. Coughlan, a Catholic priest who had associated with gangsters since his boyhood in Chicago, befriended Nelson and the others. While a chaplain at Oak Park Hospital, he had met gangster Tommy Touhy, who introduced him to Nelson.[1]

On June 25 Nelson met with Van Meter, John Dillinger, Harry Copeland, Sam Goldstein, and Clarence "Whitey" Mohler at a waterfront tavern in East Chicago, Indiana.[2] He later met with members of Dillinger's crew at a local apartment. Harry Pierpont and Nelson disliked each other almost from the start. Nelson thought the rest of Dillinger's associates were fine, especially Fat Charley Makley and robber Edward Shouse, who he believed to be "great guys."[3]

After his parole from Michigan City, Van Meter visited his uncle A. B. Van Meter and brother Harry at a summer cottage in Lake George, Michigan. One day he found his sister-in-law and another woman at the cottage when Harry was off fishing and took the ladies for a ride in his car after getting beer at a store. On a lonely road Van Meter, who often practiced his marksmanship, stopped and drew a new automatic from his pocket. "The gun was just given to me and I want to try it out," he told the terrified women. After he shot at a tree for a while, a farmer came to the road and yelled at Van Meter to stop shooting, shouting, "You might kill my livestock!" Van Meter snarled at the farmer but finally drove away. "I should have bumped him off," he told the women.[4]

Although Van Meter tried to stay in the background, he still became well known to the police. According to the press, he was busy planning robberies and finding hideouts, instead of actually robbing banks. That summer Van Meter met William Francis Finerty, a supplier of various items and services to criminals, such as hideouts, weapons, and automobiles, about fifteen times at a gambling house and other places in Calumet City, Illinois.[5]

Van Meter may have helped Dillinger rob the New Carlisle, Ohio, bank in June 1933.[6] Three months later, the two bandits, posing as tourists, visited the Peru, Indiana, police station to check out reports of a large arsenal there and the security precautions to protect it.[7] Van Meter may have cased the American Bank and Trust Company in Racine, Wisconsin, two or three times for Dillinger before he and his gang robbed it in November.[8] Melvin Purvis, special agent in charge of the Division of Investigation's Chicago office, explained the art of casing:

> Crime had become such a business to most of these barons of malfeasance that it was conducted by them in a most systematic fashion. Before a bank was robbed, one of the members of the gang always performed the job of "casing the joint." This meant

surveying the situation for the purpose of learning all hazards to be encountered when they actually robbed the bank. Homer Van Meter was said to have been one of the outstanding "casers" in hoodlumdom. He was reputed to don a derby hat, pinch-nose spectacles, spats, and to assume the air of a substantial business-man. Sometimes he would go into the bank and have a chat with the president, all the time keeping his eyes open to observe all details of the layout of the bank.[9]

A few days after the caser had completed his task, the bank would be robbed by bandits who seemed to know everything about its operation.

Shortly after his parole from Michigan City in May 1933, Van Meter met with Dillinger, Clifford Mohler, Sam Goldstein, and Harry Copeland in St. Paul to plan robberies. Mohler, an escapee from the Indiana State Prison, was recaptured on August 14, and Goldstein was nabbed for bank robbery on August 22.

The *Indianapolis Times*, quoting Indiana State Police Captain Matt Leach in an article the following year, described Van Meter's coolness and cunning in an article:

> And Van Meter not only is clever. He has, according to Captain Leach, plenty of what is commonly termed cold nerve.
> "Remember the radio incident?" asked Captain Leach.
> "Van Meter, Copeland, Goldstein and Mohler were driving in Chicago, and they had a couple of submachine guns in the car. They all had pistols, too.
> "A Chicago squad car approached and one of the gang—I think it was Dillinger or Mohler—said, 'Let's let 'em have it.'
> "All Van Meter said was 'Shut your —— head, I'll handle this.' "
> Then Van Meter, according to Captain Leach, got out of the mobsters' car and approached the Chicago police squad diffidently.
> He explained to the Chicago police that the five were "a bunch of boys from down in the sticks of Indiana" and that they would "like to see how the police radio works."
> "We're up for the World's Fair," Van Meter said glibly, "and I've been telling the boys that if we waited around here long enough that one of those squad cars with a radio in it would show up.
> "How about explaining it to us?"

The Chicago coppers said they would explain, so Van Meter beckoned "the boys from down in the sticks of Indiana" over to the car.

A pleasant three-quarters of an hour was consumed while the big-town coppers condescendingly explained the working of the police radio.

The "boys from the sticks" stood around in apparently bucolic wonder, nursing pistols in their armpits.

"Well", said Van Meter, "that's certainly nice of you boys. We always heard that you big-town cops are kind of hard-nosed, but you've certainly treated us swell. So long."[10]

Instead of joining forces with the notorious Dillinger during the summer of 1933, Van Meter linked up with the newly formed Baby Face Nelson Gang in Long Beach, Indiana. That fall he met Marie "Mickey" Conforti, a twenty-year-old brunette who worked at Scott's discount store in Chicago. Born April 14, 1913, in Chicago, Conforti had few family ties; her father was dead and her mother was an invalid in a sanitarium.[11]

Terrible Tommy

A FRIEND OF THOMAS CARROLL once said, "Tommy told his friends when he was driving a cab that someday he would be called 'Terrible Tommy.' He was spotted for a bullet the day he was born, although he never believed that he himself would get it. He had one great failing, and that was love for the spotlight and his desire to show off. . . ."[1]

Born in Red Lodge, Montana, to John and Emma Carroll on November 28, 1900, Thomas came from a poor family. His father was a day laborer who was frequently unemployed, and to make ends meet, the Carrolls took in a boarder.[2] Thomas's brother, Charles, born in 1903 in Red Lodge, also became a criminal and knew St. Paul gangster Pat Reilly. However, Thomas and Charles were not close.[3] Shortly after Charles was born, the family moved to Council Bluffs, Iowa.[4]

Emma Carroll died on November 22, 1906, in Sherman, Wyoming, and John died two years later.[5] After the Carroll boys were orphaned they were raised by their maternal grandparents, Levi and Lucinda Zentz, in Council Bluffs.[6] Levi also was a laborer, and the two youngsters were forced to take menial jobs to survive, such as selling newspapers on the streets. They also joined a juvenile gang and often skipped school.[7]

Thomas remained in school until he graduated from the eighth grade.[8] With World War I raging in Europe and sentiment rising across the nation for the United States to enter the conflict, Carroll enlisted in the U.S. Army at Council Bluffs on September 1, 1917. He served in the Quartermaster Corps and Signal Corps as a private, and when he went overseas was a motorcycle dispatch rider and expert machine-gunner. Carroll was discharged from the service at Mitchell Field, New York, on June 25, 1919.[9] After returning to Council Bluffs, the happy-go-lucky young man worked as a taxi driver, hotel clerk, boilermaker, boxer, and did odd jobs.[10]

Carroll also had some brushes with the law and by the 1920s was a paroled convict. Despite scars on his jaw and neck, his prison mug shots showed a good-looking, husky man standing five feet ten, with chestnut hair and blue eyes. He had a furrowed upper lip and a mouth that twisted to the right. A wanted poster issued in 1933 would say of him: "Neat dresser; drives an automobile well; usually resides in an apartment; gambles and is addicted to the use of intoxicants; frequents night clubs; gives his occupation as salesman; is said to be wearing a derby and a reddish mustache."

On November 25, 1925, Carroll married a woman drug addict named Viola in East St. Louis, Illinois, the couple using the names Mr. McGuire and Beulah Richard.[11]

Known for using a host of aliases—among them, James Roy Brock, George McLarken, and Frank Sloane—Carroll compiled a lengthy criminal record. He joined a car-theft ring and on January 24, 1920, was arrested by police in Omaha, Nebraska, while stealing a car. It was his first arrest, and he was sentenced to sixty days in the county jail. Upon his release, he returned to the car-theft gang.[12]

On May 24, 1921, Carroll, James Durick, and Dick Fernley stole a car in Council Bluffs and hid the vehicle in a barn in Florence, Nebraska, near Omaha. An informer told authorities in Omaha about the stolen auto, and the police staked out the barn. At 11 p.m. on May 26, a vehicle containing the three car thieves drove up. As they got out and approached the barn, the officers surprised the trio and were able to arrest Durick and Fernley. Carroll, however, escaped down a path next to the barn. One of the policemen fired shots at him but missed. The next day, a young girl found some letters and papers bearing the name "Tom Carroll" on the path.[13]

On October 21, 1921, Carroll landed in jail again at Council Bluffs for auto theft and for being drunk.[14] He was sentenced to five years at the State Reformatory at Anamosa. Received there on February 3, 1922, he served sixteen and a half months of his sentence and was released on June 18, 1923. After his release he took a job at a piano manufacturing business in Bellevue, Iowa. According to the state parole board, Carroll "conducted himself as an honorable and law-abiding person" during his parole, which finally ended on June 12, 1924.[15]

Some four months later, on November 21, 1924, Carroll was arrested by the police in Kansas City, Missouri, for a grocery store robbery, but the case was dismissed on December 10. The following year, he was arrested in connection with a slaying in Kansas City, but that charge also was dropped.[16]

Under the alias James Roy Bock, Carroll was arrested in St. Louis on August 11, 1925, on suspicion of robbery. He was released five days later because of insufficient evidence.[17] He also was suspected of robbing the Drovers and Merchants Bank in South St. Joseph, Missouri, on June 30, 1926. During that robbery, three men with handkerchiefs tied over the lower parts of their faces escaped with almost $7,000 in cash.

On August 18, 1926, Carroll was picked up by the St. Joseph, Missouri, police on a car-theft charge, but he jumped bond.[18] He was arrested under the alias Frank Sloane by the sheriff's office in Tulsa, Oklahoma, for having concealed weapons when he was found sleeping in a 1927 Nash sedan on September 20. He had stolen the vehicle eleven days earlier in St. Joseph from W. H. Laubach, and when investigators made the connection, they released Carroll to their counterparts in St. Joseph on September 29.[19]

Carroll also was accused of robbing the South St. Joseph Bank. However, he was acquitted of the charge on January 11, 1927, when the defense successfully established an alibi that Carroll was ill in Kansas City at the time of the robbery.[20] The St. Joseph car-theft charges were dropped; however, he was turned over to the U.S. marshal in Kansas City, Missouri, and charged with violating the Dyer Act, which made it a federal crime to transport a stolen car across state lines.[21] He was released on a $2,500 bond.

When Carroll tried to rob a Kansas City grocery store owned by John and Catherine Gunter on February 19, 1927, city detective Frank Rogers was in the store and fired two shots at the bandit. Both shots missed, and Carroll escaped without any loot.[22] With James Roark and Martin Wilson, Carroll robbed Kansas City soda shop proprietor Joseph Sebel of $3,340 on February 28. Later that day the three were arrested. While in custody, Carroll was charged by Justice of the Peace John M. Kennedy with the attempted robbery of the Gunters' grocery. On March 24, after a jury was impaneled in Judge Brown Harris's Court, Carroll decided to plead guilty to the soda shop robbery and was sentenced to five years in the state prison at Jefferson City. Roark and Wilson were tried and sentenced the following week.[23]

Carroll entered the Missouri State Penitentiary under the name Tom Carroll on April 1, 1927, for the crime of robbery in the first degree. On one occasion when his wife, Viola, was visiting him, she met Pretty Boy Floyd's wife, Ruby, who was visiting her husband at the facility. Three years after entering the institution, on April 26, 1930, Carroll was released.[24]

Less than a month later, on May 21, he was arrested under the alias Frank Sloane by the Tulsa Sheriff's Office for stealing the Nash in St. Joseph and was charged with violating the Dyer Act. Tried and convicted, he was given a sentence of twenty-one months and was processed into the U.S. Penitentiary at Leavenworth on June 1, 1930. He worked as a plumber at Leavenworth, and he often violated prison rules. According to his prison file: "This man is continually loitering and visiting on the gallery, especially in some other cell. He has been repeatedly warned." Released on October 26, 1931, Carroll was never again sent to prison.[25]

In February 1932 Carroll and Viola opened a restaurant in Mankato, Minnesota, or, as one writer put it, "briefly trading in his machine gun for a spatula." However, by July Carroll had become tired of the work and low income, and he abandoned his wife when he fell in love with a twenty-year-old nightclub singer known as "Radio Sally" Bennett. Viola later told the press, "When I found him with this other girl, naturally it was quite a shock to me. After he left, I took poison. I loved him. I always loved him."

Sally was great at singing Irish tunes like "Danny Boy" and playing song requests on her ukulele at John Lane's Boulevards of Paris nightclub in St. Paul. It was love at first sight when Carroll, accompanied by six men, came to the nitery and asked her to sing at his table. Every night for three weeks he went to see her at the club, where he told her he was a gambler and bootlegger. Although she rejected him when he proposed marriage, Sally agreed to live with him.

For six months during the spring and summer of 1932, the couple lived in a second-floor apartment in St. Paul. Pete and Mary Vogel, a foundry laborer and a schoolteacher, were their first-floor landlords. The Vogels had two sons, Jim and John. Whenever Sally asked Carroll what he was doing or who his friends were, he would tell her it was none of her business. They went to movies three times a week, to underworld parties at Lake Gwasso, and to the Green Lantern Saloon, a popular hangout for underworld denizens in St. Paul. Once they went to the World's Fair in Chicago, but Carroll had to leave suddenly to handle some urgent business in St. Paul.

Hoodlum friends would meet frequently in Carroll's apartment to discuss possible crimes. The heavy-smoking gangsters were "respectful" to the Vogels and their kin. A Vogel aunt, thirty-one-year-old Loretta Murphy, later recalled that "Carroll was a relentless flirt. He'd come to me and he'd say, 'Don't you think we should have a drink, you know, before you go to bed?'"

Pete and Mary Vogel thought of him as a well-dressed gentleman, who often ate with them. After a dinner of such plain fare as hamburgers and potatoes, he often would give them ten dollars, a small fortune during the Depression.

On one occasion Carroll saw police officers enter the Vogel home and, thinking they had come for him, climbed out a window to elude them. However, the police had been called to the home after local thugs stole $10 from the Vogels' son John while he was on his way to a grocery store. Carroll told the young man, "Next time that happens, you let me know, and I'll just give you the money! We don't want the police here."

It became obvious that Carroll was operating on the wrong side of the law, but the Vogels overlooked this because of his generosity. The couple and their relatives sometimes saw newspapers open to underlined articles on local robberies, hundreds of silver coins, and a vast quantity of U.S. postage stamps.[26]

Postal inspectors were looking for Carroll, Otto V. Schreck, William L. Schepers, Richard Pyes, and Charles "Chuck" Fisher in connection with a string of thirty-three mail and postal burglaries in Minnesota, eleven in Iowa, and one in Wisconsin, which had started in 1932 and ended on May 9, 1933. Most of the crimes involved blowing or punching safes and stealing government property. The crew burglarized a post office in Gibbon, Minnesota, on December 22, 1932, and on January 5, 1933, stole $79.27 in cash, $285.46 in stamps, and 275 postal savings certificates from a post office in Lakeville, Minnesota. They also burglarized post offices in the Minnesota towns of Elmore on February 13, Eden Valley on April 14, and Caledonia on May 2, and stole $700 from a post office at Ogema, Wisconsin on March 7.[27]

Carroll's luck ran out on May 17, 1933, when he was arrested by the St. Paul police during a burglary investigation. He had burglar tools in his possession and was ultimately charged by postal inspectors with the burglary in Ogema. He was released on a $15,000 bond on June 12.

On September 4 Carroll was arrested in St. Paul after an auto accident. Despite finding a loaded revolver in the car, the police released him, thanks to the so-called "O'Connor System" under which criminals who paid off local politicians, and behaved themselves while within the city limits, were protected.[28]

15

Fast Eddie

HARRY EUGENE "EDDIE" GREEN HAD a flair for planning bank robberies and finding the best escape routes, thus the expert jug marker was of great value to Baby Face Nelson and his gang.[1] Standing five feet, six and a half inches tall and weighing 146 pounds, with dark-brown hair, slate-maroon eyes, and a sallow complexion,[2] Green used numerous aliases during his criminal career, including: Eddie Green, George Green, Eugene Green, George Graham, Fred Graham, J. S. Makley, T. J. Randall, Frederick Riley, Fred Riley, Charles Ryan, and D. A. Stevens.[3]

Green was born in Pueblo, Colorado, on November 2, 1898, to John and Margaret Green, who had four other sons. His father, a steelworker, died when Eddie was just three, and in 1906 the family moved to St. Paul.[4] All of the boys eventually would have problems with the law. As Ramsey County, Minnesota, Judge J. B. Sandborn would later say, "His mother is a good woman, but the rest of the family prefer to live outside the law."[5]

Up until 1913 Eddie attended the Franklin School, where he graduated from the eighth grade. His first job immediately after school was as a credit department clerk; he later held several jobs, including iron-worker. He joined Britain's Royal Navy during World War I and during 1917 and 1918 served on a ship transporting troops.[6]

Green's first brush with the law occurred on August 11, 1916, when he was arrested by police in Milwaukee for driving a stolen car while intoxicated. On August 29 of that year he was sentenced to spend six months in the State House of Correction.[7] After his release from prison and his tour in the Royal Navy, Green seemed to live a law-abiding life until July 7, 1921, when he was arrested in St. Paul and taken to Minneapolis for deserting a wife and five children. The charges were dropped when it was found that he was not in fact married.[8]

In late 1921, however, Green joined the large, shotgun-wielding John C. Ryan gang, which robbed the Crane and Ordway Company payroll in St. Paul on December 23, 1921. Green's brother Francis (alias Jimmie), who was employed by the company, was suspected of providing inside information to the gang. After leaving the First National Bank with $2,835.40 in cash, two C&O employees, Assistant Credit Manager Richard W. Anderson and cashier Nina Z. Brownell, were robbed by two men in an automobile at 3:20 p.m. in the heart of the downtown wholesale district.

Anderson was carrying the money in a leather grip, and as he and Brownell neared an alley on East Fifth Street, a stolen touring car swung up to the sidewalk beside them. Stepping from the front seat to the running board of the vehicle a well-dressed, smooth-shaven man (Green), wearing a gray cap and dark-brown belted overcoat of English cut, ordered the pair to stop and give him the bag. After opening it and finding it full of money, the bandit got back into the car and sped away. However, Anderson and Brownell were able to provide a good description of the man, who wore no mask or other disguise, to the police.[9]

Almost a year later, on July 17, 1922, Green was arrested by the St. Paul police for robbing the Park Theater and for a burglary that netted $354.82 worth of guns and jewelry, but he was released on July 19.[10] On August 8 Green and another man were picked up by police in Des Moines, Iowa, on suspicion of being auto thieves and fugitives from Minneapolis. Green's stolen Cadillac contained safecracker tools. The city's chief of police told reporters, "They said they would return and get revenge. I informed them that I would be here when they came. Unless they have changed their attitude wonderfully, they would be a menace to society." Four days later Green was turned over to the St. Paul sheriff.[11]

Green was one of several prisoners in the Ramsey County Jail when a dozen members of the John C. Ryan gang, impersonating federal Prohibition agents, attempted to free their leader from the facility on

September 23, 1922. Newspapers called it "the most daring jail delivery ever perpetrated in an American city."

"We want Green," demanded the gangsters of the two jailers they accosted.

"You have the keys; get him," one of the jailers replied.

The gang members found Green and a criminal named Roy Freeman on the second floor of the jail, but none of the keys would work. However, they were able to find the key to the jail's hospital, where Ryan was recovering after being wounded in the legs during the attempted robbery of St. Paul's Park Theater in July. Ryan, on crutches, fell down the stairs but still managed to join his men, who fled in a large touring car after locking the jailers inside the building. Since the outlaws has cut both telephone lines to the jail, the captive lawmen had to set off the fire alarm in order to be rescued.

The next day, Ryan and six of his gang, including Green's brother Jimmie, were arrested at the rooming house of Mrs. Emma Powers, an aunt of the Green brothers.[12] On September 28 Anderson and Brownell, the two victims of the Crane and Ordway payroll job, identified Green as the robber.

Green was found guilty of first-degree robbery on November 4, 1922, despite claiming that he was sick in bed at the LaSalle Hotel in Minneapolis on the day of the C&O heist. Dr. Clayton E. May testified that Green's story was true.[13] Nine days later Green was sentenced on two counts of robbery to terms of forty years and five years. He was received on November 15 at the Minnesota State Reformatory in St. Cloud.

Green was locked in solitary confinement several times for a variety offenses, such as striking an inmate during dinner and "imitating the ladies singing" after a chapel service. According to the prison physician, the mercurial Green was "the type with criminal tendencies, selfish, impulsive, and hard to manage."[14] Because of his bad record at the reformatory, Green was transferred to the Minnesota State Prison at Stillwater on July 26, 1923. He was released on July 1, 1930, and returned to the Twin Cities, where he completed his parole on January 6, 1932.

By September 1932 Green was living with Bessie Skinner, a thirty-four-year-old with strong connections to the underworld, under the names Mr. and Mrs. Theodore J. Randall. Since leaving prison, he had been living a quiet, unassuming life as a shoe salesman in Minneapolis, and his neighbors were unaware of any criminal behavior.

A divorced woman with a son named Leonard, Bessie was above average in intelligence and had been born in North Dakota with the maiden name of Hinds. She started working as a waitress and hostess in an underworld nightclub called the Hollyhocks Inn in St. Paul, owned and operated by St. Paul underworld boss Danny Hogan. Better known as "Dapper Dan," Hogan was killed by gangsters in 1927.

Bessie was also friendly with the next underworld boss, Harry Sawyer. She later operated a haven for outlaws, especially for the Barker-Karpis Gang, called the Alamo Roadhouse on Highway 1 north of St. Paul until June 1933. She befriended such criminals as Verne Miller, Frank Nash, Jess Doyle and Doris O'Connor.[15]

Green took part in a North Kansas City, Missouri, bank robbery that netted $14,500 on the morning of January 28, 1933. Earl Doyle was the leader of the crew, which included Green, Thomas "Buck" Woulfe, and "Dago" Howard Lansdon. North Kansas City Marshall Edgar Nall and Woulfe were seriously wounded. On April 11 Woulfe died after he was captured.[16]

On the morning of April 4, 1933, Green, Alvin Karpis, Fred Baker, Dock Barker, Volney Davis, Frank Nash, Earl Christman, and Jess Doyle—armed to the teeth with three machine guns, three rifles, half a dozen pistols, and several rounds of extra ammunition—robbed the First National Bank of Fairbury, Nebraska, of $15,350 in cash and bonds. The police and local vigilantes rushed to the bank, and in the ensuing gun battle eight citizens were wounded and Christman was mortally wounded.[17] The count could have been higher, but two of the gang's machine guns jammed.

Christman was taken to Verne Miller's home at 6612 Edgevale Road in Kansas City, where he died from his wounds. Green was at his side until his death. Miller's home was considered a safe refuge for midwestern gangsters. (It was there that Pretty Boy Floyd and Adam Richetti would meet with Miller to plan what newspapers dubbed the Kansas City Massacre, the botched attempt on June 16, 1933, to free criminal Frank Nash from custody.) After Christman's death, the gang members returned to their Chicago headquarters.[18]

During the spring of 1933 Green and Bessie lived at an apartment on Kedzie Avenue in Chicago, in close proximity to the residence of members of the Barker-Karpis Gang. Later that year the couple moved to Minneapolis, where they consorted openly with Alvin Karpis, Dolores Delaney, and Dutch Sawyer, who took the money and bonds from the Fairbury, Nebraska, bank robbery and laundered them through underworld connections. Sawyer made St. Paul safe for gangsters, and his farm near the city was used as a hangout by the Barker-Karpis and Dillinger gangs.[19]

The violence of the Barker-Karpis Gang was too much for Green. For example, he did not like the August 30, 1933, payroll robbery at the South St. Paul Post Office in which one policeman was killed and one severely wounded. Green told his girlfriend "how crazy the whole plan was, as they had apparently, without necessity, shot down individuals during the course of the robbery."[20]

Green was able to establish close friendships with Harry "Dutch" Sawyer and most major hoodlums in the Midwest.[21] He personally delivered $1,500 in cash to Tom Filben for Tom Brown's campaign for sheriff of Lake County, Illinois.[22] Federal authorities believed his knowledge was "perhaps broader than that of any other prominent gangster's." Volney Davis, Alvin Karpis, Fred Barker, William Weaver, Myrtle Eaton, and Dock Barker were well known to him, and he knew of their hangouts as well as their crimes.

Green served as an "underworld post office," acting as a contact for the various members of the Barker-Karpis Gang. For example, during the fall of 1933 Jess Doyle and his paramour Doris O'Connor used Green to find members of that gang. In September, Green, using the alias Theodore Randall, rented Apartment 207 at the Charlou Apartments in Minneapolis to as a weapons storage site.

Green and Bessie seemingly lived a quiet, normal life, and neighbors thought of them as ordinary people. Green was smart enough not to make expensive purchases that would attract attention, nor did he allow several hoodlums to come to his apartment all at once. He even left home in the morning and returned in the evening to give the appearance of having a regular job.[23]

One neighbor recalled: "They almost always used the rear stairway. The woman, about forty, with red hair, never talked to us very much, not even down in the laundry. They dressed flashily but were quiet and didn't seen to want to mix at all."[24]

Making a Name
for Himself

A S THE SUMMER OF 1933 progressed, Indiana State Police Captain Matt Leach began to see the name John Dillinger associated with an increasing number of crimes. He was notified that Noble Claycomb had confessed that he, Shaw, and "Dan" Dillinger had robbed the Bide-A-Wee tavern, and Leach correctly guessed that Dillinger had been involved in the Daleville bank robbery. Employees of the Daleville bank had identified Dillinger from pictures, and reporters on the Muncie, Indiana, newspapers were calling the outlaw "Desperate Dan." This marked the first time in Dillinger's criminal career that he had received any notoriety in the media. It would not be the last.

The tall and wiry Leach was born in Croatia under the name Lichanin to a naturalized American mother. Adopted in the United States by a family named Leach, he worked as a wood finisher in Illinois, served in World War I, and finally became a lawman in Indiana. An enlightened lawman, he believed that psychology should be used in dealing with criminals, and he studied and used the most up-to-date police methods available. His rise in the Indiana State Police, which at the time had just forty-two men, including clerks, was very rapid, and he communicated directly with Governor McNutt.[1]

One of Dillinger's favorite jokes when returning from gangster movies, which always portrayed police detectives as dumb, was, "You should have been with me. Matt Leach was in the picture." He also liked to quip, "Someday that guy will try to have me indicted for shooting Abe Lincoln."[2]

According to author Toland:

> Leach . . . wore a perpetually dissatisfied look [and] . . . was a man of conflicts: hot tempered and yet capable of unusual self-control; intense, nervous, yet one who could accept setbacks with stoicism. He was a self-educated, self-polished man whom many assumed to be a college graduate. At moments of excitement or anger he sometimes stuttered badly. . . .[3]

On July 22 Frank Hope, Dillinger's parole officer, drove alone to Mooresville, where he was told at the Dillinger farm that John was visiting his older sister, Audrey Hancock, in Maywood, some fifteen miles to the northeast. From Audrey he learned that John had taken her two daughters for a ride and might be at an Indianapolis gas station operated by her two sons, but Hope did not find him there. Meanwhile, two deputy sheriffs were stationed at the Hancock home, but when Dillinger came by to drop off his nieces, the lawmen were sleeping in their car. Hope set up a personal stakeout of the Dillinger farm, hiding in an orchard armed with a gun, but he never saw the outlaw. Dillinger would never see his parole officer again.[4]

Dillinger was lucky during his next robbery, the First National Bank of Montpelier, Indiana, when he, Harry Copeland, and Hilton Crouch, a professional racing driver who was good at getaways, made a $10,110 score on August 4, 1933. Entering the bank, he yelled, "This is a stickup!" then leaped over the cashier's cage barrier and scooped up the money. When local police learned of the holdup, they set up roadblocks, but the bandits got away. A farmer saw the crooks changing license plates on their car less than ten miles from the bank.

Fortune had indeed smiled on the bandits, for the offices of Police Chief Kenneth Dewees, the town's mayor, and an attorney were located above the bank but were unoccupied at the time of the robbery.[5] All contained rifles that could have been used to thwart the robbery. In fact, two years earlier one bandit had been killed and others were captured when they attempted to raid the bank.

According to one account of the robbery:

> Three men were in the party. J. Dillinger and Copeland entered the Bank, and the third man, identity unknown [Hilton Crouch], remained in the car. This was August 4, 1933, at 2:30 p.m. At this time one of the NRA committees were meeting in Wells' & Rapp's meat market directly across the street from the Bank. . . . They were standing in front of the large plate glass window in the meat market when a large car drove up in front, and they saw two men enter the bank. In a very few minutes they saw them leave the bank, each carrying money sacks.
>
> Jim Wells, a very short, fat man says, "What in the hell do those men have in those sacks? My God, they are robbing the bank! Fred, get that gun quick!" During this excited speech Jim was jumping up and down, which was a very laughable matter later. . . .
>
> Two men, Al Wikel and John Fox, were leaning against the Kroeger store next to the Bank building, and Dillinger and Copeland passed within ten feet of these men, carrying the $6,700 that was stolen. Fox and Wikel made the remark, "Look at the money those men have. Let's hold them up," at which Dillinger only smiled. They entered their car and left town, no one knowing which way. They were not followed.[6]

Forrest Huntington, a former Pinkerton detective and Indiana State Police officer, now joined the search for Dillinger. He was employed by the American Surety Company, which was responsible for the loss at Montpelier, and his file on criminals was one of the largest in the Midwest. Huntington went to the Pendleton reformatory to talk with a very cooperative William Shaw, who told of Dillinger's hideouts and associates, including prostitutes.

Near English Lake, Indiana, in the northeastern part of the state, an abandoned blue-green Dodge car was found on August 4—the day of the Montpelier bank robbery. It had no license plates and its rear window had been knocked out to enable the criminals to fire their weapons at any pursuers. Eight pounds of roofing nails were on the back seat; the bandits would have thrown them on the road to puncture the tires of any pursuing vehicles during a chase. There also was a torn piece of paper that police believed outlined an escape route. It read:

Fleetwood.
Hy. 65.
M B on L.
House on r.
1 M B oN R.
1 big post on big refiners.[7]

Dillinger's luck changed during his next robbery, the Citizens National Bank in Bluffton, Ohio, on August 14, when he, Copeland, Sam Goldstein, and two unidentified men made off with just $2,100. Two well-dressed men entered the bank around noon, while a third remained just inside the entrance and the other two paced the sidewalk outside. One of the dapper men walked to the window of assistant teller Roscoe Klingler and asked him for change for a five-dollar bill: three singles, a dollar in nickels, and another dollar in dimes.

After pocketing the change, the man drew a gun and hollered, "Stand back. This is a stickup!"

Meanwhile, a customer entered the front door and was immediately covered by the man standing guard there. At this point Dillinger vaulted over the counter barrier and ordered cashier Elmer G. Romey and bookkeeper Oliver Locher to raise their hands. The bank employees and the customer were made to lie on the floor while the bandit shoved all the money he could find into a large sack.

"You've got more money in here. Where is it?" Dillinger said.

As Locher pointed to a large safe, the bank alarm went off.

"They're after us. Let's go!" yelled the other well-dressed bandit.

A calm Dillinger told his nervous associate there was plenty of time and demanded, "Where the hell's the drawer to this window?"

One of the hoodlums standing guard outside panicked when the alarm went off and fired several random shots to keep at bay the large crowd that was beginning to gather to check out the excitement. Bullets struck several buildings, including a dry goods store, a drugstore, and a clothing store. As the robbers began to exit the bank, one began wildly swinging a machine gun toward the crowd, looking very much like a movie gangster, but he did not fire it. Some townspeople thought the shots fired by the guard on the sidewalk were simply American Legion members setting off noisemakers as while passing through town on their way home from a state convention in Lima.

Dillinger was the last to leave, taking $2,100 in cash and a .32-caliber revolver from the cashier's cage. The robbers piled into their getaway car and roared out of town, a machine gun protruding from the vehicle's rear window. The automobile was described by witnesses variously as an Essex, a Buick, a Chrysler, a Pontiac, and a Chevrolet. From start to finish, the robbery had taken less than five minutes.

As the robbers drove off, a store security guard ran into a hardware store shouting, "Let's get out the shotguns and get them!" Postmaster Dode Murray grabbed a weapon and set up an ambush behind a large brick post in front of the post office on Main Street, but the gang drove off in the opposite direction. The town marshal did not arrive at the bank until the bandits were long gone.[8]

Still needing a substantial amount of money to break his friends out of the state prison at Michigan City, Dillinger targeted a big-city bank for his next heist—the Massachusetts Avenue State Bank in downtown Indianapolis, located near the headquarters of the state police. On September 6, the date on which Dillinger, Copeland, and Crouch chose to raid the bank, the institution was brimming with cash, as it was payroll day for the Real Silk Hosiery Company.

Just before noon Dillinger walked into the bank and approached Assistant Manager Lloyd Rinehart, who was on the telephone, telling him, "This is a stickup." Rinehart thought it was just a joke until he heard the bandit say, "Get away from that damned telephone."

A very nervous Crouch, driver of the trio's getaway car, kept shouting for his companions to hurry up as Copeland, wearing a handkerchief over his face, ordered the two patrons inside to raise their hands. However, Dillinger quickly told them to put their hands down, knowing that any passerby who saw people with their hands up would realize a robbery was in progress. The outlaws escaped with $24,800 in cash, making the heist the second-most successful bank robbery in Indiana history up to that time. A citizen in an automobile followed the gangsters as they sped away, but he soon lost them.[9]

As the number of Indiana banks raided by Dillinger and his outlaw band grew, Matt Leach launched an extensive search for the bandits. He raided several apartments, arrested several Dillinger associates, and watched the Dillinger family farm and the home of the outlaw's sister, Audrey Hancock, but had no luck. At one apartment in Gary, the state police captain was almost shot by three of his own men, who were waiting in the apartment for Dillinger to return, when Leach knocked on the door. Leach also searched for Dillinger at a local restaurant but did not find him.[10]

On August 14, the same day of the Bluffton robbery, the Indiana State Police, working on a tip, arrested several Dillinger associates at an East Chicago apartment and questioned them. One of those taken into custody was Clarence "Whitey" Mohler, an escapee from Michigan City who had drunk shellac to convince prison authorities that he had tuberculosis, which had garnered him a temporary parole for treatment. Leach told him that, if he provided useful information, he would turn Mohler over to Kentucky authorities on a robbery charge instead of returning him to the Indiana State Prison to finish his life sentence.

Mohler told Leach that the third bandit involved in the Montpelier robbery was Sam Goldstein, and that Homer Van Meter, who recently had been in Kentucky, was working with Dillinger. He supposedly said that Dillinger, Copeland, Goldstein, and Van Meter had held up the New Carlisle bank as well as a bank in Grand Haven, Michigan. He also claimed that Dillinger and company had committed twenty-four bank robberies during the preceding sixty days, and he provided Leach with the address of a seventy-five-dollar-a-week Gary, Indiana, apartment that the bandits had been using for two weeks.

Leach quickly made plans to raid the apartment. The first officer to get there was a Gary police lieutenant, who arrested Goldstein when he came outside. The gangster confessed that he and Dillinger had been in the apartment and that Dillinger, using the name John Donovan, might be staying at an apartment in nearby Hammond. A police squad visited that location, but the outlaw was not there. Nevertheless, the landlady was arrested when two .45 automatics were found on the premises. A stolen new Pontiac, with its rear window broken out and roofing nails on the back seat, was also discovered in a garage at the rear of the dwelling.

A boy told Leach that several men in a Terraplane had been at the apartment just before the police arrived. He said the men had told him to tell Goldstein to meet them at a resort in Gary. He noted that three of the men looked like Dillinger, Copeland, and Van Meter, but when police raided the resort, the bandits were nowhere to be found. The boy also had called the Gary Police Department to tell them about the suspicious men, but the cops there ignored him.

Insurance investigator Forrest Huntington learned that East Chicago was the headquarters of Dillinger, Copeland, Van Meter, and a fourth man, who were known to be driving three Terraplanes, because they were fast. Shortly afterward, Dillinger moved his base of operations to Chicago.[11]

Three months of robbing banks finally provided Dillinger with the money he needed to free his friends. According to some accounts, he gave a large bribe to a foreman at a Chicago thread-making company to allow several guns to be hidden inside one of several barrels of thread being sent to the shirt factory at the Michigan City penitentiary. The top of the "loaded" barrel was marked with a large red X in crayon.

Dillinger recruited two women—Pearl Elliott, the middle-aged owner of a combination nightclub and whorehouse in Kokomo, and Mary Kinder, Harry Pierpont's girlfriend—to help in the escape attempt. Elliott had been involved in Pierpont's Kokomo bank robbery, and since Pierpont had not told police about her, she was glad to help break him out of prison. Pearl's job was to give money to the person who would bribe the prison guards. Mary's job was to provide clothes, money, and an apartment in Indianapolis that the escapees, including her brother, Earl Northern, could use as a hideout after the prison break.

One evening in early September, Dillinger threw three loaded guns and eighteen cartridges wrapped in newspapers over the thirty-foot wall just behind the state prison's athletic field. Pierpont was supposed to pick them up, but other inmates noticed the guns and turned them in to Deputy Warden H. D. Claudy. Three convicts from Chicago were believed to be involved in the escape plot and were put in solitary confinement.[12]

At this time, Dillinger's weakness for pretty women came back to haunt him. In July he had driven to Dayton, Ohio, to visit a married girlfriend, Mary Longnaker, and her friend Mary Ann Buchholtz. He took the two women to the World's Fair in Chicago and while there amused himself by taking a picture of a policeman. He thought it was even funnier when he got the lawman to agree to take a picture of himself and Mary.

On the way home, on July 24, they stopped in Michigan City so that Mary could see her brother, Jim Jenkins, who was serving time in the state prison. The two women went inside while Dillinger waited outside. Mary carried a banana, inside of which was $50 for Jenkins to use to bribe the guards. Mary also gave $50 to a prison employee "to fix my brother's teeth."[13]

Three days later Dillinger wrote to her: "If that lousy husband of yours bothers you any more, just let me know, and he will never bother you again."

It was not an idle threat. About a month earlier Mary and John had gone to Pleasant Hill, Ohio, near Dayton, to see her twenty-four-year-old husband, Howard, whom she was in the process of divorcing. According to Ellis Cecil, manager of the village pumping station, Dillinger and Mary came to the plant and asked if he could speak with Howard. According to Cecil, the conversation between the two men unfolded thusly:

"Your name is Howard Longnaker?"

"Yes."

"You've been treating Mary like a dog. She wants to know where the children are."

"It's none of your godamned business," Longnaker replied.

"You just come out here a piece and I'll show you whether it is or not."

"Don't need to go out a piece," Longnaker said. "I'll take care of you right here!"

Dillinger jumped from the car and fought with Howard until the two were separated by Town Constable Orth Stocker and others. When Dillinger got back behind the wheel, Stocker jumped on the car's running board and ordered Dillinger to go uptown, where he would be put under arrest. Instead, Dillinger drove at high speed to the end of the town and told the marshal to get off. When the criminal drove away, he left behind his hat, about sixty cents and a fountain pen inscribed "D. M. Dillinger."[14]

Unfortunately for Dillinger, the police had been watching Mary, for her brother James was a member of Pierpont's clique at Michigan City. Dillinger also did not know that, when her divorce became final, Mary was planning to marry a wholesome young man she had recently met.

On August 25 the Pinkerton Detective Agency informed Dayton police Detective Russell K. Pfauhl that the gangster had been seeing a Dayton woman:

> Dillinger calls upon this woman regularly and, no doubt, can be apprehended at Dayton, Ohio. He is driving a new Essex Terraplane "S" sedan, black color, and probably is using Ind. License 418-673, 512-979, 703-736 or 86-9217 . . .
>
> The thought is that considering Dillinger is contacting the woman in Dayton, you could have the police be on the watch for these license numbers, or probably they could get some information concerning this woman and cause the arrest of Dillinger.[15]

Landlady Lucille Stricker was asked to look out for Dillinger, and she finally called Pfauhl. At 1:30 a.m. on September 22 Pfauhl and partner Charles E. Gross, carrying shotguns, raided the plush rooming house. They found Dillinger, standing up, showing Mary snapshots from the World's Fair. When Pfauhl aimed his shotgun at Dillinger's head and ordered, "Stick 'em up, Johnnie," Dillinger dropped the photos and raised his hands, then slowly began to lower them, perhaps to reach for a weapon. "If you do, John, I'll kill you on the spot," Pfauhl threatened.

The policemen found several guns, in addition to roofing nails and a large supply of ammunition, in Dillinger's 1933 Terraplane.

The outlaw, who had $2,604 in cash in his possession, said, "You said you were police, but I didn't know. I can only tell if they wear uniforms."[16]

Big House
Breakout

ABOUT SEPTEMBER 24, SOME TWO days after Dillinger's arrest in Dayton, the escape party at Michigan City received three automatic pistols that had been smuggled into the prison. Walter Dietrich saw the marked barrel containing the hidden weapons on a truck loaded with thread for the shirt factory. After removing the guns from the barrel and hiding them in a button box in the factory, Dietrich told Pierpont and other inmates about them.

Among those in Pierpont's clique who were told were John Hamilton, Charley Makley, and Russell Clark. Others included Joseph Burns from Chicago, who was serving a life sentence for murder; Joseph F. Fox, a bank robber sentenced to life; Edward Shouse, who began a twenty-five-year sentence in 1930 for being the triggerman in a holdup by three men of the Grand Theater in Terre Haute; James Clark (no relation to Russell), serving life for robbery; and James Jenkins, brother of Mary Longnaker, serving a life sentence for murder. Mary Kinder's brother Earl Northern also was supposed to take part in the escape, but he didn't reach the rendezvous and was left behind.

The day before the planned breakout, Pierpont, Clark, Makley, and Hamilton talked about the escape during an exercise period.[1] In August, Pierpont had been denied parole even though the judges, the prosecutor, and eleven of the original jurors (the twelfth had died) had recommended his release.[2] The trio vowed not to let themselves be captured.

At 1:30 p.m. on September 26, a cloudy and chilly day, Pierpont told the plotters, "All right, boys, if you want to go and take a chance, we will go now."

Pierpont and Clark approached G. H. Stevens, superintendent of the shirt factory, and told him he was wanted in the basement. As Stevens headed downstairs, Pierpont and Hamilton each pulled a smuggled pistol while others taking part in the escape seized him.

Hamilton said, "Turn around, Stevens. We're going home, and you're going to lead us out. There won't be any rough stuff if you just come along and mind your own business."

Meanwhile, Dietrich lured Assistant Warden Albert Evans into the basement by telling him there was a jug of wine there. Evans was also taken prisoner when he entered the basement. Pierpont stuck a pistol in his stomach and growled, "We're going home, and you're going to do what we tell you. If you try anything, you're dead where you stand. Get it, you big, brave man?"

Makley came to the defense of Evans when one of the convicts wanted to kill him.

"We need 'em. They're going to take us out. Ain't you fellows?" the gangster cooed.

The convicts and captives walked casually outside and across the yard. Stevens and Evans led the way, followed by three inmates carrying automatic pistols under piles of shirts. The others followed and were carrying concealed iron bars. They also had with them a heavy, five-foot-long steel shaft that could be used as a battering ram, if needed. No one became suspicious. One guard on the wall was even asleep. Hamilton tried to get the attention of a friend in hopes that he would join them, but the convict walked past without noticing him or the others.

At the first of three steel gates that separated the inmates from the outside world, Evans whispered to guard Frank Swanson, "They've got guns. Open the gate or they'll kill us."

Swanson unlocked the barrier and was forced to join the procession. The guard at the second gate, Guy Burklow, opened it and fell in line without any problems when guns were pointed at him. The guard at the third gate, Fred Wellnitz, was beaten unconscious when he tried to grab his rifle. Evans was also hit when he complained about the beating. Using Wellnitz's keys, the escape group opened the gate and entered the Administration Building, where they saw Lawrence Mutch, superintendent of prison industries.

"Let's get Mutch!" one of the convicts yelled, and two prisoners forced the superintendent to take them to the prison arsenal. When he refused to open the arsenal door, Mutch was beaten severely.

The prisoners rounded up eight clerks, including two women, and Warden Kunkel, whom they did not recognize, and forced them into a vault. When seventy-two-year-old Finley Carson moved too slowly, a cursing convict shot him in the stomach. Chief clerk Howard Crosby hid under his desk with a telephone and called the local police. "There's trouble out here at the prison," he whispered. "Send policemen and guns!"

Jenkins grabbed a turnkey he hated and asked Pierpont for a gun.

"Come on, buddy, we're going to kill you," he told the trembling man.

"We're out of here. Why kill anyone?" Pierpont asked.[3]

It was raining hard as the ten convicts fled through the main entrance at the same time that Harrison County Sheriff Charles Neel was delivering a prisoner. Dietrich, Burns, Fox, and James Clark forced Neel into his car and drove away. The other six escapees, led by Pierpont, ran to a Standard Oil station across the street from the prison's main gate. One of the convicts fired several shots at the prison. The proprietor of the service station, Joe Pawleski, later told the United Press about what happened next:

> I was standing beside my car in front of the station when an automobile loaded with escaping convicts dashed out of the gate.
>
> Two men were running along beside it. They came over to me. Both of them had guns—big, blue, long-barreled ones.
>
> "Give us the keys to your car, or we'll blow your brains out," they yelled.
>
> I didn't wait for any more commands but started to run, keeping the keys in my pocket.
>
> I have a neighbor living a block away who always has a gun at home, and I started for his house.
>
> One of the convicts started shooting at me while the other screamed, "Give it to him! Give it to him!"
>
> They acted like crazy men, and I guess that's why their aim was so poor.
>
> They fired three shots. One went through the sleeve of my overall jacket. The other two went past my head, or else I outran them.[4]

The six escapees flagged down a passing vehicle driven by Herbert Van Valkenberg of Oswego, ordered Van Valkenberg, his wife, and eighty-nine-year-old relative Minnie Schultz out of the car, and drove it away.[5] Pandemonium reigned when a general alarm was sounded a few minutes later. Roadblocks were set up as radio broadcasts told of the breakout. Vigilantes were called out throughout the state, and a 500-man posse was organized. There were countless reports of fugitive sightings; however, many turned out to be false. After prison officials locked down the remaining inmates, the elated convicts cheered and rattled their cell doors.[6]

The two vehicles containing the fugitives headed west on State Route 12 toward Chicago, until the driver of the car carrying Sheriff Neel turned south onto a side road. Going too fast, the driver lost control and plowed into a ditch, where the car became stuck. Taking Neel with them, the four convicts walked to a nearby farm owned by Carl Spanier and forced Spanier to drive them south in his car. When the vehicle ran low on gas and they stopped to refuel, the farmer escaped. The fugitives abandoned Spanier's car and dragged Neel into an area of thick underbrush and woods, where they hid and were plagued by rain and lack of food.

The escapees finally decided to leave Neel tied up in the woods. However, Clark argued that the elderly sheriff might die if left in the rain. Burns, Fox, and Dietrich agreed and told Clark he could stay with Neel while they moved on.

After the other three men left, at about 3 a.m. on September 29, Clark and Neel walked to Highway 6, where they caught a ride into nearby Hobart, Indiana. The lawman bought food for himself and Clark, and even gave a topcoat to the convict to hide his prison uniform. Afterward, the two caught an interurban bus to Gary, where Clark released Neel, who in turn went to a local police station. Everyone at the station thought Neel had been killed by the escaping convicts, since three companies of state militia had been searching for him but no one had seen or heard from the sheriff since the breakout.

Clark hailed a taxi and made his way to Hammond, Indiana, where he was arrested later that day after police queried taxi drivers about suspicious passengers. Clark had eluded police for three days.[7]

The other six fugitives had made their way to Indianapolis. About three o'clock in the morning on the day after the escape, they knocked at Mary Kinder's door. Pierpont insisted that Mary, who was not expecting them for another day, had to provide them with a hideout. Since her parents were in the apartment, she had to take the escapees elsewhere. Still in their prison clothes, the convicts went to the home of Ralph Saffel, a young man Mary had been dating, and forced him to shelter them before sending him downtown with Mary to buy civilian clothes.

Pearl Elliott was at Saffel's home when the two returned. Mary had made a telephone call to her before going to town and had told Pearl to bring money. For the rest of the day the fugitives kept busy washing, shaving, changing clothes, and dividing the money. Jenkins, who was said to have a "wonderful voice," sang as he moved about the dwelling. Harry Copeland came by late that night, and everyone except Saffel left for a new hiding place Copeland had found. Saffel was not harmed but was warned to keep quiet.[8]

That same day two detectives visited the Kinder apartment, but her sister, Margaret Behrens, told them Mary had not been home since the previous night. Margaret was known as "Silent Sadie" because she had not talked about a bank robbery her husband had committed in 1927 and for which he was jailed. She had been arrested during the robbery investigation but was released after a short period in custody.

The Indianapolis police, having received a tip, believed the convicts were at the home of a local woman on September 28. The convicts came into the open again late the next day and were seen in Brownstown, Indiana, south of Indianapolis. A getaway car and prison jackets belonging to Shouse and Makley were found by police at about 7 p.m. At 9 p.m., in Terre Haute, the fugitives commandeered a Franklin sedan owned by Frank M. Ratcliffe and forced him to drive several miles east of the city before releasing him.

Meanwhile, Matt Leach heard a report on radio station WIND about a woman who claimed she had been questioned by two escaped convicts concerning the location of a particular garage. In the background were the sounds of sirens and gunfire, leading Leach, like most listeners, to believe that the fugitives had been cornered and were shooting it out with police. He hurried to the scene of the "battle," only to find a director and some actors. He had the director arrested when the group admitted they were merely performing a crime drama.

Lawmen in Brazil, Indiana, spotted Ratcliffe's stolen car at about 8:45 p.m. on September 29, but the fugitives got away. At 1:30 a.m. on September 30, state police Sergeant Bert Davis, in a patrol car near Indianapolis, saw a suspicious-looking vehicle heading for the city. With siren screaming and red warning light flashing, he chased after the car at speeds of up to eighty miles an hour and was very close as the vehicles entered Ben Davis, a western suburb of Indianapolis. The driver of the fleeing auto suddenly screeched to a halt at an intersection, and Davis zoomed past. By the time he managed to turn around, the outlaws had gotten away.

The convicts smashed the rear window of their car and pointed a machine gun at some bystanders at the intersection. As the auto made a wide turn and struck a light pole, James Jenkins fell out of the vehicle. He scrambled to his feet, but the car continued to speed west—fortunate for the fugitives inside, for a roadblock had been set up on the road they had been traveling. The next day Ratcliffe's Franklin was discovered abandoned in Greencastle.

As Jenkins fled into the night, Edward Watts, a local jeweler, fired at him but missed. In the wee hours of the morning of September 30, Jenkins came upon a twenty-four-year-old man, Victor Lyle, who was getting into his car to return to his home in Indianapolis after a late date. The bandit asked if he could get a ride, telling Lyle that he was in bad shape because he had been in a fight "over on Route 40." Lyle agreed and let Jenkins into his car. Once inside, the bandit pointed a gun at him and told him to drive south and keep away from major roads.

When Lyle said he was running low on gas, Jenkins told him to stop at a filling station. While Jenkins was busy trying to get the attention of a station attendant, Lyle escaped by driving away. He contacted the police in Bloomington about 3 a.m. Despite the early hour, a posse armed with rifles and shotguns was soon formed. It was composed of state police, deputies, farmers, and men from a Civilian Conservation Corps camp.

Somehow, Jenkins eluded the posse and reached the village of Bean Blossom, Indiana, later that day. He asked a man named Will Altop if there was an auto shop in town, explaining that his car had broken down. Altop thought the man appeared suspicious and walked away. He rounded up three friends—storekeeper Herbert McDonald, Ivan Bond, and farmer Benjamin Kanter—and together they drove around looking for Jenkins in order to question him. They soon found him and told Jenkins they would help him if he would show them that he was unarmed.

Although Jenkins shouted, "Don't get out!" McDonald walked toward him with a shotgun. Jenkins jerked out his revolver and fired twice, hitting McDonald in the right shoulder. Standing just ten feet away, Kanter opened fire with a double-barreled shotgun yet somehow missed Jenkins with the first round. A second blast hit from the weapon struck the outlaw on the side of the head and he fell to the ground. He was taken to a doctor in Nashville, Indiana, where he died. The state police and Jenkins's father, the Reverend George Jenkins, a Pentecostal minister, identified the body.

The elder Jenkins said, "I'm glad it's like this. Better this than that he'd killed somebody else."[9]

After Jenkins's death, the gangsters—including Pierpont, Makley, Russell Clark, Dietrich, Shouse and Copeland, as well as Mary Kinder—hid out at the farm home of Pierpont's parents near Leipsic, Ohio. It is surprising that police did not raid the farm for several days. The fugitives also used another hideout in Hamilton, Ohio.

Pierpont and his associates decided they would return the favor and free their pal Dillinger from jail, but to do so, they would need money. Makley suggested they rob the First National Bank in St. Marys, Ohio, his hometown.

On October 3 Pierpont, Makley, Hamilton, Clark, and Shouse left their Ohio hideout and drove to St. Marys, reaching the town shortly before 3 p.m., the bank's closing time. As it turned out, the bank had been officially closed by the U.S. Treasury Department for a bank holiday and was not scheduled to reopen for several weeks. Fortunately for the bandits, however, the bank had just received a large amount of cash from the mint and was allowed to continue to make change for local businessmen, although it was not allowed to do anything anything else.

The town's chief of police, Gilbert Gerstner, who once had known Makley, had just read reports that Fat Charley might be have returned to St. Marys.

When a car bearing five of the bandits pulled to the curb in front of the bank, there was a large crowd across the street listening to a World Series radio broadcast. While one outlaw remained in the car and another took up a position in a nearby doorway, Makley, Clark, and Pierpont entered the bank. Pretending to read a road map, Pierpont approached the window of teller Roland Clausing. He then lowered the map and pointed a .45 automatic at Clausing.

"Just stand still!" Pierpont yelled as he went behind the cage.

While one bandit watched the teller, another forced three employees and a customer into the directors' room. When two more customers walked in, Makley, standing near the front door, pulled a gun, took them to the directors room, and then returned to his post by the door.

Pierpont took all the cash from the counter and then asked the bank employees to open the small safe inside the vault. He was told that only conservator W. O. Smith could open the safe. At this point, Smith, who also had known Makley but did not recognize him, walked into the bank. When Pierpont told Smith to open the safe, the conservator told him there was a time lock on the safe and that it couldn't be opened. However, when the time lock clicked off, the bandits forced him to open the safe, then herded a total of eight captives into the vault and partially closed the door.

"Wait a minute—here's another one," Makley yelled when another customer came in.

Pierpont warned that if the captives made any noise before the bandits had gone, they would "blow the side of the building in with submachine-gun fire." An alarm was turned in, but no one heard it.

Reporting on the robbery later that day, the *St. Marys Evening Leader* said: "Officials believe the bandits were all professionals. They worked quickly and with a nonchalance which amazed their victims."[10]

The outlaws drove to their Hamilton, Ohio, hideout with more than $14,000 in cash. Pierpont, Makley, and Mary Kinder then left for Leipsic, but on the way their car became stuck in a muddy ditch. A farmwoman driving by in a decrepit Ford told them she would pull their car out with a rope for $2. When Pierpont asked Mary to steer while the men pushed, she told him, "I ain't gonna get out. You know I got a sore foot."

Even after Pierpont asked again, Mary insisted, "Well, I can't get out, and I'm not getting out."

After the car had been extricated from the ditch and the bandits were back on the road, Mary explained why she did not get behind the wheel. "How in hell was I going to get out with all these guns you throwed in the back seat and the money back here?"[11]

Now it was time to free Dillinger.

A Deadly
Escape

A SEARCH OF DILLINGER AT the Montgomery County Jail just after his September 22 capture in Dayton had turned up a diagram of what looked like a prison. Dayton police Detective Russell Pfauhl told Matt Leach that he thought Dillinger was planning a prison break at Michigan City, but the state police captain would hear nothing of it.

"You've been reading too many detective novels. He ain't that big," Leach told him. "They couldn't get out of there if they tried."

Four days later, on September 26, he would be proved wrong when ten convicts escaped from the state penitentiary.

Dayton police Inspector Yendes, Leach, and others questioned Dillinger but got little information from him. It was believed he had committed several robberies, including a bank robbery at Farrell, Pennsylvania, on September 12, and he was identified as one of the men who had taken part in the recent bank robberies in Indianapolis and New Carlisle, Ohio. Indiana officials wanted him extradited.

After Dayton law enforcement authorities heard reports from informers that Dillinger was to be freed, police armed with machine guns were stationed on the rooftops near the jail and the night force at the facility was doubled. No one was allowed to see the outlaw.

A couple of days after his capture Dillinger pleaded guilty to the holdup of the Bluffton bank and was moved to the Allen County Jail in Lima, Ohio. His chances of escaping from the very old Lima jail were much better than they would have been at the newer and better-built jails in Dayton or Indianapolis. Sheriff Jesse Sarber, who, along with some deputies, had overseen Dillinger's transfer from Dayton to Lima, thought the bandit was "just another punk" and did not believe reports that the escaped convicts would try to free him.[1]

In contrast, insurance investigator Forrest Huntington believed "that Dillinger's associates will make an effort to effect his release."[2]

As soon as he was settled in the Lima jail Dillinger wrote to his father:

> Dear Dad:
> Hope this letter finds you well and not worrying too much over me. Maybe I'll learn someday Dad that you can't win in this game. I know I have been a big disappointment to you but I guess I did to [sic] much time, for where I went in a carefree boy I came out bitter toward everything in general. Of course Dad most of the blame lies with me for my environment was of the best, but if I had gotten off more leniently when I made my first mistake this would never have happened. How is Doris and Frances? I pre-ferred to stand trial here in Lima because there isn't as much prej-udice against me here and I am sure I will get a square deal here. Dad don't believe all that the newspapers say about me for I am not guilty of half of the things I am charged with and I've never hurt anyone. Well Dad I guess this is all for this time, just wanted you to know I am well and treated fine.
>
> From Johnnie[3]

Late in the afternoon on Columbus Day, October 12, 1933, Harry Pier-pont and Russell Clark called on Lima attorney Chester M. Cable to ask for his help in arranging for Dillinger's "sister" (actually Mary Kinder) to visit Dillinger in the Allen County Jail. Cable told them it would take time for him to secure permission, and he then called Sheriff Sarber to tell him about his two visitors.

Pierpont decided not to wait any longer. He and Clark had parked in front of the jail, while Makley, Copeland, Hamilton, and Shouse had parked their Terraplane a block away. The six criminals gathered in front of the courthouse, then Pierpont, Makley, and Clark headed for the Sheriff Sarber's office at the jail, while Copeland returned to the Terraplane. Shouse walked over to stand near the jail, and Hamilton moved into position by a theater behind the building. At the time, sixteen prisoners were being held in the jail.

At 6:25 p.m. it was beginning to get dark. Dinner, consisting of pork chops and mashed potatoes, had just concluded, and the forty-seven-year-old Sheriff Sarber was sitting behind his desk, reading a newspaper. Heavyset and balding, he had become sheriff after his used-car business failed. Sarber's wife was working on a crossword puzzle, and Deputy Wilbur Sharp was playing with the sheriff's dog, Brownie. Both Sarber and Sharp were unarmed, but a gun was in the middle desk drawer.

Dillinger was in a cell playing pinochle with Art Miller, who had been convicted of second-degree murder, and two other prisoners. He had told Miller his friends from Michigan City would soon be coming to free him.

When Pierpont, Makley, and Clark entered Sarber's office, the sheriff asked what they wanted. Pierpont replied they were officers from the state prison and would like to see Dillinger. When Sarber asked to see their credentials, Pierpont pulled out a .38 revolver and screamed, "These are our credentials!"

When the surprised sheriff said, "Oh, you can't do that!" and started to get up from his chair, Pierpont fired twice, one of the bullets striking Sarber in the lower abdomen and the other lodging in a wall. Falling to the floor and bleeding badly, Sarber made an effort to rise, but Makley hit him in the head with his pistol, which accidentally discharged. Although the blow had laid open the sheriff's scalp to the bone, Pierpont struck Sarber another couple of times.

"Don't kill him!" yelled Clark, whose gun also fired accidentally, wounding him in a finger.

Mrs. Sarber shouted that she would get the keys to the jail. She rushed to a hallway cupboard, retrieved the keys from where they hung on a nail, and gave them to Pierpont, who took Sarber's pistol from the desktop. He was able to open the first two doors leading to the cellblock, but when he struggled with the third door, he made Sharp open it.

Dillinger went for his coat and came out when Pierpont opened the cellblock doors. He was given Sarber's gun. Dillinger had asked Miller if he wanted to escape with him, but when Miller refused, he said good-bye to him and shook his hand.

"You other bastards get back. We want John," Pierpont yelled at the other prisoners, firing a shot down the jail corridor.

Weakly, Sarber said, "Men, why did you do this to me? Mother, I believe I am going to have to go."

Dillinger paused when he saw the dying sheriff.

An elderly couple, Mr. and Mrs. Fay Carter, heard the gunshots as they were passing by outside the jail. Shouse stepped forward and told them he had also heard shots and would go inside to see what was going on. He entered the building, saw Sarber lying on the floor, and smiling as he quickly returned, told the Carters that the noise was actually some drawers that had fallen to the floor while heavy files were being moved. When a third shot rang out, Mrs. Carter said, "Why, that sounds like they are killing each other."

Staying calm, Shouse replied, "Oh, that was another drawer that fell."

"Well," Mrs. Carter replied, "there's so darn many crooks around nowadays, when you hear a noise you don't know what to think."

Although Mrs. Sarber begged to stay with her husband, Pierpont forced her and Deputy Sharp into the cellblock and then locked the doors. As the gangsters were leaving, they were seen by a policeman and a young man, Lowell Cheney. They left in two cars for their Hamilton hideout.

After breaking a cellblock window with a chair, Sharp shouted to the young man for help. Cheney ran into the jail office and called the local police.

The sheriff's son Don soon arrived at the office, and his father said, "Turn me over on my side. My . . . back hurts."

An ambulance soon came and took Sarber to Memorial Hospital, where he died at 8:05 p.m. He had told his son his attackers were "big men."

Meanwhile, someone found a blowtorch and used it to cut through the cellblock doors to free Sharp and Mrs. Sarber.

Six posses were formed to hunt for the outlaws. Early the next morning the Pierpont home near Leipsic was raided, but no one was found. Fred Pierpont—who admitted that his brother, as well as Copeland, Clark, Shouse, Makley, and Hamilton, had used the farm as a hideout— was arrested and a stolen car found on the property was seized.

Late that night Dillinger and the other bandits reached a hideout in Cincinnati. Evelyn "Billie" Frechette, an exotic-looking, dark-haired girl-friend of Dillinger, was waiting there, as was Mary Kinder.

"It's real nice with Johnnie home and all of us sitting here," Mary said.

However, Pierpont was upset. "We had to beat up the sheriff to get Johnnie out," he said.

Although Clark thought Sarber was not seriously hurt, Pierpont believed he was dead. Pierpont asked Mary if she would still stay with him, given the circumstances. She told him, "I can't go now. I know too much. No, it wouldn't be right, me leaving you boys just because you're in trouble."[4]

The following day Deputy Sharp and Mrs. Sarber both identified Pierpont through photos. On November 3 Pierpont, Hamilton, Copeland, Shouse, and, erroneously, Joseph Burns were indicted in Lima for the murder of Sheriff Sarber.[5]

Shortly after Dillinger's breakout from the Lima jail, the *Mooresville Times* ran an interview a reporter had obtained from the father of the town's most notorious resident:

> Stopping in the midst of sawing wood for Winter use, John W. Dillinger, farmer living on the Mooresville Pike, told a representative of the *Times* Thursday he believed his son John, paroled gunman who was liberated last week from the Lima, Ohio, jail at the cost of a sheriff's life, would never have figured in major crimes had the judge who sentenced him for the first offense been more lenient.
>
> The father, who has been besieged by squads of police, deputy sheriffs, constables and newspaper men since a report spread that his son was taking refuge at the Mooresville home, has gone quietly about his work—for he says despite all the trouble that can come to a family, he realizes that corn must be shucked and wood must be cut.[6]

Nelson Gang
Up North

T HE SUMMER AND FALL OF 1933 were also a busy time for Baby Face Nelson and his gang. On August 18 the Nelson Gang robbed the Peoples Savings Bank in Grand Haven, Michigan, of $14,000. The holdup crew included bank-robbery guru Edward Wilhelm "Eddie" Bentz, Earl Doyle, Chuck Fisher, Tommy Carroll, William S. "Three-Fingered Jack" White, and Nelson. When the bank alarm was triggered, one of several townspeople who rushed to the bank spotted the gang's getaway car and its driver, White, waiting at the rear of the bank. When White saw the crowd, he drove off, leaving his fellow criminals behind.

When the thugs came out of the bank, using hostages as shields, they discovered their getaway car had vanished. During the gunfight that ensued, Earl Doyle was wounded and captured, and four hostages—two citizens and two bank employees—were wounded. The gunmen flagged down a passing auto and forced two women and four children from the vehicle before fleeing town in it. The car was later abandoned, and the gang commandeered another one; however, it blew a tire and crashed into a tree. The robbers stole yet another vehicle and were finally able to elude the massive manhunt that had been mounted. Nelson swore he would kill White for deserting the gang.[1]

The next month Carroll thought the Union Bank in Amery, Wisconsin, a town he had traveled through many times, would be easy to plunder. Fisher, Thomas Gannon, and Van Meter joined him in the robbery on September 13. When assistant cashier Clifford Olson came to work at 7:50 a.m., the four masked men came up to him. One of them had a sawed-off shotgun, another carried a rifle, and the other two held pistols.

"That's right, lock the door!" one of the gunman yelled after Olson had let them inside the bank. "Now get away from the window!"

Olson was told to open the vault, but when he was unable to do so on the first try, a nervous Van Meter gave him several hard kicks. Just after the vault was finally opened, head cashier Vincent Christenson walked through the bank's rear door, calling out to Olson that the lock appeared to have been jimmied.

"That's all right," one of the bandits said, stepping toward Christenson and pointing a pistol at the cashier's head. "Come in and lie down on the floor."

The robbers loaded two black satchels with $11,000 in cash and $35,000 in securities and fled across the Minnesota state line.[2]

In October, Nelson and his gang split into two groups and laid low in cabins at the Sebago Resort on Round Lake and on Louge Lake, both some fifteen miles from the central Minnesota town of Brainerd, where they planned to rob the First National Bank. Nelson himself had cased the bank, and early on the morning of October 23 Nelson, Homer Van Meter, John Paul Chase, Tommy Carroll, and Chuck Fisher left their respective cabins and headed for Brainerd.

At 6 a.m. three of the gang members surprised the bank's janitor as he arrived for work and forced him to let them into the building. Two other bandits stood guard outside, with a machine gun hidden under a bushel basket. The crew inside, waiting for the time lock on the vault to open at 8:45 a.m., herded fourteen employees who entered the building between 6 and 8:30 a.m. into a washroom and forced them to lie on the floor. The robbers even knew the employees' names and allowed them to smoke as they waited.

About 8 a.m. Nelson, positioned near the entrance, grabbed seventeen-year-old employee Zane Smith as he came into the bank. "He jumped to his feet . . . took hold of the collar of my topcoat and swung me around and hit my jaw with his fist," Smith said later. "He . . . dragged me across the bank lobby floor to an office where they had the bank guard and janitor."

When the time lock clicked open, the outlaws snatched up $32,000 in cash and exited the building. As they fled, they sprayed the interior of the bank and adjoining buildings with machine-gun fire.[3]

The First
Dillinger Gang

I N MID-OCTOBER 1933 DILLINGER AND his associates set up their headquarters in Chicago. Not the leader of the group but merely a member
among equals, Dillinger was able to promote trust, loyalty, and confidence among the gang's members, as well as restore calm when they
became angry.[1] According to Opal Long, Harry Pierpont was "the
thinker" of the gang, and her husband, the handsome Russell "Boobie"
Clark, who was a traveling companion of Dillinger,[2] was "the talker."

Closest to being the leader of what most historians view as the "first
Dillinger Gang," Pierpont was the most daring, courageous, and intelli-
gent of the lot. But his impulsiveness was a serious weakness. The ven-
erable John "Red" Hamilton offered the wisest advice. According to
Mary Kinder, "Hamilton was the oldest. He was nice and quiet as could
be . . ."[3] But he, too, had a serious problem. "Somebody forgot to give
John a memory," Opal Long would say later. "He'd forget addresses of
the places we were staying, and he'd even forget the aliases he was
using. He'd stumble into trouble and stumble out of it somehow."[4]

In general, the bank jobs the gang pulled were well planned and pre-
cisely timed. While casing a bank for a robbery, two of the gang posed

as journalists and were given a red-carpet tour by the bank's president, who showed them all of the security arrangements.[5]

Sometimes, however, the gang members made mistakes. While en route to rob the biggest bank in Muncie, Indiana, at closing time, Harry Copeland, who was driving, made a wrong turn arrived at the bank just after it had closed. Pierpont threatened to kill Copeland, and the other gangsters wanted to get rid of him.[6]

The female members of the entourage now included Pierpont's girlfriend Mary Kinder, Hamilton's girlfriend Patricia Cherrington, Opal Long, and Billie Frechette, Dillinger's attractive, raven-haired girlfriend, who was part Menominee Indian and had high cheekbones and large brown eyes. Pat Cherrington had recently introduced Dillinger to Billie, a hatcheck girl in a Chicago cabaret where Pat was a dancer.

A Division of Investigation report would later comment on Billie's "use of a great deal of profanity" and surmise that she was "the 'hard-boiled' gangster moll type of woman . . . the thrill-seeking type." According to one account, "Dillinger claimed she was the best bed partner he'd ever had." Her husband, Walter Sparks, was serving a long stretch in Leavenworth Penitentiary.

Billie was born in 1907 to a French father and Menominee mother on a Wisconsin reservation, where she remained until she was about thirteen. For the next four years she attended an Indian school in Flandreau, South Dakota, and then went to live in Milwaukee and Chicago, where she worked as a nursemaid and waitress. Dillinger did not approve of Billie drinking and at one point told told Pierpont: "She's an Indian. It's not good for her—or for us—if she drinks."[7]

Mary Kinder would later note that, "Sometimes we had separate apartments, but mostly two couples stayed together. John and Harry and I stayed with Billie—Evelyn Frechette—for a while, then we'd change. . . .

"We'd all go to dances, taverns, restaurants, and prizefights. Nobody hid around. We'd read different stuff, listen to the radio and everything. . . . We lived four or five places in Chicago, paying in advance for a month. We'd stay in a place until we thought we had to move because we were seeing too many strangers or something. I just cooked day and night—frog legs, chicken, and stuff. They'd eat anything I'd cook."[8]

Boobie Clark found his wife through friends in Chicago. Commenting on their life together, Opal said, "I'd had a pretty rocky time of it while he was gone. I was glad to see him, and I was scared of what was going to happen to him."[9] Often Makley and Shouse resided with them.[10] Opal once found machine guns in a closet and became terrified, but Clark told her to forget about what she saw and ask no questions. The couple lived at four or five different addresses in the uptown district of Chicago's North Side.[11]

Hamilton and Pat Cherrington had also become involved recently. Pat, who was born September 26, 1903, had had a short-lived union with Chester Young, whom she had married at the age of fifteen. In 1930 she met bank robber Robert "Bob" Cherrington, but in August 1932 he was sentenced to fifteen years at Leavenworth for mail robbery. She took up with Harry Copeland and then with Hamilton after Copeland was arrested. Pat worked as a waitress and then as an interpreter of Russian and Egyptian dances. While working as a specialty dancer in a Chicago nightclub, she was introduced to Hamilton, whom she thought was "a nice-looking man," by Dillinger. The very courteous and gentlemanly Hamilton said he was an unmarried bond salesman.

After a brief courtship Hamilton asked Pat to marry him. Although she did not wish to marry, in part because she was still wed to Bob Cherrington, Pat agreed to live with the gangster, but not for money, for she was making $100 a week at the nightclub. When she saw a picture of her lover in a Chicago newspaper, Pat finally became aware of who Hamilton really was.[12]

The male members of the gang were careful not to become overly intoxicated and chose to drink only beer. They frowned upon the women's habit of consuming hard liquor, since the girls acted as the gang's advance agents, renting houses and apartments and buying cars and even guns. They also served in the important role as messengers and liaisons between the Dillinger Gang and other criminals. Although the men and their women were lovers, the gangsters were always aware that they could be betrayed by their sweethearts.[13]

The gang planned several major bank robberies, but to increase their chances of success, Dillinger, Pierpont, and Makley raided the Auburn, Indiana, police station on October 14 to obtain weapons and bulletproof vests. Dillinger and Pierpont entered the station, while Makley stayed outside as a lookout. Brandishing a gun, one of the outlaws walked up to a desk where Henry West, one of the two officers on duty, was sitting and said, "You might as well sit still. We don't want to kill anyone unless we have to. Have you got any guns?" Fred Krueger, the other officer, replied in the affirmative.

The policemen were quickly disarmed, forced to give the bandits the keys to the gun cabinet, and then locked in a cell. A restaurant owner later released the officers with a cell key he found on the premises.[14]

The outlaw trio made off with two steel vests, a submachine gun, six pistols, three rifles, and more than a thousand rounds of ammunition.

Seven days later, on October 21, gang members pulled a similar heist when they surprised officers at the Peru, Indiana, police station. A month earlier, pretending to be tourists, Dillinger and Van Meter had entered the station and asked officer Ambrose Clark what measures the police had taken against Dillinger and his mob. Clark and a desk sergeant eagerly gave the pair a tour of their facility.

At about eleven o'clock on the night of October 21, Dillinger, Pierpont, and Walter Dietrich entered the station and took four policemen captive. In a cold voice Pierpont told them, "I haven't killed anyone in a week, and I'd just as soon shoot one of you as not. Go ahead and get funny." No one tried anything. After forcing the four men into the basement, the gangsters grabbed six bulletproof vests, two machine guns, a pair of Winchester .30-30 rifles, four super .38 police specials, two sawed-off shotguns, three police badges, and a cache of ammunition. Wrapping the weapons in blankets, they ran to their car, jumped in, and headed for Chicago.[15] When Mary Kinder, who was in the back seat serving as a lookout, saw the extent of the haul, she exclaimed, "My God! What are you going to start—a young army?"

Armed to the teeth with weaponry and a sophisticated plan of action, the so-called first Dillinger Gang was ready to attempt its first bank job. On October 23, 1933—the same day the Baby Face Nelson Gang robbed the bank in Brainerd, Minnesota—Dillinger and his cohorts pulled their black Studebaker to the curb near the Central National Bank in Greencastle, Indiana. While Russell Clark remained behind the wheel and John Hamilton acted as lookout at the bank's entrance, Dillinger, Harry Pierpont, and Fat Charley Makley, holding a stopwatch, entered the building.

Walking to the fifth teller window, Pierpont, who with Dillinger had cased the building a few days before, posing as newsmen, gave Assistant Trust Officer Ward Mayhall a twenty-dollar bill and asked for change. When Mayhall told him to go to the second window instead, Pierpont, opened his overcoat and produced a machine gun. "Keep your hands at your sides and don't move. We're not advertising," he said.

Makley herded a dozen employees and about ten customers into the vault room, and while he held guns on the group, Dillinger made a flashy leap over a small railing separating the bank's lobby from the

In just a few years, young John Herbert Dillinger, left, became America's most notorious criminal, a man of violent deeds and many faces, below.

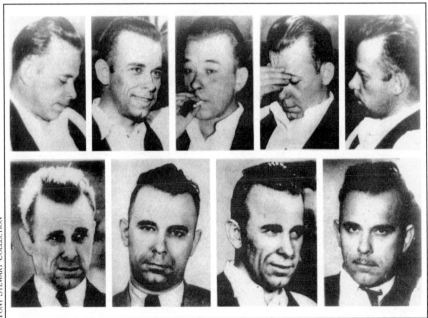

The First Dillinger Gang

Key members of the First Dillinger Gang included, clockwise from above, John Dillinger, Harry "Pete" Pierpont, John "Red" Hamilton, Russell Lee "Boobie" Clark, and Charles "Fat Charley" Makley.

Gangster gals Evelyn "Billie" Frechette, above left, Dillinger's girlfriend; Opal "Mack Truck" Long, Russell Clark's wife; and Patricia Cherrington, left, with boyfriend John Hamilton.

U.S. NATIONAL ARCHIVES

Dillinger Gang members at their arraignment in Tucson, above from left, Harry Pierpont, John Dillinger, Billie Frechette, and Mary Kinder. Below, a period editorial cartoon depicting the wave of "motorized bandits" using new technology to outpace American law enforcement.

WILLIAM J. HELMER COLLECTION

The chummy photo at left, taken at the Crown Point jail, ruined prosecutor Robert Estill's career. Dillinger's fingers appear to be in the shape of a gun. Below, a Division of Investigation identification order issued shortly after the outlaw's daring March 3, 1934, escape from the facility.

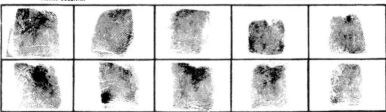
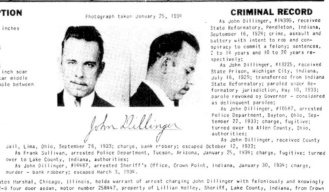

IDENTIFICATION ORDER NO. 1217
March 12, 1934.

DIVISION OF INVESTIGATION U. S. DEPARTMENT OF JUSTICE
WASHINGTON, D. C.

Fingerprint Classification

$$\frac{12\ \ 9\ \ R\ \ 0}{14\ \ U\ \ 00\ \ 9}$$

WANTED

JOHN DILLINGER, with alias,

FRANK SULLIVAN

NATIONAL MOTOR VEHICLE THEFT ACT

DESCRIPTION

Age, 31 years
Height, 5 feet 7-1/8 inches
Weight, 153 pounds
Build, medium
Hair, medium chestnut
Eyes, grey
Complexion, medium
Occupation, machinist
Marks and scars, 1/2 inch scar
  back left hand; scar middle
  upper lip; brown mole between
  eyebrows
Mustache

Photograph taken January 25, 1934

John Dillinger

CRIMINAL RECORD

As John Dillinger, #14395, received State Reformatory, Pendleton, Indiana, September 16, 1924; crime, assault and battery with intent to rob and conspiracy to commit a felony; sentences, 2 to 14 years and 10 to 20 years respectively;

As John Dillinger, #13225, received State Prison, Michigan City, Indiana, July 16, 1929; transferred from Indiana State Reformatory; paroled under Reformatory jurisdiction, May 10, 1933; parole revoked by Governor - considered as delinquent parolee;

As John Dillinger, #10587, arrested Police Department, Dayton, Ohio, September 22, 1933; charge, fugitive; turned over to Allen County, Ohio, authorities;

As John Dillinger, received County Jail, Lima, Ohio, September 28, 1933; charge, bank robbery; escaped October 12, 1933;

As Frank Sullivan, arrested Police Department, Tucson, Arizona, January 25, 1934; charge, fugitive; turned over to Lake County, Indiana, authorities;

As John Dillinger, #14487, arrested Sheriff's Office, Crown Point, Indiana, January 30, 1934; charge, murder - bank robbery; escaped March 3, 1934.

The United States Marshal, Chicago, Illinois, holds warrant of arrest charging John Dillinger with feloniously and knowingly transporting Ford V-8 four door sedan, motor number 256447, property of Lillian Holley, Sheriff, Lake County, Indiana, from Crown Point, Indiana to Chicago, Illinois, on or about March 3, 1934.

Law enforcement agencies kindly transmit any additional information or criminal record to the nearest office of the Division of Investigation, U. S. Department of Justice.

If apprehended, please notify the Director, Division of Investigation, U. S. Department of Justice, Washington, D. C., or the Special Agent in Charge of the Office of the Division of Investigation listed on the back hereof which is nearest your city.
(over) Issued by: J. EDGAR HOOVER, DIRECTOR.

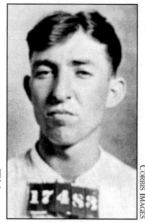

The Second Dillinger Gang

Key members of the so-called Second Dillinger Gang, above from left, George "Baby Face" Nelson (Lester Gillis), Harry Eugene "Eddie" Green, and Homer Van Meter, and Thomas Carroll, below.

STATE OF MINNESOTA, BUREAU OF CRIMINAL APPREHENSION

STATE CAPITOL BUILDING · ST. PAUL, MINNESOTA

Record from _____ PD _____ (Address) _____ St. Paul, Minn.

On the above line please state whether Police Department, Sheriff's Office, or County Jail

Date of arrest __ May 17, 1933

Charge _____ Investigation

Disposition of case _____

Residence _____ St. Paul, Minn.

Place of birth ___ Red Lodge, Mont.

Nationality _____

Criminal specialty _____

Age 37-Nov., 1933 Height 5'10"

Weight 166 Hair Dk. Ch.

Build Med. Eyes Lt. blue

Comp. Med.

Marks and Scars I 2 vac cics upper l ar
II Sev pit scrs upper r arm.
III From scr on r lower jaw bone; scr
on neck front; furrow upper lip;
brows heavy and dist; scr center back
of neck in hair; mouth turns to right

CRIMINAL HISTORY

11/28/33
Pal of Chas W Fisher –
Richard Pyes and Otto Schreck. all men wanted for P.O. robbery at Superior - Wis

6/7/34 Shot in gun battle with police at Waterloo, Ia. Died 6/8/34

The Little Bohemia Resort, above, site of an April 22, 1934, shootout between the Dillinger Gang and federal agents. A jaunty Dillinger, below left, at his father's home. Billie Frechette, below right, after a June 1934 court appearance in St. Paul, Minnesota.

WANTED

JOHN HERBERT DILLINGER

On June 23, 1934, HOMER S. CUMMINGS, Attorney General of the United States, under the authority vested in him by an Act of Congress approved June 6, 1934, offered a reward of

$10,000.00

for the capture of John Herbert Dillinger or a reward of

$5,000.00

for information leading to the arrest of John Herbert Dillinger.

DESCRIPTION

Age, 32 years; Height, 5 feet 7-1/8 inches; Weight, 153 pounds; Build, medium; Hair, medium chestnut; Eyes, grey; Complexion, medium; Occupation, machinist; Marks and scars, 1/2 inch scar back left hand, scar middle upper lip, brown mole between eyebrows.

All claims to any of the aforesaid rewards and all questions and disputes that may arise as among claimants to the foregoing rewards shall be passed upon by the Attorney General and his decisions shall be final and conclusive. The right is reserved to divide and allocate portions of any of said rewards as between several claimants. No part of the aforesaid rewards shall be paid to any official or employee of the Department of Justice.

If you are in possession of any information concerning the whereabouts of John Herbert Dillinger, communicate immediately by telephone or telegraph collect to the nearest office of the Division of Investigation, United States Department of Justice, the local addresses of which are set forth on the reverse side of this notice.

JOHN EDGAR HOOVER, DIRECTOR,
DIVISION OF INVESTIGATION,
UNITED STATES DEPARTMENT OF JUSTICE,
WASHINGTON, D. C.

June 25, 1934

WANTED

LESTER M. GILLIS,

aliases GEORGE NELSON, "BABY FACE" NELSON, ALEX GILLIS, LESTER GILES,

"BIG GEORGE" NELSON, "JIMMIE", "JIMMY" WILLIAMS .

On June 25, 1934 HOMER S. CUMMINGS, Attorney General of the United States under authority vested in him by an Act of Congress approved June 6, 1934 offered a reward of

$5,000.00

for the capture of Lester M. Gillis or a reward of

$2,500.00

for information leading to the arrest of Lester M. Gillis

DESCRIPTION

Age. 25 years; Height, 5 feet 4-3/4 inches; Weight, 133 pounds; Build, medium; Eyes, yellow and grey slate, Hair, light chestnut; Complexion, light; Occupation. oiler.

All claims to any of the aforesaid rewards and all questions and disputes that may arise as among claimants to the foregoing rewards shall be passed upon by the Attorney General and his decisions shall be final and conclusive. The right is reserved to divide and allocate portions of any of said rewards as between several claimants. No part of the aforesaid rewards shall be paid to any official or employee of the Department of Justice.

If you are in possession of any information concerning the whereabouts of Lester M. Gillis communicate immediately by telephone or telegraph collect to the nearest office of the Division of Investigation, United States Department of Justice, the local offices of which are set forth on the reverse side of this notice.

The apprehension of Lester M. Gillis is sought in connection with the murder of Special Agent W C Baum of the Division of Investigation near Rhinelander, Wisconsin on April 23, 1934.

JOHN EDGAR HOOVER, DIRECTOR,
DIVISION OF INVESTIGATION,
UNITED STATES DEPARTMENT OF JUSTICE.

Federal wanted posters were issued June 25, 1934, for Dillinger, facing page, and Baby Face Nelson, above. Nelson was miffed that the reward for Dillinger was twice the amount offered for him.

GET·DILLINGER!
$15,000 Reward

═══ A PROCLAMATION ═══

WHEREAS, One John Dillinger stands charged officially with numerous felonies including murder in several states and his banditry and depredation stamp him as an outlaw, a fugitive from justice and a vicious menace to life and property;

NOW, THEREFORE, We, Paul McNutt, Governor of Indiana; George White, Governor of Ohio; F. B. Olson, Governor of Minnesota; William A. Comstock, Governor of Michigan; and Henry Horner, Governor of Illinois, do hereby proclaim and offer a reward of Five Thousand Dollars ($5,000.00) to be paid to the person or persons who apprehend and deliver the said John Dillinger into the custody of any sheriff of any of the above-mentioned states or his duly authorized agent.

THIS IS IN ADDITION TO THE $10,000.00 OFFERED BY THE FEDERAL GOVERNMENT FOR THE ARREST OF JOHN DILLINGER.

HERE IS HIS FINGERPRINT CLASSIFICATION and DESCRIPTION. ——— FILE THIS FOR IDENTIFICATION PURPOSES.

John Dillinger. (w) age 30 yrs., 5-8½.
160½ lbs., gray eyes, med. chest, hair, med.
comp., med. build. Dayton, O., P. D. No.
10587. O. S. B. No. 559-646.

F.P.C. (12)

$$\frac{M \quad 9 \quad R \quad O \quad O}{S \quad 14 \quad U \quad OO \quad 8}$$

13	10	OO	O	O
u	R	w	w	w
5	11	15	I	8
u	U	u	w	u

FRONT VIEW

Be on the lookout for this desperado. He is heavily armed and usually is protected with bullet-proof vest. Take no unnecessary chances in getting this man. He is thoroughly prepared to shoot his way out of any situation.

GET HIM

DEAD
OR ALIVE

Notify any Sheriff or Chief of Police of Indiana, Ohio, Minnesota, Michigan, Illinois.

or **THIS BUREAU**

SIDE VIEW

ILLINOIS STATE BUREAU OF CRIMINAL IDENTIFICATION

The governors of Indiana, Ohio, Minnesota, Michigan, and Illinois added $5,000 to the $10,000 federal bounty offered for Dillinger.

At left, Dillinger in the spring of 1934. Below, the St. Paul home of sisters Lucy Jackson and Leona Goodman where Eddie Green was ambushed and mortally wounded by G-Men hiding behind first-floor windows as he returned to his car after picking up luggage the maids had kept for him.

GANGSTER'S CAR

Dillinger was gunned down on the evening of July 22, 1934, outside Chicago's Biograph Theater, above. DOI (later FBI) Director J. Edgar Hoover, at right below, with Melvin Purvis, special agent in charge of the agency's Chicago field office, who set up the ambush.

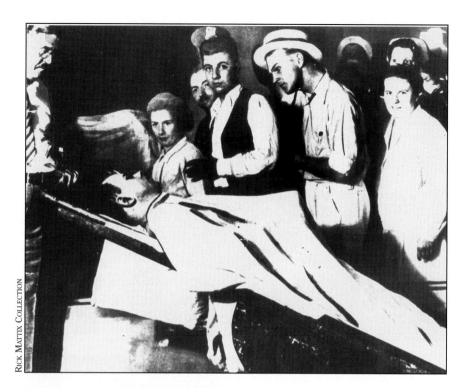

Dillinger's body was seen by more than 15,000 people at the Cook County Morgue, above. "Lady in Red" Anna Sage, left, Dillinger's betrayer. Below, Dillinger's personal effects after his death included a hat, eyeglasses, and a cigar.

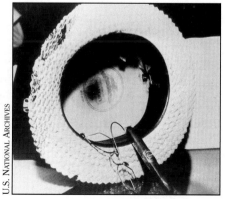

Homer Van Meter, below, was killed by police in St. Paul. His sheet-covered corpse attracted a large crowd, above, before it was ferried to the morgue to await an autopsy, right.

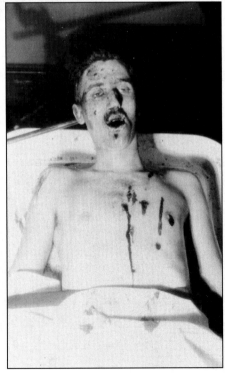

For Baby Face Nelson, left, with wife Helen and son Ronald, the end came several hours after a November 27, 1934, gun battle with federal agents in Barrington, Illinois. His body, displayed at the Cook County Morgue, below, was viewed by some 2,000 people.

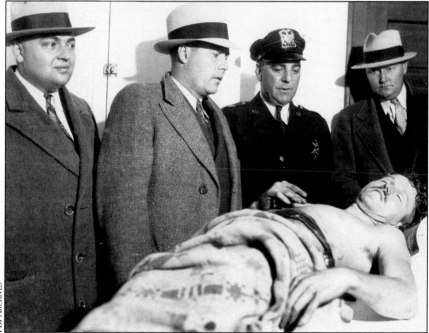

Editorial cartoon depicting public sentiment surrounding Dillinger's demise.

tellers' area. Pierpont followed him, and the pair quickly stuffed $18,428 in cash from the cashier's cage into a sack. They also took bonds valued at $56,300.

One of the employees managed to slip outside. After trying in vain to find large tacks to place under the gangsters' getaway car, he called the police station. No one thought to contact the sheriff's office, located across the street from the bank, where a deputy and a state policeman were on hand, as well as high-powered rifles.[16] Hamilton saw an elderly, foreign-born woman come out of the bank, and he demanded that she go back inside until the robbers left. Confused, she told him, "I go to Penney's and you go to hell," and continued on her way.[17]

"It's five minutes," Makley yelled. Dillinger, who had almost finished filling the bag with loot, immediately jumped back over the railing. When he saw a farmer standing in front of a teller's cage and a small amount of money on the counter, he asked, "That your money or the bank's?"

"Mine," the farmer said.

"Keep it. We only want the bank's," the outlaw replied.[18]

In its coverage of the robbery, the *Chicago Tribune* noted that, "for some reason the invaders ignored piles of silver and paper currency lying on counters within easy reach." However, as news of the bank heist spread, many across the Depression-ravaged nation began to look at Dillinger as a sort of latter-day Robin Hood, believing the legend that he only wanted to steal from the rich.[19]

Many were unaware that, as the gangsters were leaving the bank, a customer entered the building and apparently made a gesture that gave the appearance he was reaching for a gun. In very un-Robin Hood-like fashion, one of the robbers slugged the man so hard that he collapsed to the floor.

By the time the police arrived, the outlaws were gone. The gang easily avoided roadblocks by traveling on predetermined side roads. It was a very happy group, for the score was the largest that Dillinger or any of his crew had every made.[20]

The recent spate of robberies and jailbreaks and Sheriff Sarber's slaying caused a furor throughout Indiana and Ohio, spurring demands by citizens and the press that something be done to stem the rising tide of crime. The *Indianapolis Times* made an informal request to U.S. Attorney General Homer Cummings for federal assistance, and to Division of

Investigation Director J. Edgar Hoover to give limited aid to the Indiana State Police.[21]

Ohio Congressman Frank L. Kloeb asked for help from J. W. Brabner Smith of the Justice Department, and he in turn asked the DOI to assign an agent to the case.[22]

An October 25 editorial in the *Evansville Courier* stated that Indiana Governor Paul Vories McNutt had officially asked for federal assistance. "Uncle Sam has promised aid, and for that promise many citizens are devoutly thankful," the paper said.[23]

That same day, Indiana State Police Captain Matt Leach visited Special Agent Bliss Morton of the DOI's Indianapolis field office for the first time, to brief Morton on the Dillinger case.[24] However, DOI Director Hoover at the time considered Dillinger to be to be of minor importance. Although the director ordered that "any and all possible assistance" be given to state authorities, he did not want DOI agents "to take the initiative."[25]

On October 26 Governor McNutt called up the National Guard, which wanted to use everything it had—airplanes, tanks, and poison gas—to fight the Dillinger mob. Indianapolis police patrolled city streets in armored cars equipped with machine guns, and the Indiana Bankers Association suggested that a statewide one-way police radio network be established. Roadblocks were set up throughout the state. The Indiana American Legion planned to arm 30,000 of its members to patrol the state's roads,

Not everyone viewed Dillinger as evil incarnate, however. Many people throughout the Midwest and the nation, particularly those beaten down by the Depression and looking for salvation from any source, saw him as a latter-day Robin Hood. Believing in the legend that was growing around the outlaw, many saw in Dillinger someone who would indeed take from the rich—in this case bankers, whom countless citizens blamed for the country's economic chaos—while giving a break to the "little man," such as the farmer at the Greencastle bank. Letters to the editor, and sometimes editorials, supported Dillinger and his gang. One reader wrote:

> I am for John Dillinger. Not that I am upholding him in any of his crimes; that is if he did any.
>
> Why should the law have wanted John Dillinger for bank robbery? He wasn't any worse than bankers and politicians who took the poor people's money.
>
> Dillinger did not rob poor people. He robbed those who became rich by robbing the poor. I am for Johnnie.[26]

Another reader, in response to an editorial castigating Dillinger, wrote:

> This person [the editorial writer] calls Dillinger cheap. He isn't half as cheap as a crooked banker or a crooked politician because he did give the bankers a chance to fight, and they never gave the people a chance.[27]

Dillinger had a close call in Chicago in mid-November, thanks to minor gang member Arthur McGinnis, who had informed police that Dillinger was being treated by local physician Charles Eye for "barber's itch," or ringworm, which he had contracted in the Lima jail. On the night of November 15, 1933, law enforcement officers set a trap for the outlaw.

The police arrived in several unmarked cars but parked many of them facing the wrong way on the street outside Dr. Eye's office. The cops expected to nab Dillinger as he left the doctor's office, but when the gangster looked out the window and saw all the cars and the manner in which they were parked, he knew something was amiss.

With Billie Frechette in tow, Dillinger stealthily made his way to his car—his favorite, a Hudson Terraplane, noted for its high speed and durability—and roared away, followed by a squadron of police vehicles. Exhibiting great driving skill, Dillinger managed to elude all of his pursuers except Sergeant John Artery and his partner, Art Keller. Narrowly missing streetcars, autos, and pedestrians, both cars careened along Irving Park Boulevard at speeds approaching eighty miles an hour. Finally able to draw even with Dillinger, Artery poked a shotgun out a window and fired at the Terraplane.

"Hey, somebody's shooting at you!" Billie frantically cried out. Smiling at her, Dillinger stepped on the gas and pulled ahead. Although the car was moving at terrific speed, Dillinger deftly cranked the steering wheel sharply and maneuvered the big car onto a narrow side street. Artery could not make the turn and continued down Irving Park. By the time he was able to reverse his course, Dillinger's car had vanished. "That bird can sure drive," Keller marveled. The next morning, when police found Dillinger's abandoned car on the Far North Side, they discovered the vehicle had twenty-two bullet holes in it, but none had penetrated the Terraplane's thick bodywork.[28]

Newspapers falsely reported that Dillinger and Billie had fired on the pursuing police officers. According to an editorial in the *Chicago American*:

And last Wednesday night John Dillinger, Indiana bad man and escaped convict, emerged from a doctor's office on Irving Park blvd., climbed into his automobile and drove away from many Indiana and Chicago squad cars filled with policemen. Dillinger, incidentally, also had a girl friend. She earnestly strove, with a large pistol, to destroy pursuing policemen. The ideal of "sex equality" seems to have been attained in the criminal world . . .

Last Wednesday night's clowning seems to have been particularly inexcusable. It was known that Dillinger was in a doctor's office. Why didn't a couple of policemen simply walk in and arrest him? Or has that old-fashioned method of taking criminals been abandoned by our modern police strategists?[29]

Relationships between most of the gang's members were good in the fall of 1933. Matt Leach, hoping to create friction between Pierpont and Dillinger, began to refer to the gang as the "Dillinger Mob." But since neither Dillinger nor Pierpont cared who was credited with being the leader, the ploy failed.[30]

Dillinger was supposedly so megalomaniacal that, after his breakout from the Lima jail, he telephoned Leach, telling the state police captain, "This is John Dillinger. How are you, you stuttering bastard? . . . We'll get you. Watch your ass." Captain John Stege, who by year's end would be named head of the Chicago Police Department's new Dillinger Squad, later said he also received a similar call.[31]

The day after Halloween, Leach received a copy of a 1896 paperback entitled *How to Be a Detective*. Many thought Dillinger was the sender, but it was actually a prank by two Indianapolis newsmen.[32]

As the weeks passed, however, the outlaws began to chafe. Copeland was drinking too much, and Shouse was trying to seduce Billie. There was reason for concern, for some women found Shouse, who liked to wear the best clothes, quite handsome. After arguing with Shouse the day after escaping from Dr. Eye's office, Dillinger accused Billie of being unfaithful to him and even threatened to kill her.

Mary Kinder came to Billie's defense, saying, "There ain't no sense to it, Johnnie. That girl likes Shouse. So what?" She insisted that Billie could have any man she wanted.

At that point the angry Dillinger stormed out, saying he was taking Billie for "a one-way ride." Three hours later, however, the subdued gangster returned with his girlfriend, telling Mary, "I didn't have the heart to do it."

Pierpont wanted to keep Shouse and kick Copeland out of the gang. However, it was decided to get rid of Shouse when Mary Kinder overheard the outlaw asking Hamilton to help him and another outlaw pull a bank job the next day. Mary told the pair, "You ain't going to do a damn thing. There ain't nobody going no place until we all talk it over. This has always been a friendly bunch, and you ain't going to take no two or three and go to rob a bank."

The following morning, November 18, the gang members threw money at Shouse, and Dillinger told him, "There's your money. Now get your ass out." Shouse took the cash, then stole Clark's car and headed for California.

The Dillinger Gang's next robbery, the American Bank and Trust Company in Racine, Wisconsin, on November 20, 1933, included a new man, Leslie Homer, among the crew. Pierpont drove through the town several times before the robbery, checking the lay of the land and plotting possible escape routes, and it is believed that Homer Van Meter may have visited the bank two or three times at 2:30 p.m., the time the heist was scheduled to take place. A gang member planted a spare can of gasoline along the primary escape route, so the outlaws wouldn't have to stop in public to refuel.

On the day of the holdup, Makley and Dillinger entered the bank first, followed in a few seconds by Pierpont, Clark, and Hamilton. It was almost closing time, and the employees were puzzled when Pierpont pasted a huge Red Cross poster in the middle of the bank's large picture window. Once it was in place, blocking the view from outside, Makley pulled a pistol and told head teller Harold Graham, "Stick 'em up." Believing the portly man was joking, Graham replied, "Go to the next window, please."

"I said stick 'em up," Fat Charley repeated.

When Graham made a sudden movement, Makley fired, hitting the teller in his elbow and hip. As Graham fell, he hit the alarm button, which sounded at Racine's police headquarters. Pierpont told everyone inside to drop to the floor, and then he, Dillinger, and Hamilton entered the teller area and began gathering up the money behind the cages.

As Pierpont entered the vault he pointed his machine gun at young employee George Ryan, who begged, "For God's sake, mister, point that gun the other way!" Laughing, Pierpont replied, "As long as you are a good boy, you don't have to worry."

Since there had been many false alarms at the bank, officers at police headquarters took their time responding. When officers Wilbur Hansen and Cyril Boyard finally arrived, Pierpont disarmed them as soon as they entered the front door. When Hansen was slow in giving up his machine gun, Makley shot him. As the women captives screamed, Dillinger came out of the vault saying, "I've got all of it." With $27,789 in hand, the bandit brandished his gun at an off-duty police officer who was just entering the bank and said, "Come on in and join us."

Using bank President Grover Weyland and several women, including bookkeeper Mrs. Henry Patzke, as human shields, the gangsters hurried out the front door and ran to the parking lot behind the bank, where Clark was waiting in a big Buick. Police officers fired at the group but had to aim high to avoid hitting the hostages and the large crowd that had gathered to see what the commotion was. As the bandits drove away from town along the predetermined escape route, Makley started to curse but stopped when Pierpont told him, "Cut it out, Mac, we got a lady in the car."

Looking at the bookkeeper, Dillinger mused, "Maybe we ought to take you along. Can you cook?"

"After a fashion," Mrs. Patzke replied.

"Some other time," he said.[33]

When the gang stopped to retrieve the gasoline can that had been hidden before the robbery, Pierpont ordered Weyland and Mrs. Patzke from the car. When Mrs. Patzke complained of the cold, the gangster gave her his coat and Weyland his hat, and then led the captives into the woods. He politely let Mrs. Patzke stop and tie her shoes, and when he spied a large tree, he had the two hostages stand on opposite sides of the tree and then tied their hands together with shoelaces. The two were afraid at that point that they would be shot, but Pierpont simply took back his coat from Mrs. Patzke and told Weyland, "Sorry, mister, I'll have to have my hat."

The gang then headed for their hideout in Milwaukee. Mary Kinder was doing laundry when the robbers arrived. As she would later recall: "They all come in kidding Harry because he took off his overcoat to put around the girl. And they said to me, 'You didn't give a damn whether we got killed or not. You ain't even got the radio on.'"

Soon afterward, witnesses looking at police photographs identified Pierpont, Dillinger, Makley, and Clark as the bank robbers.[34]

Interlude

From June to November 1933 Tommy Carroll used the Minneapolis duplex of Radio Sally's brother Joseph Bennett as a hideout, and Homer Van Meter and Baby Face Nelson visited him there. Some five packages containing weapons, including machine guns, arrived from Dillinger and his pals during October.

On November 11 Carroll barely escaped from two Minneapolis police officers who tried to arrest him for the Brainerd bank robbery. After kicking one officer in the face and punching the other and stealing his gun, Carroll fled barefoot, leaving behind $1,600 in crisp bank notes, a rifle, a machine gun, and a shotgun.

After his daring escape Carroll dumped Sally and took up with a twenty-one-year-old waitress named Jean Delaney Crompton, a recent divorcée whom he'd met at a Minneapolis dance hall. The sister of Alvin Karpis's girlfriend Dolores Delaney, Jean left her mother's home and would live with Carroll in Minneapolis until April 1934. She would later tell federal authorities, "From the way Carroll talked, I believed he was a gambler—he always seemed to have plenty of money." She said she did not ask questions about Carroll's business "for fear that Tommy would slap me down." Carroll was very jealous, according to Jean, and often wanted to "beat up college boys who would pass us in cars and holler, 'Hello, Blondie' and 'Hello, Cutie' at me."[1]

In late November, Nelson and wife Helen, Van Meter, and Marie Conforti, Van Meter's girlfriend, had Thanksgiving dinner with gunsmith H. S. "Hymie" Lebman and his wife in San Antonio, Texas. Van Meter placed a personal order for a custom-made .45-caliber pistol. Tommy Carroll, using the name Tom McLarkin, was also in San Antonio with his partner Chuck Fisher, who was using the name H. L. Keith.[2]

Police were alerted to to Carroll and Fisher's presence in town when Grace Poole, the operator of a local "assignation house," noticed that two of her customers were armed and told her concerns to Chief of Detectives Audry Hopkins. Believing one of the armed men to be Carroll, Hopkins ordered three detectives—H. C. Perrow, Alfred Hartman, and Lee Jones—to lay a trap for the outlaw.

On the afternoon of December 11, detectives waited for Carroll to arrive and pick up a hooker named Blanche Bowman on South Street. They were expecting the outlaw to be driving a car with Illinois license plates, but he pulled up in a taxicab instead. It wasn't until Blanche had run from the house and jumped into the cab, and the vehicle was speeding away, that the officers realized Carroll was inside. With Hartman driving, the detectives followed the taxi, pulling alongside when it stopped at an intersection. Seeing the lawmen, Carroll bolted and ran down the street. Jones sprang from the squad car and gave chase, while Hartman and Perrow followed in the vehicle.

Carroll ducked into a dead-end alley at 430 East Commerce Street. When the two detectives pulled up by Levinson's Market, a woman shouted that a man had just run into the alley. As Hartman and Perrow rushed from their car, Hartman fired a single shot from his revolver into the air and ordered the gangster to halt. With a gun in each hand, Carroll fired at Hartman, hitting him in the right arm and knocking the gun from his other hand.

Racing back to East Commerce Street, Carroll shot twice at Perrow, who returned fire with a sawed-off shotgun. During the exchange Perrow was wounded in the head and later died at a local hospital. Jones arrived at the alley just as Carroll, who was unscathed, fled down East Commerce. The lawman squeezed off several shots, but all of them missed Carroll, who fired back. One bullet passed through Jones's coat, whereupon the detective fainted.

Carroll ran toward a slow-moving car and jumped on its running board. When the driver pushed him off, Carroll fell into the street but jumped up immediately and raced away. He ran toward Hymie Lebman's gun shop, where he changed his clothes and then disappeared.

Fisher was arrested that night at the Aurora Apartments by DOI Special Agent in Charge Gus Jones and was returned to Minnesota, where, on January 16, 1934, he would be sentenced to an eight-year prison term for a series of post office robberies. Nelson and the remaining gang members fled back to the Midwest.[3]

On the Lam

AFTER THE RACINE BANK ROBBERY the Dillinger Gang decided to split up for three weeks to let the "heat" die down and then meet again in Chicago. Russell Clark and Opal set out for Texas, drove around the periphery of the Gulf of Mexico, and ambled through the South en route to Florida. In Atlanta they picked up a couple of hitchhikers who told them that cars were being searched at the Mexican border for fruit and vegetables. Since they were loaded down with guns, Clark and Opal decided to head back to Chicago.[1]

Charley Makley, using the alias William Martin, went to Denver and on December 9 rented an apartment there. Two days later, he saw someone who knew him, and fearing that the man would call the police, Makley hurried to the bus station. His instincts were correct, for soon after, a pair of investigators from the district attorney's office, surmising that the portly criminal would try to leave town quickly, showed up at the bus station to arrest Makley for selling spurious stock. However, just seven minutes before the lawmen arrived, the outlaw had left town aboard a bus.[2]

Several other members of the gang weren't so lucky. Harry Copeland was nabbed in Chicago on November 19 when policemen Edward McBride and John Ryan saw the drunken gangster and a girl sitting in a car arguing. When Copeland began waving a revolver at the woman, the officers arrested him and took him to the police station. Although he insisted he was John Santon, fingerprints revealed his true identity and he was subsequently returned to the Indiana State Prison.[3]

On November 24 Leslie Homer was arrested along with a criminal named Jack Liberty in Chicago. In the satchel he was carrying, police found a bulletproof vest and a loaded pistol with two extra clips.[4] Homer, who had only $511 of his share of the Racine bank loot on him when arrested, told lawmen:

> I have been in trouble before. I have spent sixteen out of the last seventeen years in prison. I am under parole. I came out of prison with very little money. I was approached by one of these men to simply run a few errands, for which I was well paid. I was guilty of aiding and abetting criminals. As time went, and certain things occurred, I wished to withdraw from the connection, and I found myself in the position of the man who couldn't let go. In other words, I got in the position where I knew too much.[5]

In fact, Homer, who had finished three years of high school before dropping out to work for himself, had been imprisoned for burglary in 1917 and was released in 1928. That same year he was rearrested for armed robbery and sentenced to five to twenty-one years. He was paroled on October 10, 1933, and four days later Pierpont asked him to join the gang.[6]

On December 23 gang member Hilton Crouch was arrested by five policeman at his Chicago apartment and charged with bank robbery. For his part in the holdup of the Massachusetts Avenue State Bank in Indianapolis, he was sentenced to twenty years.[7]

On January 6, 1934, gang member Walter Dietrich, one of the convicts who had escaped in the breakout from the state prison at Michigan City, was captured in Bellwood, Illinois.[8]

According to some accounts, the Dillinger Gang may have been responsible for the robbery of Chicago's Unity Trust and Savings Bank on December 13, 1933. A few days earlier, while the bank was closed,

Dillinger and Harry Pierpont, posing as burglar-alarm salesmen, had learned the particulars of its alarm system from a seventy-three-year-old male attendant.

At 2 p.m. on the day of the heist, Fat Charley Makley, serving as lookout, stood outside the bank dressed as Santa Claus, soliciting charitable donations. Unsuspecting passersby put money into his pot, which concealed a pair of .45 automatics. Dillinger, Pierpont, and John "Red" Hamilton entered the bank and in just ten minutes looted $220,000 in cash and negotiable bonds from safety-deposit boxes, before exiting the building and disappearing into the holiday crowds.[9]

The next day, Chicago Police Detective Sergeant William T. Shanley and Patrolman Frank Hopkins were working a stakeout at a Broadway garage where Hamilton's green automobile reportedly had been seen. Shanley and Hopkins were hiding in the garage, while Patrolman Martin Mullin was hunkered down in a squad car about a block and a half away. About 4 p.m. Shanley told Hopkins to walk to the squad car and tell Mullin to take the vehicle back to headquarters and send out a relief team of officers. Just after Hopkins left, Hamilton and his new girlfriend, Elaine Dent, entered the garage.[10] A mechanic, Sam Tower, later told reporters what happened next:

> They walked over to the car. Sergeant Shanley walked up to them and asked, 'Is this your car?' Hamilton told him, 'No, it belongs to my wife.' The woman took out a vehicle receipt and handled it to the officer. Shanley told Hamilton, 'Keep your hands out of your pockets!' And began to pat his [Hamilton's] hip pocket for a gun. As he did so, Hamilton pulled a gun from a shoulder holster and shot Shanley twice.
>
> Sergeant Shanley yelled, 'I'm shot! Call the police.' Then he fell down, with the license receipt still in his hand. Hamilton grabbed the woman by the hand and ran out the front door, dragging her behind him.[11]

Hopkins, returning to the garage, saw the two running and chased them. As Hamilton left Elaine behind and fled across a vacant lot, Hopkins seized the struggling and cursing woman and took her back to the garage. She theatrically told the detectives she was an innocent victim who did not know Hamilton was a criminal. She insisted, "He was good to me, brought me this coat and the car. He certainly deceived me, as I thought he was a rich man's son. Why, I never heard him say 'damn.' And clean! He'd take two baths a day."

Shanley, a *Chicago Tribune* Hero award winner and the thirteenth policeman killed on duty that year, died at Edgewater Hospital. At first police thought Pierpont was the killer.[12]

The day after Detective Shanley's murder, the gang members again left Chicago and went in three different directions. They were to meet in Chattanooga, Tennessee, three days later. Before leaving town, Clark, who had dyed his hair dark brown, and Opal bought a new car. After stowing a suitcase full of machine guns and pistols in the back seat, they headed south.

While driving along slick roads near Evansville, Indiana, Clark struck a truck broadside. The front of the car was caved in and the truck was seriously damaged. Opal was knocked out and was bleeding from a large cut across her face. After the truck driver called the police, several lawmen and an ambulance arrived. Although Opal told Clark she would not go to a hospital, Clark insisted that she go and said he would come later and get her. Opal had hidden $4,500 in her shoe and was worried that someone would find the cash at the hospital and ask questions.

Clark, wearing a slouch hat and smoking a pipe, did not put up a fuss when the officers asked him to accompany them to the police station. He took the suitcase with the guns out of the wrecked car, put it in the police vehicle, and rode with the officers to the station. When they arrived, Clark simply left the suitcase on the sidewalk, walked into the station, admitted that the wreck was his fault because he was not paying attention to the road, and settled up financially with the truck driver. The police captain pumped Clark's hand, told him he was a "square-shooter," and then let him go. He even offered to help Clark out some day. The bandit was glad to get out outside, for he had recognized several policemen in the station, where he had once been locked up. He quickly headed for the hospital.

Meanwhile, Opal was having a miserable time. Afraid she would talk under anesthesia and get the gang arrested, she refused ether when the doctors sewed up the cuts on her face, gritting her teeth as they repaired her wounds. After treating her, the medical staff took her to a room and wanted to put her to bed, but Opal was not about to stay. When Opal took off her shoes and laid them on the bed, a nurse tried to take them away. But since the $4,500 she had secreted under the inner sole was all the money she and her husband had, she fought fiercely until the nurse allowed her to put the shoes under her pillow.

By the time Clark got to her room, Opal was very tense. Clark took her out of the hospital and checked them both into a hotel for the night. Since they could not wait for their car to be repaired, they boarded a plane the next morning for Chattanooga. They were unable to locate the other gang members there or in Nashville but finally caught up with them in Florida.[13]

When Matt Leach received a tip that Edward Shouse would be at the Paris Hotel in Paris, Illinois, on December 20, the Indiana State Police captain set up an ambush.

As Shouse, returning from California and accompanied by another man and two young women, pulled up to the hotel and stepped out of his car, Leach's men ordered him to surrender. Instead, he jumped back into the car and started shooting, giving up only when Trooper Eugene Teague fired into the rear of the vehicle. But as Teague sprang from behind the car to arrest Shouse and the others, Lieutenant Chester Butler fired his riot gun and accidentally hit Teague, killing him. In the confusion, Shouse's male companion escaped.

Taken into custody, Shouse was interrogated. When asked about the Dillinger Gang, he told his questioners, "They are kill-crazy, and that is why I left them."

Holidays and Homicide

TWO EVENTS OCCURRED DURING THE latter part of December 1933 that would profoundly affect Dillinger and his cohorts. On Dec. 16, the Chicago Police Department formed its Dillinger Squad, a special unit headed by Captain John Stege and comprising forty men whose primary task was to locate the outlaw and bring him to justice—one way or another.

Nearly two weeks later, on December 28, the Illinois Crime Commission, which had produced the nation's first official Public Enemies list on April 24, 1930, issued its latest roster of most-wanted criminals. The list contained twenty-one names, with John Herbert Dillinger declared Public Enemy Number One and Baby Face Nelson listed last.[1]

With Christmas approaching, Dillinger and the remaining gang members decided to spend the holiday season in warmer climes and traveled to Daytona Beach, Florida, where they rented cottages near the ocean. On the drive south, Harry Pierpont and Mary Kinder stopped in Nashville, where Pierpont bought Mary a diamond ring and a wedding ring from a jewelry store.[2] Two days after arriving in Florida, the couple were in the lobby of their hotel when a host of police swarmed through it. Despite their initial concerns, the two were relieved to find that the police were there because a guest had leaped from an upper-level window.[3]

Dillinger and Billie and Clark and Opal rented a hundred-dollar-a-month beach house, while Makley and Hamilton took up separate residences nearby. The beach house was described later by a DOI agent as "a mansion . . . with a beautiful round living room that contained four fireplaces." The outlaws took it easy and enjoyed swimming, playing golf and cards, listening to the radio, fishing, and going to shows and movies. They even traveled to Miami to see the air races. The women, the DOI agent noted, rode "in their bathing suits on horseback."[4] They also reluctantly cooked the men steak and potatoes.

Despite the pleasant surroundings, it wasn't long before Pierpont and Dillinger became upset when Mary and Billie got drunk on champagne. During an argument on Christmas Day, Dillinger hit Billie around the eyes and forced her to leave town. Later, gifts were exchanged, and Opal insisted on cooking the entire Christmas dinner. On New Year's Day the gangsters celebrated by shooting machine guns at the ocean.[5]

Shortly after the first of the year, several of the gang members decided to go to Tucson, Arizona. Makley, Clark, and Opal drove out in one car, arriving about January 9, while Pierpont and Mary traveled in another, arriving about the middle of the month.

At 2 p.m. on January 14, 1934, Dillinger and Hamilton left Florida. Driving throughout the night, they returned to Indiana and robbed the First National Bank in East Chicago of $20,736 the next day. It was there that Dillinger committed his only known murder: that of policeman William Patrick O'Malley.

At 2:45 p.m., shortly before closing time, Hamilton and Dillinger, armed with a machine gun, entered the bank. As the latter yelled, "This is a holdup!" bank Vice President Walter Spencer pressed the silent alarm. While Hamilton was scooping money into a sack, Dillinger saw a policeman at the front door. "There's a cop outside!" he shouted. But he calmly added, "Don't hurry. Get all that dough."

Actually, four policemen had arrived outside, but they thought the situation was just another false alarm. When Patrolman Hobart Wilgus entered the building, Dillinger took him hostage. As the two gangsters left the bank, they used Wilgus and Spencer as human shields. Patrolman O'Malley was able to get a clear shot at Dillinger when Wilgus jumped aside, and while several bullets struck the criminal, he was saved from serious injury by his bulletproof vest. Dillinger returned fire, striking O'Malley in the leg. As O'Malley slipped to the floor, he fired again, but that volley also failed to penetrate Dillinger's vest. A low burst from Dillinger's gun struck the patrolman in the heart, killing him instantly.

Carrying the money, the unlucky Hamilton was hit by a bullet that ripped thought a weak spot in his armored vest. Dillinger bravely scooped up his fallen partner—and the money—and continued to move away from the bank. With Hamilton in tow, Dillinger hurried toward their getaway car. Police fired several shots, but all of them missed Dillinger, even though his back was completely unprotected as he moved toward the vehicle.

Upon reaching Chicago, Dillinger took the seriously wounded Hamilton to an underworld doctor.[9] Hamilton had been shot seven times, with six of the bullets entering his shoulders and left arm. A bullet also had passed through his body just above the pelvic bone. A wound in his left shoulder and arm made that limb practically useless; Hamilton was unable to raise it above shoulder level and could not straighten it to its full length.

The day before the robbery Pat Cherrington, who was in Detroit, had received a telegram from Dillinger telling her to go to a Chicago hotel. Pat left Detroit by train that evening, arrived in Chicago the next morning, and checked into the hotel about 3:30 p.m. Dillinger came to her room and told her that Hamilton was in the car, badly wounded. Pat quickly left the hotel and drove away with the two gangsters in an attempt to find another "discreet" physician. They tried many doctors but were not able to find an outlaw-friendly practitioner until 11 p.m. That doctor, who thought Hamilton's condition was hopeless, still charged $5,000 to treat him.

Dillinger, Hamilton, and Pat checked into an apartment hotel on the night of January 15 for five days, paying a steep $500 for the accommodations. Two days later, on January 17, Dillinger left the couple to travel to Tucson, Arizona, where the remaining gang members had decided to continue their winter vacation.

Hamilton was nursed by his girlfriend at the residence of Hazel Doyle in Chicago's Lincoln Arms Apartments. Hazel was a hostess at the 225 Club and the wife of gangster Earl Doyle, who was serving time in the Michigan State Penitentiary for robbing the Peoples Savings Bank in

Grand Haven. Pat became ill and was admitted to a local hospital, where she subsequently had an operation and recuperated for two weeks. She then convalesced for about seven weeks at the Detroit home of Russell Clark's mother.[7]

While driving to Tucson, Makley, Clark, and Opal Long were stopped at the New Mexico state line by police looking for a stolen auto. The car in which the three were riding was not the one the cops were seeking, and they were quickly allowed to continue on their way. Makley, who wanted to call on a girl he knew in Tucson, and his two companions were the first of the gang members to arrive, pulling into the southern Arizona town about January 10.

They registered at the three-story Congress Hotel and kept busy by sightseeing and going to nightclubs and gambling rooms in Tucson and across the Mexican border in Nogales with Madge Ritzer and Florence Reeves, who had once been a nightclub entertainer in Nogales. With the easygoing Clark cracking jokes, the group had a lively time, but they spent too much and talked so much that someone told the local police two suspicious-looking men and their dates were carousing in a nightclub.[8]

A fire at the Congress Hotel on the morning of January 23 brought even more attention to the gangsters. Two firemen saw Makley and Clark, with trousers over their pajamas, maneuvering a ladder under a window on the building's third floor. Asked by the firefighters what they were doing, the outlaws said they were trying to retrieve their belongings. The firemen agreed to try to save their clothing and baggage, including a two-foot-long, heavy fabric box in which several machine guns were hidden.

When Makley gave the pair a $50 tip—an exceptionally generous offering during the Depression—they became suspicious. The next day, one of the firemen saw a picture of the Dillinger Gang in *True Detective Magazine*, recognized Clark and Makley, and called the police.

After the fire, Makley, Clark, and Opal moved into a rented house near the University of Arizona campus. Makley, who was going under the name Mr. Davies, impressed the owner, Hattie Strauss, who thought he was a well-dressed, self-confident, successful businessman. She said something looked familiar about him, but Makley smiled and denied that he had been in the news or in Tucson before. Police soon learned of the trio's whereabouts from the drayman who had moved their luggage, and arrested them.

Harry Pierpont and Mary Kinder took their time motoring west and did not arrive in Tucson until about January 16. Shortly thereafter, while Pierpont was driving aimlessly around town, he ran a stop sign. When he spotted a police car nearby, he boldly went to it and told the two officers inside that he was afraid another car was following him. When the officers told him there was nothing to worry about, he made small talk about the weather, talked about buying some property in the area, and even said he was staying at a cabin on South Sixth Street. The officers, who thought Pierpont was a college professor, told him to contact the police if he had any trouble. After thanking them, the bandit told them, "I certainly feel better knowing no one is following me."

On the afternoon of January 24 Dillinger and Billie Frechette, with a Boston bull terrier puppy, drove into town and registered as Mr. and Mrs. Frank Sullivan at a motor court. A few hours later Pierpont and Mary, who had no idea where Dillinger was staying, checked into the same place. When she saw a Hudson parked in front of the cabin next door, Mary asked, "Isn't that Johnnie's car?" Pierpont refused to believe that could be the case, but later that day Mary heard a dog barking next door and then glimpsed Dillinger and Billie through a window. Pierpont still was not convinced until he answered a knock on the door and found Dillinger standing there. "I recognized your Buick, Pete," Dillinger said.

It was agreed that everyone would meet the next morning near the Veterans Hospital close to the main highway about two miles from Tucson. When the outlaws arrived, they decided that, to avoid suspicion, they would rent different houses and act like quiet, well-behaved tourists. Mary said she felt uneasy and urged everyone to leave town. It would turn out to be a prescient hunch.

Makley, Clark, and Opal returned to the Strauss home, where May Miller, a local nightclub singer whom Makley had been dating, had lunch with them. About 1:30 in the afternoon Makley and Miller left to go downtown to pick up a radio Makley had taken to an electronics store to be repaired. Three policemen in a car, who had been watching the Strauss home, followed them to the Grabe Electric Company store.

The policemen followed the couple inside and took them into custody without any resistance. The store's owner facetiously asked the officers if they were looking for a group of criminals. Makley, insisting that he was J. C. Davies, demanded he be taken back to the Strauss home to get his identification papers. However, the cops took the gangster directly to the Tucson jail.

Meanwhile, at the Strauss home, police Sergeant Chet Sherman, wearing a Western Union cap and posing as a messenger, knocked on the front door. Officer Dallas Ford was stationed across the street to back up the diminutive Sherman, and Sergeant Frank Eyman and another officer were behind the house, ready to break through the back door. Clark, who was drinking a bottle of Schlitz Repeal Special beer, decided to play it safe and went into the bedroom while Opal answered the door. Sherman said he had a telegram for Mr. Long and, when Opal tried to sign for it, insisted that he had to deliver it to Long personally.

When Clark came forward, the lawman drew his gun. The much larger gangster grappled for it, forcing Sherman inside and toward the bedroom. When Opal saw Ford running toward the door, she slammed it on the officer's hand, breaking a finger, but he still managed to barge inside. Ford hurried into the bedroom, where Clark had pinned Sherman on the bed and was using both hands to try to take the sergeant's gun from him. Ford hit Clark on the head with his gun butt as Clark reached under a pillow to retrieve his own pistol, but it wasn't there. Opal had thought it would be safer to put the gun under the mattress. Eyman finally crashed through the back door and rushed to Sherman's aid, but he accidentally hit Sherman with his gun when he tried to club the gangster. Clark gave up after Sherman wrestled his own gun free and slugged him.

Pierpont and Mary became aware of the police hunt when they stopped by the Strauss home and saw blood, overturned furniture, and kicked-up rugs. Although the couple fled immediately, a neighbor took down their license number and called the police. As the two were driving out of town, they were pulled over by three police officers in a car, who pretended that the stop was only a minor traffic check for all cars from Florida. Acting unconcerned, Pierpont decided to play along and let Sergeant Frank Eyman get in the back seat to give him directions to the police station, while the other two officers drove behind them. When Pierpont adjusted the rearview mirror to keep Eyman in sight, the nervous policeman quietly took out his gun and placed it on his lap.

Thinking he could bluff his way out of the situation, Pierpont played it cool until he saw Clark's luggage when he entered the office of Chief C. A. Wollard. As Pierpont went for his gun, three officers grabbed him and quickly disarmed and handcuffed him. The police found two handguns on Pierpont, including the service revolver of the murdered Sheriff Jesse Sarber, as well as a machine gun in his luggage.

Until fingerprints proved his identity, the gangster denied who he was. "These cops out here ain't like the kind in Indiana. They pull [their guns] too fast for us," he said. The morose Mary told reporters she'd had a feeling the gang should not have gone to Tucson.

When Dillinger and Billie pulled up in front of the Strauss residence, the rest of the gang members had been taken into police custody, although the outlaw had not heard any of the radio broadcasts concerning the arrests. Three officers were waiting for them. Going to the porch to check out the address, Dillinger turned when he heard footsteps. In the dim light he initially thought the short, stocky man approaching him was Makley, but the portly figure drew a .38 revolver just as another man came out the screen door and shouted, "Stick 'em up!" The other officer approached Dillinger's car and told Billie to get out. Dillinger's hands began to drop slowly, but the gangster obeyed when one of the cops commanded, "Reach for the moon, or I'll cut you in two!"

"My God, how did you know I was in town?" a perplexed Dillinger asked. "I'll be the laughingstock of the country! How did I know that a hick town police force would ever suspicion me?"[9]

Initially taken to the Tucson jail, the outlaws were soon moved under heavy guard to the larger Pima County Jail. In hopes of preventing a breakout, police placed fifteen armed officers around the building. Searches of the gangsters' vehicles, residences, and possessions turned up more than $30,000.

Securely behind bars, Dillinger raved at his captors, "You can't keep me in any two-by-four jail like this! I'll get out and kill you all!" Later, when much calmer, the bandit told Sergeants Eyman and Sherman, "Where you were smart was getting one of us at a time."

Four states put in claims for the Dillinger Gang members. Indiana State Police Captain Matt Leach wanted custody of all four gangsters, but that decision ultimately resided with Arizona's governor.

There was great excitement in the local community, and about 1,500 citizens were allowed to see the outlaws in the county jail. Ironically, Dillinger first gained national notoriety as a result of his capture in Tucson.

On January 26 the four male gang members and their women were given a preliminary hearing before a justice of the peace. When his name was called, the surly Dillinger refused to rise, claiming, "I ain't John Dillinger." When he was forced to stand by the husky guards, he growled, "I'm being framed."

Pierpont cracked jokes until ordered to be silent. When his name was called, he stood, laughing, and said, "That must be me." As the clerk called the name Anne Martin, the alias under which Billie had been booked, Pierpont laughed again and said, "There ain't no such animal."

Charged with being fugitives from justice, bond for each of the men was set at $100,000. Bond for Opal Long, Billie Frechette, and Mary Kinder was set at $5,000 each on charges of obstructing justice. Later, Mary's bond was increased to $100,000 because of her role in the Michigan City breakout.

Later, Jack Weadock of the *Indianapolis Star*, a friend of Makley during his boyhood, went to see him at the county jail. Makley had once shoed horses in the blacksmith shop run by his friend's father.

In high spirits, Fat Charley said, "So you're George's kid?" He then told Weadock he had met a mutual friend during the St. Marys bank robbery and warned the reporter that Pierpont was the most dangerous member of the gang. "If anything happens here, you watch out for Pete," he said. "He's a wild man." Dillinger, he said, was a man who could be trusted, but he was not quite as tough as Pierpont.

Makley told other newsmen that he was not present when Sheriff Sarber was shot, and that he was in Jacksonville, Florida, when the East Chicago robbery took place. He became angry when asked about the recent kidnapping of wealthy St. Paul banker Edward G. Bremer. (Bremer had been abducted January 17 by the Barker-Karpis Gang and was held until a $200,000 ransom was paid.) "What kidnapping?" Makley barked. "That's too low a business for a good gunman. I would never stoop to that. Bank robbery's my trade!"

When Arizona Governor B. B. Moeur visited the jail, Makley eagerly talked with him about such things as the weather and the Old Pueblo. "When I get out of here," he told Moeur, "I'll be hotter than ever. I've gotten out before." Pierpont's mood also improved with the governor's visit. The outlaw quipped that he was sorry to see Moeur in prison.

Pierpont chattered to reporters about the gang's stay in Chicago and claimed they had paid a thousand dollars a week in protection money while there.

Matt Leach also visited Pierpont, but when the lawman appeared, Pierpont stopped being friendly and "raged and swore." "I should have killed you when I had the chance, you dirty ———," he screamed. "You put my mother in jail in Terre Haute, you ———. If I ever get out of this, the first thing I'm going to do is kill you, you rat!"

(After an automobile accident in November, Pierpont's mother and brother Fred had been hauled in for questioning about the gang's whereabouts. Leach had nothing to do with it, but Pierpont still blamed him. Once, Pierpont and Dillinger had been walking in downtown Indianapolis and spotted Leach on Capitol Avenue. Dillinger had a great deal of trouble preventing Pierpont from killing the state police captain.)

Disturbed by the Pierpont's tirade, the other prisoners in the cellblock had to be quieted by the sheriff.

After Leach's visit, Pierpont refused to talk to anyone. An enterprising young Texan being held on a minor charge told visitors he was Pierpont and collected money from them in a tin cup. Makley cooperated in the deception. The next day, the Texan had enough cash to pay his lawyer and his fine, and was freed.

Pierpont also requested that he be allowed to wed Mary, but the nuptials never took place, for officials were unsure if Mary was actually divorced.[10]

Robert Estill, who would be the prosecuting attorney if Dillinger were extradited to Indiana for the killing of patrolman Patrick O'Malley, arrived at the jail to help Leach. With him was patrolman Hobart Wilgus, who identified Dillinger as the killer of the East Chicago police officer. Dillinger refused extradition to Indiana, but nonetheless Arizona authorities released him to Indiana lawmen who would take him to Crown Point to await trial for O'Malley's murder.

The other gangsters wanted to go to Wisconsin, since it did not have a death penalty.[11] Instead, they too were initially sent to Indiana and then to Lima, Ohio, to stand trial for the murder of Sheriff Sarber. Mary Kinder was to be taken to the jail in Indianapolis. Billie and Opal were released.

On January 29 several Indiana lawmen arrived in Tucson to accompany Dillinger on an airplane flight to Chicago, and then by car to the town of Crown Point. When the sheriff told the outlaw he was being taken to Indiana, Dillinger yelled, "You're shanghaiing me!" He had to be subdued and put in handcuffs before he could be led away.

"I won't forget it," Dillinger snarled as he left the jail. "I'll come back here and get the whole damn bunch of you."

He was taken to a waiting car, with Estill inside, and was driven to a nearby airport, where the gangster fought like a wild animal as the lawmen tried to put him aboard a small chartered plane. After a fifty-minute flight the plane landed at Douglas, Arizona, where the group transferred to an American Airlines flight bound for Dallas. During the flight Dillinger admitted to robbing the Greencastle and East Chicago banks. Surprisingly, he also confessed to killing O'Malley, although he said he would deny it in court.

"It was self-defense," he said. "He was going to stop us. He shot first."

The plane also stopped at Fort Worth, Little Rock, and Memphis, where the group boarded another plane that flew to St. Louis and then Chicago. Huge crowds met the aircraft each time it landed.

At 6:10 p.m. on January 30, the lawmen and their charge touched down at Chicago's Midway Airport. Awaiting the group's arrival were Captain John Stege's Dillinger Squad and eighty-five heavily armed police officers.

As Sergeant Frank Reynolds led Dillinger to a row of thirteen police cars that would escort the prisoner to Crown Point, he snarled, "You yellow son of a bitch, if anyone tries to stop us, you'll be the first dead man." Dillinger was forced into the back seat of Reynolds's car and shackled between two Indiana police officers. Reynolds sat next to the driver and told the outlaw, "Just start something."

As a large crowd watched, the procession of police cars and a dozen motorcycles pulled out of Chicago for the trip to the Lake County Jail in Crown Point, where the caravan arrived just before 8 p.m.[12]

In Tucson on the morning of January 30, Makley, Clark, Pierpont, and Mary Kinder were put on a train to Chicago in the custody of Matt Leach, who let Pierpont and Mary share a seat. Mary was taken off the train the next day at Kansas City and was subsequently sent to a women's correctional facility in Indianapolis. She would soon be released.

In an attempt to protect Red Hamilton, Pierpont told newsman Tubby Toms of the *Indianapolis News* that the bandit had died from wounds he sustained during the East Chicago bank robbery, and that his body had been thrown into the Calumet River. When a senator from a western state talked with the three outlaws, they had no comment when asked if the gang had paid the Chicago police a thousand dollars a week for protection during November and December 1933.

Several Chicago lawmen, led by Dillinger Squad head John Stege, met the train in Chicago at 10 p.m. on February 1, and escorted the three gangsters directly to the state prison at Michigan City in a motorcade that included 115 police officers.

"Every day for years something has happened to make me hate the law," Pierpont said during the trip. The quiet Clark, who said he hoped "to die soon," was hard and angry.

"Do me a favor," Makley told Sergeant Reynolds as they approached the prison. "Shoot me through the head so I won't have to go back in there."

Upon their arrival at the institution, the three were immediately placed in solitary confinement and given only bread and water to consume.

Clark, Pierpont, Makley, and Harry Copeland ultimately would be indicted for the murder of Sheriff Jesse Sarber in Lima, Ohio. All but Copeland, who would remain in Indiana to stand trial for robbing the Greencastle bank, would be extradited to Ohio.

The Party's Over

SOME FIVE HUNDRED SPECTATORS WERE on hand when Dillinger entered the Lake County Jail. Inside, a festive atmosphere developed as the huge throng of reporters and lawmen drank beer and conversed with the friendly and talkative gangster. Among those in the crowd were Lake County Prosecutor Robert Estill and Sheriff Lillian Holley, the widow of the former sheriff (who had been killed by a drunken farmer) and who was in charge of the Crown Point jail. "I like Estill," Dillinger told the crowd. He added that, "Mrs. Holley seems like a fine lady."[1]

One reporter asked Dillinger if he was "going collegiate" when he saw his bare head. "Hell, no," the outlaw quipped. "Somebody swiped my hat in Tucson, just as they did my money."[2]

Dillinger insisted he was innocent of the murder charge. "I never killed O'Malley. I never had anything to do with that stickup. I was in Florida when the East Chicago job was pulled, and I can prove it. They can't hold me for that."

He told the reporters that Art Ginnis had set him up to be captured at Dr. Eye's office in Chicago. He also blamed Russell Clark and Charley Makley for drawing unwanted attention to the gang in Tucson by giving such a large tip to the firemen who saved their luggage from the burning hotel. "If the saps had made it only a couple of bucks," he said, "we'd still be safe—and happy."

When reporters asked about John Hamilton, Dillinger, who knew the outlaw was still alive, responded, "Poor Red! He died from the wounds he received in East Chicago. Caught a whole flock of bullets in his stomach. I wasn't with him when he got it, but one of the boys told me about it. I think they dumped his body in the Calumet River. Hamilton has some kids, and before he died he sent me some money to take to them. That was the dough that was in the sacks that the Tucson police took away from me."

The cocky Dillinger was asked if he had really sent a copy of the book *How to be a Detective* to Matt Leach as a Christmas present. "Well," he said, "I was there when it was sent." Everyone burst into laughter.

When someone remarked that it was President Roosevelt's birthday, Dillinger replied, "You can say that I'm for him all the way, and for the NRA—particularly for banks." Again there was laughter.[3]

Dillinger's new home was supposedly so "escape-proof"—inmates had to pass through six steel doors—it was thought that only master magician Harry Houdini might be able to make a successful breakout. And now, dozens of men armed with shotguns and machine guns surrounded the building, just in case Dillinger tried to escape or his gang attempted to free him.

The *Lake County Star* editorialized that the jail was "now as impregnable as the Rock of Gibraltar or granite quarries of the Old World. There will be no jail delivery; there will be no kidnapping; there will no repetition of the Lima, Ohio, jail delivery in which Dillinger was liberated, as long as the 'boys' around the jail can keep their powder dry."[4]

When newspapers published pictures of Prosecutor Estill with his arm around Dillinger, whose fingers appeared to be in the shape of a gun, there was national outrage and Estill's political career was ruined. The picture made DOI Director J. Edgar Hoover furious.

The reaction of Frank J. Loesch, president of the Chicago Crime Commission, was typical:

"I was shocked at seeing newspaper photographs of a prosecutor who is about to prosecute a vicious murderer posing with his arm around the murderer's neck, both of them smiling and exhibiting friendship. For a state's attorney to put himself in such a familiar attitude with a criminal is to install in the mind of the criminal the hope of escape or of avoiding the death penalty. Perhaps it is not unethical, but it is certain that such familiarity breeds contempt for law enforcement in the minds of criminals."[5]

When Dillinger's father was told of the gang's capture he said, "I'm glad he is alive. I've been haunted by the thought of having to bury my boy in frozen ground."

On February 1 he appeared at the jail with attorney Joseph Ryan to help his son. The gangster apologized to his father, who gave him $10, for all the attention the elder Dillinger was receiving.[6]

Seven days later, on February 8, Dillinger was positively identified by five men as the killer of Officer O'Malley. The following day Dillinger was arraigned in the courtroom of Judge William J. Murray. If convicted of O'Malley's murder, the gangster would receive the death sentence. Instead of retaining Ryan, Dillinger chose as his attorney the flamboyant middle-aged Louis Piquett, who was famous for his dramatic courtroom performances in which he dazzled the jury with emotional and melodramatic speeches.

Piquett, who had not attended law school but had taught himself while working as a waiter and bartender, had to take the Illinois bar exam more than a dozen times before he passed it. He became the city prosecutor of Chicago and then a defense attorney. The lawyer demanded that he be given at least four months to prepare for the case. When Judge Murray asked why he wanted so much time, Piquett said, "I've got forty thousand dollars in bonds from the Greencastle robbery, and I'm waiting to fence it to get my fees." Trial was set for March 12.[7]

Dillinger, quiet and well behaved, was put in a cell with three other prisoners. He played cards and read the bible, magazines and books, but he was not given any newspapers. He was, however, allowed to write to and receive mail from his father and sister.[8] Several visitors were allowed to see Dillinger, including Billie Frechette, who called herself Mrs. John Dillinger; Piquett and two other attorneys from his office; and Meyer Bogue, a friend from Michigan City.[9]

The six-foot-five police chief of Valparaiso, Indiana, Jerome Fraker, also visited the gangster, who told him that he and other members of the gang had once passed him in a car as he was directing traffic around a dead horse.

Laughing, Dillinger told the lawman, "You big Indian, you don't know how lucky you were, or how many guns were trained on you."

Dillinger desperately wanted to escape. Estill attempted to have the prisoner moved to a more secure prison, such as the state prison in Michigan City, but Judge Murray rejected the idea because he thought it would be a sign of weakness.[10] Dillinger devised a plan whereby his gang, headed by Hamilton, would dynamite the jail and free him. He asked Billie to be his go-between, but when she returned, she told Dillinger that Hamilton had rejected the idea. Most of the gang members were themselves in jail, and those who were not knew it would be suicide to attempt a breakout at the heavily fortified jail. Dillinger understood he would have to do it himself.

Through attorney Piquett, the outlaw managed to bribe jail officers (most accounts implicate Deputy Sheriff Ernest Blunk) to smuggle a wooden gun into the facility, and Edwin J. Saager, a garage mechanic, who was to provide a fast car for the escape.[11] There is also an unlikely story, according to author Toland, that Piquett met a judge on the grounds of the Chicago World's Fair and gave him a bribe of several thousand dollars to smuggle a real gun into the jail.[12] However, a real gun would suggest that someone had been bribed, so by bringing in a fake weapon, a cover story could be devised that Dillinger had somehow gotten a razor and used it to carve a crude pistol from a piece of wood, which he then darkened with bootblack to make it appear authentic.

Red Hamilton asked Homer Van Meter and Baby Face Nelson to loan the money needed for the bribes. The bribes were actually distributed by Tommy Carroll, since he was not that well known in law enforcement circles.

The breakout was originally planned for Friday, March 2, 1934. However, Piquett had not yet acquired the wooden gun. About noon on that day Piquett assistant Arthur O'Leary received the bogus weapon, and someone subsequently passed it to Blunk. Early on the chilly, rainy morning of March 3, Blunk gave the wooden gun to Dillinger, who was waiting for his chance to escape from the "escape-proof" jail.

"Can Dillinger
Take Orders?"

B Y MID-FEBRUARY 1934, THE ONLY members of the Baby Face Nelson
Gang who remained free were Nelson, Homer Van Meter and Red
Hamilton. Nelson was suspected of killing of William S. "Three-Fingered
Jack" White on January 23 in his Oak Park, Illinois, apartment, in retaliation for deserting the gang at the bank robbery in Grand Haven. However, the diminutive bandit was elsewhere at the time of the slaying, and
most authorities believe that White was murdered by gangster Fred
Goetz, also known as "Shotgun George" Zeigler, because he had been
talking to federal agents.[1]

Hamilton was being sought for the murder of Peter de Young, a
watchman at the South Holland Trust and Savings Bank in Chicago. De
Young had been shot in the head and body when he surprised three
men inside the bank early on the morning of February 10. Before he
died late that evening, de Young was shown a picture of Hamilton and
told police he believed the man in the photo was the leader of the robbery crew.[2]

Now it was Van Meter who asked Nelson if he wanted to join the Dillinger Gang. With Dillinger set to break out of the Crown Point jail and wanting immediate action so that he could repay Nelson and Van Meter some of the money they had fronted for bribes, Nelson was ready to pull two big bank jobs—in Sioux Falls, South Dakota, and Mason City, Iowa—that had been set up by jug marker Eddie Green.

But when Nelson asked, "Can Dillinger take orders?" the two outlaws became furious at the diminutive bandit's impudence. However, Van Meter and Hamilton nevertheless meekly agreed to let Baby Face be the gang's leader.[3]

Van Meter and Marie Conforti, who had moved to Minneapolis in late December 1933, first met Eddie Green that month through Dutch Sawyer. During January and February 1934 the couple lived in Apartment 201 at the Josephine Apartments, 3310 Fremont Avenue South, in Minneapolis, under the aliases Mr. and Mrs. John Ober. They met frequently with Green and his girlfriend, Bessie Skinner, who lived next door, at 3300 Fremont Avenue South, in an apartment Green had rented under the name T. J. Randall.[4]

Van Meter frequented the Green Lantern Saloon in nearby St. Paul and liked to go to the movies, especially Eddie Cantor films.[5] He donated $1,000 to St. Paul Chief of Police Thomas "Big Tom" Brown's re-election campaign. Van Meter, who had been using the name John L. Ober, told Marie his "real" name was Ted Ancker, giving her an alias for an alias. Marie would later tell federal authorities that the gangster "never told me what his business was. He never told me the address of any business he was connected with, and never introduced me to any of his friends."[6]

Frank McCormick's Town Talk Sandwich Shop in downtown St. Paul was also a popular hangout of Van Meter. According to fry cook Charles Reiter, "Van Meter would want the special center cut of the ham, the best. He'd tip me a quarter, which was an hour's wage!"

In spite of the manhunt that had been mounted for Van Meter, he often drove to the Hollyhocks restaurant with his girlfriend to enjoy its great steaks, and would eat in his car for security. According to Opal Long, "Homer Van Meter was more or less a lone wolf. He kept to himself as much as possible."

As March arrived, the surviving Nelson Gang members continued to lay low, waiting for Dillinger's breakout and the bank robberies that lay ahead.

Just Like Houdini

J UST AFTER NINE O'CLOCK ON the morning of March 3, 1934, attendant Sam Cahoon, carrying soup, and trusties entered the lower tier of cells at the Crown Point jail as Dillinger and fourteen other prisoners were exercising nearby. As the group passed by Dillinger, the gangster thrust the wooden gun into Cahoon's side and snarled, "Do as I tell you, or I'll blow you apart. Call Blunk."

When Deputy Sheriff Blunk came over, Dillinger jammed the gun into his stomach. Then the gangster told the trusty, "Now call Baker."

"John, I can't do it," Cahoon replied.

"All right. You don't have to," Dillinger said. "I'm not going to hurt you. Blunk will do it. But I'll have to lock you up. Blunk, give me a hand here!"

After Blunk opened the door to the cell tier, Cahoon was locked into one of the cells. Blunk then called for Warden Lou Baker, who also was quickly taken prisoner.

Dillinger told the latter, "I don't like to have to do this, Mr. Baker. I'll put you in where Cahoon can keep you company."

Blunk was made to continue to call for guards Kenneth Houk, Marshall Keithley, and Mack Brown, who Dillinger locked into cells. Herbert Youngblood, a black man jailed while awaiting trial for the murder of a Gary fruit peddler, agreed to go with Dillinger. As they left the cell tier they encountered trusty John Kowaliszyn, who offered no resistance and was taken prisoner.

After Dillinger took a full set of keys from the trusty, he, Younglood, and Blunk entered the jail office, where guns and ammunition were stored. Dillinger walked up to a guard who was dozing in a chair with his back to the door, and put the wooden gun to the back of his head. With his other hand the outlaw took a machine gun from a nearby rack, telling the guard curtly, "This is Dillinger. If you move a muscle, I'm going to blow your head off your shoulders."

At Dillinger's command, Youngblood grabbed a machine gun that was in the guard's lap. With two machine guns now in their hands, the escaping prisoners were in a powerful position. Dillinger toured the first floor of the jail, forcing his prisoners to march in front of him. When they encountered an Indiana National Guardsman, the man was relieved of his .45-caliber pistol. With too many to hostages to handle, Dillinger took his captives back to the cellblock.

Then Dillinger, Youngblood, and Blunk went into the kitchen, where three more guards, the warden's wife, and her mother, Mary Linton, were taken prisoner. Dillinger put on a hat and overcoat belonging to Cahoon that had been hanging on the wall.

"Don't be frightened, Mrs. Baker," Dillinger said. "We're not going to hurt anybody. You two be good girls, and nothing will happen to you."

The women were locked in the basement laundry, and the guards were taken to the cellblock where Dillinger had deposited the other captives. A through search of the jail by the escaping inmates turned up another five guards, who were also taken to the cellblock. Dillinger, Youngblood, and Blunk finally went outside and slipped into the jail garage, where there were two cars, but no keys were available. They returned to the jail, and Dillinger went through the warden's desk.

"We're liable to need some money. Let's see what the boys upstairs have got in their pockets," he said. Once in the cellblock, he told the surprised imprisoned guards, "I'm afraid we need to take up a collection. I want all of you to give, and give generously."

After getting $15 from the group, Dillinger laughed and rapped the wooden gun on the cell bars.

"See what I locked all of you monkeys up with?" he taunted. "Nothing but a little piece of wood. Well, so long, boys. I'll have to be moving on."

He told Warden Baker, "I'm sorry to have to do this to you, Mr. Baker. But you can see how it is."

"Yes, John, I can see how it is."

After Dillinger had locked several doors behind him, he, Youngblood, Deputy Blunk, and three trusties who had joined the group walked through the jail's kitchen door into the side yard. Dillinger and Youngblood, each armed with a machine gun, led the group about fifty yards across the yard and entered the back door of the public Main Street Garage. No guards were around, although many were stationed in front of the jail, but none apparently heard the clamor of more than thirty jail employees yelling from the facility's windows to be let out.

It is interesting to note that the sister of the garage's owner, Clyde Rothermel, was married to a brother of Red Hamilton. Rothermel knew there was going to be an escape attempt, but he wanted to have nothing to do with it, since he would be a obvious suspect, so he stayed away. Oddly, no one seriously investigated him. Mechanic Edwin Saager and Robert Volk, a mail truck driver, were the only people inside the garage. Although Volk had a pistol, he offered no resistance.

"What's the fastest car in the joint?" Dillinger asked.

Saager showed him Sheriff Holley's Ford, all ready to go. Dillinger allowed the three trusties to return to the jail, while he got into the car's passenger seat and motioned Blunk into the driver's seat, and Youngblood and Saager piled into the back. Holding a machine gun on his lap, Dillinger ordered Blunk to drive out of the garage.

"Maybe I ought to go back and tell Mrs. Holley I'm leaving," the gangster said. "She seemed like an awfully nice lady, and I don't want her to feel hurt about all this."[1]

As the car sped away from the jail, Blunk came close to hitting a passing motorist and drove through a red light. Dillinger would later say that he was tempted to rob a nearby bank.

Mail truck driver Volk immediately called the police, then ran out of the garage and yelled at a volunteer guard of the Farmers Protective Association stationed across the street, telling him what had transpired.

"You don't mean it! Dillinger's got away?" the guard said.

"Sure! Can't you hear all the hollering over at the jail?"

Volk hurried next door to the prosecutor's office, where numerous guards had been stationed to prevent a raid on the jail, yelling, "Dillinger's escaped."

"You're nuts," one guard replied. "You want us to lock you up?"

Deputy Prosecutor Floyd Vance walked up, and Volk told him, "Dillinger escaped."

"Is that right?" Vance replied.

Several volunteers tried unsuccessfully to enter the jail, and it took nearly ten minutes before they could gain access and release the imprisoned jail employees.[2] Sheriff Holley was first told of the escape by John Hudak, a trusty, and immediately notified the state police. She thought the escape was "too ridiculous for words" and later told reporters:

"Dillinger took one chance in a million, and all the breaks were with him and against me. Ordinarily I would have walked out of this room into the jail just about at that time. In the six weeks he's been here, though, I have been on the job until 3 a.m., and haven't tried to sleep until 4 a.m. At 5 a.m. I had gotten to sleep.

"I was dressing when a trusty ran into my room with a shotgun and said, 'Dillinger's out!' I thought he had gone mad. Then I saw he hadn't. He said, 'Have you got a gun there? I can't shoot with this thing.' I handed him my pistol and said, 'Kill him.' But they had gone. . . . How this could have happened I don't quite see."[3]

The sheriff denied a report that she had said the job was too big for a woman. "Oh, hell's fire, of course not," she scoffed, adding, "If I ever see John Dillinger again, I'll shoot him dead with my own pistol."[4]

As the escapees left Crown Point behind, Dillinger worried about roadblocks as they passed through the town of St. John and then traveled on gravel roads. He had Blunk stop once to remove the red light from the front of the sheriff's car, then told the deputy as they proceeded, "Take your time, take your time. There's no hurry. Thirty miles an hour is fast enough."

As they drove along the muddy backroads, Dillinger sang "I'm Heading for the Last Roundup." At a rural crossroads known as Lilley's Corner, about two miles from Peotone, Illinois, the car skidded into a ditch filled with water. It took Saager half an hour to put chains on the rear wheels so the vehicle could be extricated from the ditch.

Dillinger remained calm and said, "What's time to me?"

After Saager had finished, the outlaw set the two hostages free, giving them $4 for carfare and food.

"I'd give you guys more, but that's all I can spare," Dillinger told Saager and Deputy Blunk.

Suspecting that a black man and a white man traveling together would look too conspicuous, Dillinger told Youngblood to hunker down in the back seat of the car. Then, waving at the two men he'd left on the side of the road, the gangster drove off toward Chicago, twenty-five miles away.

A farmer picked up Saager and Blunk and took them into town, where they explained what had happened and called Sheriff Holley.[5]

"I was never scared of Dillinger," Blunk said. "I knew he wouldn't hurt me. He was too nice for that."

Since there was no extensive radio system that could quickly alert police throughout the region about the escape, Dillinger and Youngblood reached Chicago without incident. The police in Indianapolis learned of the escape from local newspapers.

Greatly helping Dillinger and Youngblood was the fact that authorities had given out the wrong license number for the stolen car. Nevertheless, Lorimer Hyde, a Chicago detective, saw the sheriff's car and followed it, but he lost his quarry twice during the afternoon.

Piquett learned of the escape from a telephone call at about 9:45 that morning, while Billie Frechette was in his office. At about four o'clock that afternoon Piquett met Dillinger and Youngblood for a couple of minutes in a car on Belmont Avenue, after which Youngblood went off on his own. Four hours later the lawyer again met Dillinger, who was now with Billie and another woman, on Halsted Street, just half a block from the Town Hall police station. Dillinger pulled out a wooden gun that he said he had used in the jail escape.

"I told him," Piquett would say later, "that it was impossible for him to defeat the law. I told him it was my duty to advise him to surrender and let me take him to Town Hall station. He said he would do it later."

Acting Chicago Police Commissioner Ira McDowell warned that, "If Dillinger sticks his head inside Chicago, he will be shot at first sight. Those are my orders."

Sheriff Holley's abandoned car was finally found on March 5 on Chicago's North Side.[6]

Aftermath

ILLINGER'S BREAKOUT FROM A SUPPOSEDLY "escape-proof" jail caused a sensation throughout America and much of the world. One man wrote to an Indianapolis newspaper, "I'm for Johnnie. Dillinger never robbed poor people—he robbed those who became rich from robbing the poor." Even President Franklin Roosevelt, in a radio "Fireside Chat," told the nation he was "shocked by the public adulation of a vicious criminal. . . . It permits police to be corrupted and intimidated, and romanticizes men who are nothing but insane murderers."[1]

J. Edgar Hoover called the event "a damnable outrage" and said, "Someone is guilty either of nonfeasance or malfeasance. Either negligence or corruption must be at the bottom of this. That is true of nearly all jailbreaks. Escape from a good jail is impossible if the jail authorities are both diligent and honest." Republicans strongly criticized the Democratic governments of Indiana and Lake County.

Many thought it was humorous. A letter from California addressed to "Harry Meyers, Wooden Gun, Indiana," was actually delivered. Some people thought Crown Point should be renamed Clown Point.

Dillinger's friends and relatives were relieved. His father said in Mooresville, "It makes a fellow feel a little better, but of course they may catch him. . . . Guess I'll start listening to the radio again now. When he was out before, that's about all I did when I wasn't working." Mary Kinder was delighted to hear the news and was glad she could prove she had nothing to do with the escape.[2]

The *Chicago Tribune* told its readers that Dillinger, "aided only by his desperate courage and a little toy pistol he had made himself escaped yesterday morning from the heavily guarded jail at Crown Point." Although Colonel Henry Barrett Chamberlin, operating director of the Chicago Crime Commission, said he was "speechless," he continued to say, "It's just one of those impossible—why, I'm speechless. The idea of a man with a record like this getting away! There should have been a competent, trustworthy, proven guard assigned to watch Dillinger day and night. I can't understand it."

Clarence Marley, the Mooresville justice of the peace who had arranged for Dillinger to be held for trial for the robbery of Mr. Morgan ten years before, put a notice on a bulletin board in the city hall, which read:

JOHNNY ISN'T WITH THEM ANY MORE.

At least one news report commented on the "half-comic exploit of Dillinger in taking complete possession of the fortress-like prison," which was "typically Dillinger-like. It was marked by desperate courage, unhurried precision, and an occasional laugh for punctuation."

Many letters to the editor supported Dillinger. One writer said, "Governor McNutt, why not give Dillinger a gold medal and a pardon? He deserves both. Hurray, for you, John. May you never be caught!" Only a few letters criticized the gangster and disagreed with the idea of Dillinger being a Robin Hood. Many investigations were made of the escape, but nothing was ever proven. According to the *Crown Point Register*, publicity helped Dillinger "because it caused to build up an unwholesome fear of him and made his toy pistol a dangerous weapon. What would have been just a plank in the hands of an ordinary prisoner helped to bring an instant compliance to Dillinger's commands."[3]

A washboard that had been whittled on was found under Dillinger's mattress, and wood shavings lay nearby.[4]

On February 13, some three weeks before the Crown Point breakout, Harry Pierpont, Charley Makley, and Russell Clark had been taken from Michigan City to Lima, Ohio, to be arraigned for the murder of Sheriff

Sarber. After Leo M. Larkins, police chief of Findlay, Ohio, who was serving as a guard, refused to loosen Makley's handcuffs at the Indiana State Prison, Makley would not come out his cell. Larkins was forced to drag the gangster out. On the trip to Lima, Makley was shackled to Larkins.

When he arrived at the Ohio jail, Makley told reporters, "Tell the world I don't like it."

He told Larkins, "I'll get you when I get out, and if I don't get out, I'll have some of my friends get you!"

When the police chief challenged Makley, the gangster barked, "You know I'm handcuffed." Unruffled, Larkins, a former football player, shot back, "Take 'em off, and I'll give you the licking of your life."

Makley loudly protested his treatment at the county jail. He complained about not being permitted to communicate with the outside, referred to the jail as a dungeon, and said the prisoners had been treated like a "pack of wolves."[5] On February 17 they were arraigned in Lima. All three were granted trials and entered not-guilty pleas to charges of killing Sarber.[6]

When Dillinger escaped from the Crown Point Jail on March 3, the three men, expecting to be rescued soon, put on their best clothes. Residents and town officials in Lima, terrified that an attempt would be made to free the prisoners, asked that the National Guardsmen be called out to protect them. The number of guards at the jail was doubled, and sandbag emplacements containing heavy machine guns were set up outside. Ohio Guard Brigadier General Harold M. Bush announced that Dillinger was headed toward Lima.[7]

No breakout attempt was mounted, however, and on March 8 Harry Pierpont became the first of the outlaws indicted for Sheriff Sarber's slaying to go on trial before Judge Emmit E. Everett in common pleas court. The atmosphere was much like a carnival with a great sense of panic. Special passes were required to enter the courtroom, which was kept locked during the trail, and even jurors were searched as they entered. Armed guards stood around the courtroom, even though Pierpont was shackled hand and foot. Don Sarber, who had succeeded his slain father as Allen County sheriff, sometimes carried a machine gun in court.

Pierpont's attorney, Jessie Levy, asked jurors if they were influenced by the "veritable fortress" in the courtroom. "The career and character of John Dillinger" justified the precautions, prosecutor Ernest Botkin replied. The prosecutor demanded the death penalty because "it was necessary, to accomplish their purpose in a few minutes, that they act viciously, cruelly, murderously, as they did, to secure the possession of the keys so that John Dillinger could be liberated. Death was part of the plan for this crime."

The testimony of Pierpont's mother, Lena, that the outlaw was "at my house eating supper" at the time of the murder carried little weight when measured against Mrs. Sarber's and Deputy Sharp's identification of Pierpont as the sheriff's killer. According to Lena, when the police raided her home at midnight on the day of the killing, all of the gang had left except for her son Harry and his "wife" Mary, who were hiding in a secret room above the kitchen.

Pierpont testified that Sarber's gun, which had been found on the gangster when he was captured in Tucson, had been given to him by Dillinger on Christmas at Daytona Beach, Florida. He insisted that Edward Shouse, who had testified against him, was insane. When Prosecutor Botkin declared that Pierpont had stolen more than $250,000, the gangster replied that if he had, "at least I wasn't elected a president of a bank first." The courtroom roared with laughter. But on March 11 he was found guilty of murder in the first degree, with no recommendation for mercy, which meant a mandatory death sentence.

When Pierpont walked past Makley's cell after the trial, Makley asked, "Well, what was it?"

"Well, what would it be?" Pierpont replied.

Charley Makley's trial commenced on March 12. As the gangster, whom the press referred to as "rotund and slow-moving," left the jail for court, Pierpont cried out, "Good luck, Charley!" Makley's sisters, Florence and Mildred, and his half-brother Fred, the only defense witness, attended the trial, during which Judge Everett ominously intoned, "We have received direct word that Dillinger is on his way here with armed men."

Governor White and his daughter, who were on hand for the trial, were placed under rigid security when rumors circulated that Dillinger might kidnap them and use the two to ransom his fellow gangsters. Three heavily armed men, led by Dillinger, were reportedly seen driving in northwestern Ohio. When the defense attorney entered a motion for a change of venue, because the heavy military presence was prejudicial to his client, the judge summarily overruled it.

During the proceedings, which lasted six days from jury selection to verdict, the pleasant-faced Makley had his hands in iron cuffs, and his legs were placed in chains as soon as he was seated. Ed Shouse refused to testify against Makley. After the closing arguments, the jury deliberated throughout the night of Friday, March 16, and the following morning at ten o'clock found Makley guilty of first-degree murder. There was no recommendation of mercy, meaning Makley would also face the death penalty.

According to author G. Russell Girardin, "There is small need to mourn the ranting, cursing, violent Pierpont, but sympathy for the genial and mild-mannered Charles Makley is not totally out of place. There was no stain of murder upon his record, and no thought of murder in his mind when he went to take Dillinger from the Lima jail. It was solely the act of the trigger-happy Pierpont that was now sending him to his death."

Russell "Boobie" Clark was the last to be tried. His wife, Opal Long, paid Louis Piquett to help defend Clark, but when the flamboyant lawyer went to Lima he was harassed and even jailed by the local police. Finally he just gave up.

Clark's trial began on Monday, March 19. Jury selection took two days, and testimony began on Wednesday. Clark's attorney Jessie Levy asked Judge Everett for a directed verdict of not guilty on the basis that Clark "doesn't believe in capital punishment."

"That is utterly silly for you to say," the startled judge replied, "because he is on trial for murder, that he don't believe in capital punishment."

Levy answered, "Well, it may be utterly silly, but nevertheless, there are certain guarantees under the Constitution that this defendant is entitled to, and he does not believe in it, and he makes this motion and he deserves that the court rule on it."

The judge rendered an adverse ruling.

Shouse testified that, "Clark only fired one shot that night, and that wounded him [Clark] in the hand." Clark's mother, May, insisted that her son had been in Detroit at the time of the murder. A brother-in-law, Andrew Stracham, and a sister, Mrs. Beulah Stracham, also testified on Clark's behalf. Once again the number of guards around the jail was increased.

The outlaw, often yawning and dozing off, thought a death sentence was a foregone conclusion. But while the jury found him guilty of first-degree murder on March 24, there was a recommendation for mercy, which meant he might receive a sentence of life imprisonment instead of death. The verdict caused Clark to be affected for the first time and he cried.[8]

That same day, both Pierpont and Makley were sentenced to die on Friday, July 13; the date was later changed to October 17. The death sentences were the first ever handed down in Allen County, and newspaper accounts described Pierpont as "brazen and defiant." Clark received a life sentence on March 26.

Lawyer Jessie Levy said he would appeal Pierpont's and Makley's verdicts to the U.S. Supreme Court on the basis of prejudice, citing the infamous case in Scottsboro, Alabama, in which nine black men had been condemned to death for raping a white woman.

"The facts are entirely different," said Judge Everett.

Levy responded, "The only fact different is color."[9]

In a sleet storm on March 27, 1934, the three criminals were taken from Lima to the Ohio State Penitentiary at Columbus in a caravan led by forty-five armed officers. National Guardsmen in two trucks trained machine guns on a crowd of spectators at the prison.[10] That day Homer Van Meter called a lawyer in Fort Wayne, Indiana, to "talk about the Dillinger Gang," but the attorney refused to help the outlaws. Van Meter also hired an attorney to get funds from his estate, but the lawyer was unsuccessful.[11]

The Second
Dillinger Gang

ALTHOUGH THE FEDERAL DIVISION OF Investigation had helped local law-men in the hunt for Dillinger for months, the agency officially became involved in the search when Dillinger drove Sheriff Holley's stolen police car from Indiana to Illinois. By crossing the state line, he had violated the federal Dyer Act.[1]

After the breakout Director J. Edgar Hoover called Melvin Purvis, special agent in charge of the division's Chicago field office, to express surprise that the office "had done practically nothing in this matter," although Hoover previously had ordered that they were "not to take the initiative." He insisted there would be no more inaction and told Purvis to "take immediate steps" and "put forth every effort" to appre-hend the criminal.[2]

On March 4 in St. Paul, Nelson may have shot and killed a Theodore W. Kidder, a thirty-five-year-old paint salesman with the National Lead Company. Kidder and his mother-in-law were returning home from a children's party in Minneapolis when, at the intersection of Lake Street and Chicago Avenue in that city, a Hudson sedan containing Nelson and other criminals had a traffic altercation with Kidder's vehicle. Kidder sped away, but the gangsters tailed him to his home in St. Louis Park.

As Kidder's wife watched, the driver called her husband by name and one of the car's occupants jumped out and murdered Kidder by shooting him several times with a .32-caliber handgun as he approached. It is a mystery why Kidder, who worked at a sporting goods store and sold guns and ammunition, was killed. It may have been because of an arms transaction.

Police investigators got a good description of Nelson and his vehicle, as well as its California license number, G-H-475, which the DOI "traced to James Rogers, the alias used by [Lester] Gillis when he purchased the Hudson sedan." The incident was big news in the Twin Cities area, but it was soon forgotten because it was overshadowed by Dillinger's sensational escape from the Crown Point jail the previous day.[3]

On March 5 Nelson went to a St. Paul hideout where Dillinger, Billie Frechette, Red Hamilton, Homer Van Meter, Eddie Green, and Tommy Carroll, who was suspected of attempting to rob the National Bank of Topeka, Kansas, in February, were gathered around a table planning a bank heist.

Desperate to add another member to the gang, Dillinger curtly asked Nelson if he wanted to join his crew and told him that any money stolen would be split equally. Baby Face immediately accepted the offer and joined the discussion. Van Meter laughed when the bantam gangster suggested they should go through the bank's front door shooting. Moving angrily toward Van Meter, Nelson was stopped by Dillinger, who was able to calm things down.[4] Van Meter was close to Dillinger, so close that an FBI informer once reported that "Van Meter seemed to dominate over Dillinger," who "would ask the advice of Van Meter about different things."[5]

Referred to by many historians as the "second Dillinger Gang," the outfit was actually an enhanced version of the Baby Face Nelson Gang, since its members included Nelson, Green, Carroll, and Van Meter. Hamilton also joined the crew. Dillinger detested the psychotic Nelson, but he needed him and his confederates. He also needed money to finance a permanent escape, pay back Nelson and Van Meter for the bribe money they had advanced, and to pay legal expenses for Pierpont, Clark, and Makley.[6]

In early March, Dillinger and Billie moved into Apartment 106 of the Santa Monica Apartments in Minneapolis, where they lived under the names Mr. and Mrs. Irwin Olson. Just one block away was the apartment Eddie Green shared with Bessie Skinner.[7] Dillinger told Green not to take Bessie to see the movie *Fashions* because it would put ideas into her head.[8] Dillinger and Bessie did not like each other, and Bessie also detested Billie because she thought Dillinger's girlfriend was too vulgar and drank too much.

Smart enough to know it was not wise to live near the notorious John Dillinger, Green would soon move to an apartment in St. Paul, using the name D. A. Stevens. A few days later, however, Dillinger and Billie would move into an apartment nearby, eliminating any need for Green to retain his apartment in that city; he would ultimately let Van Meter live there. During the spring of 1934 the Greens were frequent visitors to Nelson's apartment in Minneapolis.[9]

Also that spring, the gang members traveled to Louie's Place, a roadhouse in Fox River Grove, Illinois, some forty-five miles north of Chicago, where they had dinner. They were grossly overcharged by the management to get rid of them.[10]

Just before 10 a.m. on March 6, three days after Dillinger's daring escape from the Crown Point jail, a car slowly pulled to the curb near the Security National Bank and Trust Company in Sioux Falls, South Dakota. As several men in long overcoats quickly emerged and began to head for the bank's front door, a female employee looking out the window said, "There's a bunch of holdup men. I don't like the look of this."

Upon entering the bank, Nelson, carrying a machine gun, screamed, "This is a holdup! Everyone on the floor!" An alarm suddenly began ringed loudly outside the bank, prompting the angry and nervous Nelson to poke his machine gun at several employees and demand, "I'd like to know who set that alarm off! Who did it? Who?"

"If you want to get killed, just make some move!"

Meanwhile, Dillinger and Van Meter calmly went about cleaning out the bank's vaults, ultimately grabbing some $49,000.

Everything was going smoothly until Nelson spotted off-duty policeman Hale Keith getting out of a car and hitching up his pants. Jumping on a desk, Nelson fired several shots through the bank's front window, four of which struck Keith. He would later recover.

"I got one of them!" shouted a jubilant Nelson. "I got one of them!"

As police and townspeople attracted by the clanging alarm bell began to arrive, Carroll, armed with a machine gun, took several officers captive, including the Sioux Falls police chief. When the crowd of about a thousand mostly good-natured citizens began to press in too closely,[11] he fired several shots into the air to move them back.

Dillinger, Green, and Van Meter finished their tasks and emerged from the vault area as Nelson was selecting a group of bank employees and customers to serve as human shields when the gangsters made a break for their getaway car. Nelson saw a man approaching the entrance and squeezed off a volley from his machine gun that shattered the glass above his head.

With the bank manager and four tellers as hostages, the gang erupted from the bank and joined Carroll, who was standing in the middle of the street guarding several policemen he had taken prisoner. On nearby rooftops several lawmen, hoping to shoot down the robbers as they exited the bank, held their fire as the hostages moved between them and their targets.

Upon reaching the getaway car, the bandits scrambled inside, forcing six of the hostages to stand on the vehicle's running boards to protect the gang from gunfire. The local sheriff managed to fire several rounds into the car's radiator as it slowly drove out of town. When the outlaws noticed two vehicles pursuing them, they pulled over and spread roofing nails across the pavement, which punctured the cars' tires.

After commandeering a farmer's car, the gangsters transferred their loot, extra weapons, and spare cans of gasoline into the vehicle and piled inside, telling their hostages to walk away. Traveling down countless back roads in hopes of eluding roadblocks and pursuers, the gang made it back to Minneapolis, entering the city after dark.

One newspaper noted that in Sioux Falls, despite "the apparent ruthlessness of the gang, small groups of citizens gathered in the street, others peered from doorways or behind poles or other available shelter to watch the proceedings." One resident took a snapshot of the robbery and sold it to the Associated Press syndicate, which published it with the caption: "Here's a real hold-up in action."[12]

At Eddie Green's apartment in Minneapolis, Green attempted to divide the loot, but the infuriated Nelson, who strongly disliked Green, grabbed a machine gun, pointed at the gangster, and asked him who the hell had given him the job of gang counter. Diplomatically, Dillinger told Green to let Nelson count the loot, saying, "It'll come out just the same."

Taking his time, the petulant Nelson divided the cash into neat piles. John Paul Chase was to get a portion of Nelson's share, and there were also expenses for such things as bulletproof vests, weapons, and protection.

Jug marker Eddie Green found a real plum in the First National Bank of Mason City, Iowa, whose vault held almost a quarter-million dollars. At 7 p.m. on March 12 Green went to the home of Harry Fisher, the bank's assistant cashier, to make sure he could recognize the man responsible for opening the main vault each morning. When Fisher came to the door, Green asked if the address was 1228 North President. Fisher told him that address was a few doors up the street. Looking intensely at the assistant cashier, Green simply said, "Oh" and walked off in the wrong direction.

The next day, after having lunch and checking out of the local YWCA, Green and Van Meter drove in a big Buick to a rural school, where they met a car containing Dillinger, Carroll, Hamilton, and Nelson. The four gangsters transferred to the Buick and headed toward the First National Bank. It was a cold day, with flurries of snow.

As the gangsters were getting out of the Buick in front of the bank at 2:20 p.m., cameraman H. C. Kunkleman was filming downtown Mason City for a documentary. He put away his equipment when one of the robbers yelled at him to stop filming. Carroll, armed with a rifle, remained at the car, while Nelson took up a position in the rear alley next to the bank. The others—Dillinger, Van Meter, Green, and Hamilton—entered the bank.

This time things went badly. One of the gangsters fired into the ceiling, and the bandits ordered, "Hands up! Hands up! Everybody on the floor."

Willis Bagley, the bank president, thought "a crazy man was loose" when Van Meter, who knew Bagley had the key to the vault, fired several rounds through the door of an office after Bagley had run into the room and locked the door. When he couldn't gain access to the office or force Bagley out, the outlaw stalked across the lobby to help clean out the teller cages.

Green was hit in the back and almost knocked down by a tear-gas shell fired by bank guard Tom Walters from a specially equipped seven-foot steel and bulletproof-glass cage above the main lobby. Green sprayed the cage with machine-gun fire, wounding the guard as some of the bullets passed through the small gun slot.

A female customer who had apparently lost a shoe as she ran from the bank and down the alleyway toward Nelson, screamed at the bandit, "Get to work and notify somebody! The bank is being held up!"

"Lady, you're telling me!" Baby Face shouted, waving her back with his machine gun.

When Nelson saw a man—R. L. James, the local school board secretary—crouched over and moving toward him, he ordered him to stop.

James did not hear the command, and when he continued to approach the bandit, Nelson shot him twice in the leg.

As tear gas swirled inside the bank, Hamilton pushed cashier Harry Fisher toward the rear of the building, where Fisher unlocked a steel gate leading to the vault and stepped inside. The gate snapped shut before Hamilton could enter, and Fisher, claiming he could not open the barrier from his side, began passing stacks of one-dollar bills through the bars to the gangster.

Hamilton, who could see many stacks of bills, many of them larger denominations, began waving his machine gun at Fisher, threatening to shoot him if he didn't open up the vault gate. "I can't," the cashier reiterated. "I already told you, I don't have the key. All I can do is continue to shove the money out through the bars."

As Fisher continued to hand Hamilton several more bundles of dollar bills, Van Meter yelled, "Let's go!"

"If you don't hurry up, I'm going to shoot you," Hamilton threatened.

"C'mon!" yelled Van Meter, who was anxious to exit the area.

"Just give me another minute," Hamilton pleaded, then ordered Fisher to "Gimme the big bills!" But Fisher continued to hand him bundles of one-dollar bills.

When Van Meter screamed, "We're going now!" the frustrated Hamilton finally decided to join him. His sack contained a mere $20,000 in small bills; Fisher's quick thinking had caused the bandits to leave behind more than $200,000. "It's hell to leave all the money in there!" Hamilton said as he ran to join the others. Fisher quickly closed the vault door.

Dillinger, who had led a group of hostages outside and had them line up in front of the bank, was pacing the sidewalk, expecting the police to arrive at any moment. When he saw James lying on the ground, bleeding, he looked at Nelson and asked, "Did you have to do that?" Nelson merely shrugged.

Judge John Shipley, watching the action unfold from the window of his third-floor office in the bank, fired an old pistol at Dillinger when he saw the bandit beginning the herd the hostages toward the getaway car down the street. Dillinger was struck in the right shoulder and turned to unleash a machine-gun volley at his assailant in the bank building, but Shipley had retreated.

After telling the hostages to move closer to him, Dillinger continued down the street and Shipley returned to his window. When Hamilton caught up with the group as it was approaching the Buick, Shipley fired again and wounded Hamilton in his right shoulder.

The bandits forced several of the hostages to climb onto the vehicle's running boards, fenders, and back bumper, where they held on to a glassless back window frame. Lawmen dared not shoot as the car crept down the street, observed by hundreds of spectators. With Carroll at the wheel, the car headed out of town, stopping about a mile outside the city limits to release some female hostages while Nelson scattered tacks across the road. When a pursuing police car approached, the bantam bandit fired several shots at it from a large-caliber rifle, causing the lawmen inside to give up the chase and turn back. Two hours later the last hostage was released and the gang headed for St. Paul.

Reflecting on Fisher's ruse with the stacks of one-dollar bills, the brooding Hamilton said, "I should have killed that man." Still, when all was said and done, the gang had stolen an impressive $52,000.

The outlaws arrived in St. Paul in two cars just before midnight. Bandages were put on the shoulder wounds of Dillinger and Hamilton, and Green promised to get a doctor for the pair because of the fear of infection. He found his friend Pat Reilly at the Green Lantern Saloon on Wabasha Street. Reilly agreed to take the two gangsters to his family doctor, N. G. Mortensen, the city's health officer. After Van Meter made a point of showing his machine gun to Mortensen, the nervous doctor treated the gangsters, told them their wounds were minor, and did not dare to call the police.[13]

The gang decided to split up for a while as Dillinger and Hamilton recuperated from the shoulder wounds inflicted by Judge Shipley. Carroll and Jean Crompton stayed in St. Paul for several days before going to Chicago. Nelson, who was disappointed with the $52,000 take from the bank job,[14] met Helen in Chicago and the couple went to Minneapolis before fleeing to Bremerton, Washington—accompanied by their son, Nelson's mother, and John Paul Chase—to stay at the home of Helen's sister. Nelson knew lawmen would look for him there, so he and the others drove to Reno, Nevada, to find shelter with friends.

Shortly after the group arrived, James McKay and William Graham, the two gamblers who had helped Nelson after his escape from custody in early 1932, asked Nelson and Chase to eliminate a witness who was slated to testify against them. Since Baby Face owed the pair a debt, and because the pay was very good, he and Chase agreed.

According to one account, on March 22, with Chase driving Nelson's car, Baby Face kidnapped the witness—a banker named Roy C. Frisch—killed him, and disposed of his body. Nelson then ordered Chase to drive the vehicle to San Francisco and get rid of it. Nelson and his family drove back to Bremerton and later took a train to Chicago, where they were to meet Chase.[15]

Herbert Youngblood, who had escaped with Dillinger from Crown Point, lasted less than two weeks on his own. On March 16 he was trapped by three deputy sheriffs in a tiny tobacco and candy store in Port Huron, Michigan. During a furious gun battle one lawman was killed and the other two were wounded, while Youngblood was struck by six bullets and later died. He claimed Dillinger had been with him the day before. After that meeting the gangster was believed to have crossed the St. Clair River into Canada with two companions.[16]

Shootout in St. Paul

I N MID-MARCH DILLINGER AND BILLIE returned to their apartment at the
Santa Monica in Minneapolis, but they didn't stay there long. Shortly
after their arrival, Hamilton, still recovering from his shoulder wound,
paid a visit. According to Billie, "Hamilton was taking off his coat one
night when he pulled his pistol from its shoulder holster. The weapon
clattered to the floor and discharged. We packed our clothes and were
on our way in less than ten minutes."[1]

The next day, March 19 Dillinger and Billie moved into Apartment
303 at the Lincoln Court in St. Paul, where they lived under the aliases
Mr. and Mrs. Carl Hellman. They were visited frequently by Eddie Green,
his girlfriend Bessie, and Homer Van Meter.[2]

A fourteen-year-old boy who lived nearby, Louis Schroth, often saw
Billie hanging laundry on a clothesline behind the apartment building.
He would later recall that Billie "was an attractive woman. She wore red
shorts and a halter top when she did the laundry. We kids in the neighborhood, we'd never seen women in shorts and halters before, so we'd
whistle at Dillinger's girl from the distance."[3]

To pass the time while laying low, Dillinger and his girlfriend had seen two movies, while Red Hamilton and Pat Cherrington had gone to three movies in the past week—but not together. The number of visitors who came to the apartment at all hours raised the suspicions of the building's landlady, who on March 30 alerted police, who in turn alerted the DOI. That evening two agents, R. C. Coulter and R. L. Nalls, were sent to stake out the apartment, but they were not noticed as they sat in their car the next morning when Hamilton, Pat, and Opal Long, who had spent the night in Dillinger's apartment, went for a ride and to buy groceries.[4]

About 10 a.m., while Dillinger and Billie remained in bed, Coulter and St. Paul police Detective Henry Cummings entered the building and knocked on the door of Apartment 303. A sleepy Billie cracked open the door and, when asked, said that her husband, "Carl Hellman," was not home. When the men asked to speak with her instead, "Mrs. Hellman" replied that she was not dressed and closed the door while she ostensibly went to put on clothes.

She quickly ran to the bedroom and shook Dillinger awake, telling him that two policemen wanted to see him. The two dressed quickly and Billie packed a bag as they prepared to flee the apartment.

Meanwhile, Van Meter arrived and was climbing the stairs, en route to Dillinger's apartment, when Coulter noticed him and asked, "Who are you?"

Smiling as if nothing were wrong, the outlaw answered, "I'm a soap salesman."

"Yeah? Where are your samples?" Coulter asked suspiciously.

Van Meter told the agent his samples were in his car and said Coulter could follow him outside if he wanted to see them. When the outlaw reached the first floor, he turned around and pulled a pistol, growling, "You asked for it, so I'll give it to you!"

Van Meter fired two shots but missed, enabling the DOI agent to dart by him and flee outside. The two exchanged volleys as Coulter ran toward his car, which Agent Nalls had just exited. When both lawmen began firing at him, Van Meter quickly spun around and ran back inside the apartment building.

Meanwhile, when Dillinger heard the commotion downstairs, he flung open the apartment door and loosed a machine-gun burst that forced Detective Cummings to seek cover. The bandit and Billie quickly ran downstairs, Dillinger spraying machine-gun bullets at Cummings as the detective followed. Cummings emptied his weapon at the fleeing couple, one round hitting Dillinger in the left calf just below the knee. Nevertheless, the bandit and Billie were able to make it to their Hudson

Terraplane, which Dillinger backed down an alleyway at high speed, leaving the lawman behind.[5]

For his part, Van Meter slipped out a rear door of the apartment building and managed to elude his pursuers. Coming upon a horse-drawn delivery wagon a few blocks away, the outlaw, according to one account, put on the driver's cap and made a bizarre escape, whipping the horses as the wagon raced down the street.

Less than half an hour later Van Meter turned up at Green's apartment, followed shortly by Billie, who explained that Dillinger had been wounded and was sitting outside in the Hudson.

Green hurried downstairs to see Dillinger, who told him, "The police raided us. Have you got a place where we can hole in? I caught a slug in the leg."

"We'd better get you a doctor." the jug marker told him.

"It's not bad. Do you know a doctor that will stand up?"

"I'll get Doc May. I've known him for years. He's a right guy."

Dr. Clayton May had been an alibi witness for Green at his trial for a 1921 St. Paul payroll robbery. Green rushed to May's office and told him a friend needed medical help, and the two drove to an alley where Dillinger was waiting. After May treated the wound, the gangster was taken to a private nursing home in Minneapolis to mend. Green paid May $1,000 for his services,[6] and by April 4 Dillinger had completely recovered.

When Hamilton, Pat, and Opal returned to the apartment an hour after the raid, a crowd had gathered in front of the building. Pat got out of the car to find out what had happened. She hastily returned, and they drove to Van Meter's apartment.[7] Van Meter introduced them to a man they did not know who had arranged a hideout for the gang at a resort some 200 miles away, in Wisconsin.

That night Hamilton and Pat, Opal, Nelson and Helen, Van Meter and Marie Conforti, and Tommy Carroll and Jean Crompton drove to the resort but found it closed. The group returned to St. Paul, and Opal soon left for Detroit. The next day Hamilton and Pat went to Harry Sawyer's farm cottage, where the couple would remain until the night of April 4, when, fearful of a police raid, they drove back to St. Paul.[8]

Meanwhile, on April 2, Van Meter and Carroll, who used the alias Mr. Holmes, took Dillinger's car to Clements Auto in Mankato, Minnesota, for repainting, new taillights, and license plates attached with wing nuts for easy removal. Someone recognized Carroll and called the town's chief of police and federal agents. However, friends tipped off Carroll, and he and Van Meter were able to successfully flee.[9]

Hamilton, Pat, and Van Meter next traveled to Nashville, Tennessee, where they stayed at a tourist-camp cottage for about one week. The two gangsters went into town to purchase some things on the night of April 10, while Pat stayed behind. As the two men were sitting in their car drinking soda pop, a policemen pulled up in a patrol car, having been summoned by the store owner, who had called the police station about several other suspicious men. A very stout officer jumped from his car and asked the two their names. The gangsters gave fake names to the policeman, who asked if they had any credentials to prove their stories.

Hamilton raised a machine gun and pointed it at the officer, telling him, "Here's our credentials. You better get in your car and get away."

The policemen stumbled and fell on his car's running board before scrambling into the vehicle and driving away.

When Hamilton had been gone for an hour or so—longer than expected—Pat had a premonition that something was wrong and immediately packed their bags and put them near the cottage door. A short time later Van Meter and Hamilton drove by the cabin at terrific speed, then slammed on the brakes and hurriedly backed up. Pat immediately started carrying the bags toward the car. The gangsters got out to help her put the baggage in the vehicle, explaining that they had been "jumped up" and had to get out of town immediately.[10]

The Death of
Eddie Green

EANWHILE, AT DILLINGER'S FORMER APARTMENT in Minneapolis, federal agents had discovered a slip of paper listing the telephone number of the St. Paul apartment rented by Eddie Green. It was the same apartment where Green had stored weapons for two weeks and where Van Meter had stayed up until the shootout at the Lincoln Court. On April 3, DOI agents and St. Paul Police Chief Tom Dahill raided Green's apartment, where they found machine-gun clips, shotgun shells, three notebooks labeled "Get Away Charts," and two feet of dynamite fuse.

Lucy Jackson and Leona Goodman, sisters who worked as maids for the Barker-Karpis Gang, arrived at the apartment while the agents were still there. The two black women told the DOI men that Green had asked them to clean up the apartment and hold his bags at their home at 778 Rondo, where the gangster said he would pick up his belongings.

The agents told the maids to carry out their task, and proceeded to lay a trap for the outlaws at the women's home. The plan called for agents armed with rifles, automatic shotguns, and machine guns to hide inside the sisters' house, as well as other nearby homes, and wait until

Green came to pick up his luggage, which was stored on an enclosed side porch. An agent in the bedroom would then fire a .30-caliber rifle into the engine block of Green's car to disable it. Orders came down from on high that, "This man should be shot. . . . Kill him."

At 5:30 p.m. Green and Bessie calmly parked their Terraplane across the street. Going alone to the kitchen door, Green took his baggage from Goodman and began walking back to the car. Only then did he realize something was wrong, and he started to run. According to DOI reports, Green made a "threatening" or "menacing" gesture, although he was unarmed. "Let 'im have it!" yelled Agent E. N. Notesteen. Another agent inside the house fired through a window, hitting Green in the shoulder and head. The seriously wounded Green was rushed by police ambulance to St. Paul's Ancker Hospital, where he was admitted in a semi-conscious state at 6:20 p.m. Doctors gave him one chance in seven of surviving.

The agents took Bessie Skinner into custody and found $1,155 on her person. She would not disclose Dillinger's whereabouts, provide any information, or cooperate in any way. Bessie thought Green had been shot down by the DOI men "without being given a chance." She would later say that she believed Green was a salesman, who would leave at times and not tell her where he was going. He sometimes traveled to Kansas, she said.[1]

Green had Dillinger's keys and $83 in cash in his pockets when he was admitted to the hospital. He slipped into a delirious fog and told the DOI agents all about the Dillinger Gang, as they kept an around-the-clock watch at his bedside. Agents searched Green's apartment and found a mini-arsenal, including a machine gun and fully loaded fifty-round drum, another machine gun, a .45 automatic pistol, a high-powered rifle, a bulletproof vest, a machine-gun butt, several drums of machine-gun ammunition, and ammo for the other weapons. Agents later discovered that Green also had safety-deposit boxes in two Minneapolis banks that respectively contained $4,000 and $4,700.

Agent Thomas Dodd sat at Green's bedside, taking down everything the delirious criminal said. When the outlaw began to mumble, his mother, who was usually nearby, would attempt to prevent him from incriminating himself and the others by reading aloud from her prayer book and asking Eddie to "say your prayers." His brother Frank also would interrupt, saying "Don't talk, Eddie. Don't talk." As a result, the DOI men had Frank barred from the hospital for a time.

A memo to DOI Director J. Edgar Hoover stated that "Green couldn't see and was in a state of delirium and half the time subconscious and talking." The bandit apparently thought he had been hit over the head during a robbery attempt, and the agents, acting out the part of doctors, gangsters, and others, were able to trick him into telling gang secrets.

Green admitted participating in five or six bank robberies; planning bank jobs with the Barker-Karpis Gang, including one in Newton, Iowa, that had fallen through; and that he had received $3,000 from the bank robbery in Racine, Wisconsin, to cover his expenses. He claimed he had been present when Dillinger escaped after the shootout at the Lincoln Court Apartments. He also admitted his participation in the Sioux Falls and Mason City bank robberies and told who else was involved.

The DOI "doctors" assured the semi-conscious Green, whose eyes remained closed, that no police were present. When Green asked if the "doctor" would perform plastic surgery on Dillinger, the man responded that he would, but only if Green could tell him where Dillinger could be found. Once, mistaking a nurse for Bessie, the bandit told her to remove Dillinger's possessions from an apartment and take them to him.

When the questioning became too intense, Green said, "Doc, you sure are a nosy fellow. Give me a shot so I can sleep." But the faux physician insisted that Green would have to tell him about Dillinger before any injection could be given. In his delirium, the outlaw gave the DOI agents the names of all of the Dillinger Gang members, the name of underworld doctor Clayton May, and the locations of the gang's hideouts in Minneapolis.

On the night of April 10 Green, who now exhibited partial paralysis of his face and arm, slipped into total unconsciousness. At 12:55 the next afternoon, he died of meningitis after his temperature reached 105 degrees. Green was buried on April 12 in St. Peter's Cemetery in Mendota, Minnesota. Getaway charts and maps were found hidden in Green's apartment after his death.

While the *St. Paul Pioneer Press* had "no unfavorable comment" on the Green case and had quoted "verbatim the release which was furnished," the rival *St. Paul Dispatch* demanded that the propriety of the ambush be examined by a Ramsey County coroner's inquest. DOI officials wanted to take measures "to prevent any adverse publicity" and attempted to withhold the identities of the agents involved in the ambush so that they could not be subpoenaed. Director Hoover approved a recommendation by an agency official that, "in view of the fact that the *St. Paul Dispatch* has been exerting itself to try to embarrass us, that a confidential tip be given to the rival paper."

DOI officials knew it would be hard to justify Green's killing in any official investigation, so every effort was made to not have one. There was great "concern over the fact that a gangster was shot down, probably from the back." If the inquest into the killing of Green were "not held until May 2, the date at which it is now set, it would be given very little consideration, and it would probably be a mere formality; that there was a possibility that there would not even be one," one DOI report stated.

In fact, no inquest was ever held, although the federal agency told the press that there indeed had been an inquest and that it had concluded Green's death was a "justifiable homicide."[2] Reactions to the news were mixed. One man wrote the DOI: "I am glad to read that Federal agents opened fire on Eugene Green without stopping to ask foolish questions."[3] The St. Paul police, on the other hand, had little respect for the DOI. One local lawman questioned whether there "was any danger of the man getting away from us at the hospital."[4]

Under intense interrogation by Melvin Purvis in Chicago, Bessie Skinner told the DOI all about the Dillinger and Barker-Karpis gangs, and especially about the activities of St. Paul crime bosses Dutch Sawyer and Jack Peifer, both stalwart guardians of the city's O'Connor System. A DOI memo regarding Bessie stated, "There appears to be some friction between this woman and Dillinger."

On May 23, 1934, a federal judge in St. Paul sentenced Bessie to fifteen months at the Industrial Reformatory for Women in Alderson, West Virginia, for harboring Dillinger.[5]

Midwestern Sojourn

ILLINGER VISITED THE FAMILY FARM IN Mooresville on April 7. During a
picnic he told his father he was going on a long trip and that there
was no need to worry about him anymore. He even posed for pictures
with his wooden gun. John's half-brother, Hubert, took him for a ride in
a big Hudson but fell asleep at the wheel near town and smashed into
another car. The Hudson plowed almost a hundred yards into a wooded
area but miraculously didn't hit any trees. No one was hurt in the
mishap, and after John apologized to the occupants of the other car,
Hubert went for another vehicle. Nobody bothered to tell the DOI
agents watching the Dillinger farm about the outlaw's visit.

The next day, April 8, Dillinger and Billie Frechette left for Chicago.
The following evening Billie was arrested at a Chicago restaurant.
Dillinger, who was waiting outside in a car, noticed the commotion but
simply drove away unnoticed.

On April 13 Dillinger and Homer Van Meter raided the Warsaw, Indiana, police station, making off with several guns and bulletproof vests.
The bandits had forced night watchman Judd Pittenger to admit them

to the building and open the room where the guns and body armor were kept. As they were leaving, Pittenger fled outside and watched as the two gangsters drove away.[1]

On April 17, driving two cars, Dillinger, Red Hamilton, and Pat Cherrington went to Sault Ste. Marie, Michigan, to see Hamilton's sister, Mrs. Anna Steve. When Anna answered the door about 8:30 p.m., Pat told her not to be afraid or excited and not to say a word, but there was someone in the vehicle who wanted to see her. Anna walked toward the car, saw her brother, and greeted him very cordially—and immediately recognized Dillinger, although Hamilton introduced his traveling companions merely as friends.

Both gangsters wore bulletproof vests and had revolvers. Hamilton also had an automatic pistol tucked under his belt, and a holster could be seen protruding from the front-right side of Dillinger's vest. The two men carried a machine gun and a rifle wrapped in a blanket into Anna's home. A boarder named Matt Brown, who occupied an upstairs room, heard the gangsters come in and saw Hamilton and the rifle.

When the outlaws requested some food, Anna said she would go to the store. Both Dillinger and Hamilton objected, saying they didn't want her to go anywhere and would eat anything she had on hand. She cooked bacon and eggs and made them toast as the pair kept a constant vigil at doors and windows to ensure that no one was approaching the house. Hamilton told his sister she could have his share of their deceased mother's estate.

When Anna's son, Charles Campbell, came home about 9 p.m., he saw the two men sitting at the kitchen table and recognized Dillinger. Startled by his entrance, the gangsters reached for their guns but put them away when Anna told them the young man was her son. Hamilton, who now recognized the youngster, introduced him to his partner, saying, "Charles, this is Johnnie." He introduced the young woman simply as "Pat." As they entered the living room next to the kitchen, Campbell saw a machine gun on a sewing machine partially covered with a blanket and a rifle on a chair. The bandits mentioned that Chicago had become "too hot" for them and that they would not be returning there.

Hamilton sent Campbell to the home of a former close friend named Paul Paukette to bring him to the Steve home. A few minutes later Campbell and Paukette entered by the kitchen door and noticed Dillinger was limping. Hamilton told them Dillinger had been shot in the leg and then showed them the bulletproof vests he and Dillinger were wearing and the machine gun, which was kept within easy reach at all times. The gangsters also showed off their bullet wounds.

"Now you can say that you have had a machine gun in your hands," Hamilton told Campbell and Paukette after he had allowed them to hold the weapon.

About 11 p.m. the gangsters left, leaving behind a Ford V-8 sedan that was too "hot" to use any longer. The next morning Anna told Matt Brown that the visitors the night before had been her brother and the infamous John Dillinger. Paukette also told his wife whom he'd seen, and someone informed the local sheriff, who in turn called the DOI.[2]

Bohemian Brouhaha

THE SAME DAY DILLINGER AND his companions went to Sault Ste. Marie, John Paul Chase went to see Baby Face Nelson and told him that Dillinger wanted to see him. When the gang met at Louie's Place in Fox River Grove, Illinois, two days later, Dillinger and Hamilton were still recovering from their shoulder wounds, Van Meter and Carroll were indecisive, and nobody except Nelson himself wanted to accept the leadership of the psychotic bantam bandit.

It was obvious things were getting too hot for the gang members. They needed time to think, and decided to rest and recuperate at a resort called Little Bohemia in the northern Wisconsin woods.

Louis Cernocky, the owner of Louie's Place, had told the gang about the resort, which was located in a region noted for its hunting and fishing, but which would not open officially until May.[1] Built in 1931, Little Bohemia was about thirteen miles from Mercer, Wisconsin, and was named for the native land of its proprietor, Emil Wanatka, who may have once used the services of Dillinger's attorney Louis Piquett.[2]

Wanatka and his wife had owned a club in Chicago but had to give it up after several murders by gangsters took place there. He would later tell federal agents that he wanted "to get away from the situations

175

existing in Chicago, particularly conditions requiring me to furnish free meals and beer to policemen, etc."[3]

The lodge was a large two-story building, the lower part of which was constructed of logs and the upper part consisting of white-painted wood siding. To the north of the building were several guest cottages, and behind the lodge lay the small White Star Lake. A long, narrow road connected the main highway with the lodge.[4]

On Friday, April 20, three carloads of gangsters and their women arrived at Little Bohemia. Arriving first, at about 1 p.m., were Homer Van Meter, calling himself Wayne; his girlfriend, Marie Conforti, who carried a Boston bull terrier; and St. Paul gangster Pat Reilly. It would be Van Meter's job to make sure the lodge was safe, to make arrangements for rooms, and to check out escape routes. After the group had lunch, Wanatka showed Van Meter around the resort while the others tried their luck at the lodge's nickel, dime, and quarter slot machines.

Later that afternoon, Dillinger, Red Hamilton and Pat Cherrington pulled up, and at about 5 p.m. Tommy Carroll arrived. With him were his girlfriend, Jean Crompton, and Nelson and his wife, Helen. Dillinger was introduced as Johnnie, and Nelson, using the alias Jimmie, gave Wanatka a short letter of introduction signed by Cernocky that said the group were friends of his. The resort owner, knowing Cernocky's background, surmised that his guests were connected to the underworld.

Nelson and Helen and Carroll and Jean were assigned to a three-room cabin next to the lodge, while the others were given rooms on the second floor of the main building. Dillinger and Reilly roomed together. When Van Meter told Wanatka he wanted a cabin because the lodge was too public, Nelson, who had overheard the conversation, came up to Wanatka and told him that he gave "all the orders."[5]

Van Meter later asked Wanatka if he knew of anyone with a cottage for rent where they could stay for about two weeks, saying he would be willing to pay plenty. Wanatka replied that he knew of no one. As Van Meter walked away, Nelson asked Wanatka what Van Meter had said.

He told Nelson, and the gangster snapped, "If there is any renting of cottages to do, I'll do it."

Nelson wanted the second-floor room of the lodge that Dillinger and and Reilly had been given, not the cottage he and Helen were shown. When Pat Cherrington told him the room was Dillinger's, he responded, "Well, who in the hell does he think he is? We'll put him in the cottage."

Nelson and Dillinger had a slight argument over the room, but Dillinger refused to give in to the dictatorial and officious bandit. He later told Pat that is Nelson had asked him nicely, he would have let him have the room.[6]

When George Baszo and Frank Traube, two young men who served as bartenders, carried the gangsters' heavy bags to their rooms, Baszo told Wanatka, "There must be lead in this one. What are these guys, hardware salesman?"[7]

After a steak dinner prepared by Wanatka's wife, Nan, Carroll set up a poker game in the bar with some of the gang members and Emil Wanatka. Carroll and Nelson were very talkative, while Dillinger, Hamilton, and Van Meter said little.

Van Meter and Hamilton were close friends, but the only member of the gang who could get along with the contentious Nelson was Carroll. Thoroughly disgusted with Nelson, Dillinger planned to break away from him soon. He voiced his displeasure to Hamilton about the diminutive bandit's brash manners and brazen tactics. Both men distrusted Nelson and feared that he might even go so far as to turn a machine gun on them when counting loot after a bank job and seize the entire haul for himself.[8]

Interestingly, Baszo, Traube, and the three girls who worked in the kitchen liked Nelson, who joked with them and gave them big tips. The outlaw was quite personable when around the employees and even bought drinks for them as well as others, mostly regular customers, who came into the bar.

While playing cards, Wanatka noticed that the men had not removed their jackets and were carrying guns in concealed shoulder holsters. He also noticed that Johnnie resembled a certain newspaper photo he had seen. It was at that point, he would later claim, that he became alarmed and realized he was surrounded by the notorious John Dillinger and his gang.

The next morning Pat Cherrington woke up feeling ill. Hamilton and Dillinger suggested that she ride back to St. Paul with Pat Reilly, who was going there to get $2,500 in cash and more ammunition. Hamilton told her that if something should happen to the others, she should remain in St. Paul until they contacted her.

Wanatka asked to talk with Dillinger alone after breakfast. When they entered his office, he confronted the bandit, saying, "You're John Dillinger."

"You're not afraid, are you?" Dillinger replied. "I'll pay you well, and then we'll all get out. Don't worry about anything."

Wanatka apparently accepted the situation, but afterward he and his wife and the other employees were constantly watched by the gangsters. Whenever someone came to the lodge, one of the gang would ask Wanatka who the person was. The outlaws also eavesdropped on the family's and employees' telephone calls, fearing they might alert authorities to the gang's presence. Dillinger would later remark, "You couldn't whisper your own thoughts to your pillow without Mrs. Wanatka knowing all about it ten minutes afterwards."[9]

Later that morning the gangsters, Wanatka, and Traube staged a shooting match behind the helps' quarters. After some of the outlaws fired pistols at a tin can, six men tested their skill with rifles at a range of about eighty yards. Only Wanatka and Van Meter hit the target.[10]

"The boys wasn't very good marksmen," Wanatka said, "but I guess they were good with the sprayer [machine gun]."[11]

Afterward, the men played tossed around a baseball with ten-year-old Emil Jr.[12]

That afternoon Wanatka wanted to take his son to a cousin's birthday party, and Van Meter went along to make sure he did not "say anything smart to anybody." After dropping Emil Jr. off, he and Van Meter took some laundry to a local woman to wash. Looking at the large bundle, the woman joked, "You haven't got Dillinger over there, have you?" Wanatka explained to an upset Van Meter on the way back to the resort that the woman was only joking and that there had been a lot of stories about the gang in the papers.[13]

That evening, Nan left in the family car, saying she wanted to join Emil Jr. at the birthday party. After driving a while, she noticed she was being followed and suspected it was one of the gang members. She would later claim it was the violent Nelson who tailed her. She stopped at the home of her brother, Lloyd LaPorte, telling him that Emil believed their visitors were none other than the Dillinger Gang. The two then drove to the party, which was being held at the home of her brother-in-law, Henry Voss, owner of Birchwood Lodge some two miles south of Little Bohemia. After explaining the situation to Voss and her sister, the family members decided they would first clandestinely ask Emil's opinion, and then contact federal authorities.[14]

When Nan left for the party she had secretly carried a letter Emil had written, at her urging, to Assistant U.S. Attorney L. E. Fisher, a friend from Chicago. The letter was more for the sake of appearance—if lawmen raided the resort, the Wanatkas could claim they had been forced to provide food and lodging for the gangsters—because it would not be delivered before Monday, and by then it might be too late. Her brother mailed the letter at the train station in Mercer en route to the party. It said:

> I am in an awful position here and I hope I can trust you, and that you won't show this to nobody.
>   John Dil is here since yesterday. . . . I never squaked [sic] in my life but I don't want to be the fall guy for somebody else. If you

come up, come at night and stop to Vosses, Birchwood Lodge—
that's a mile before you get to my place. I have all the dope for you
there. Come well prepared if you do come . . .
Don't call up. I'm wached [sic].

                                                              Emil
Whatever you do don't put my name into this. I hope I can trust
you.[15]

Lloyd LaPorte visited the lodge the next morning, and as he was
leaving Nan slipped him a package of cigarettes containing a note saying that Henry Voss should contact federal authorities about the gang.
To avoid any chance of detection by the outlaws, LaPorte drove Henry
and Lloyd Voss fifty miles to Rhinelander, Wisconsin, where Henry
called the U.S. marshal in Chicago. The marshal listened to his story,
then telephoned Melvin Purvis at his home about 1 p.m. to tell him that
a Henry Voss claimed he knew where Dillinger was. Purvis dialed the
number he had been given.

"The man you want is most is up here," said Voss nervously.

"Who is that?" Purvis asked, finally adding, "You mean Dillinger?"

Voss insisted the bandit was at Little Bohemia, and Purvis asked
Voss to meet him later that day at the Rhinelander airport. Purvis had
all available agents in the Chicago field office report immediately, and
chartered a pair of six-passenger planes to ferry them to Rhinelander.
He then called Hoover, who told Purvis to contact the agency's St. Paul
office and DOI Assistant Director Hugh Clegg to have agents from that
office sent to Rhinelander as well. Clegg dispatched Werner Hanni, special agent in charge of the St. Paul office, and three other lawmen by car
to the small Wisconsin town, while he, Inspector W. A. Rorer, and three
agents chartered a plane for the 190-mile trip.

The plane carrying the St. Paul agents and Clegg, who outranked
Purvis and would be in charge of the raid, arrived late in the afternoon.
Henry Voss related Nan Wanatka's story to Clegg and told him that
Dillinger would be leaving the resort the next morning, Monday, April 23.[16]
He also drew a crude map of the resort, leaving out several key features.

Clegg and a couple of agents rented two cars from a Rhinelander
auto dealership, returning to the airport as the planes carrying Purvis
and the heavily armed contingent of Chicago agents arrived. Clegg's
plan called for the lawmen to discreetly circle the lodge, alert the
Wanatkas and the employees to hide in the basement, and then assault
the building at dawn.

Meanwhile, all was quiet at the Little Bohemia resort. "Everything went smooth until Sunday," Wanatka would say later. "Then, about 10 o'clock in the morning, Dillinger called me to the side. He paid me five hundred dollars and said, 'We'll be leaving in the morning.' He told me how nice everything was, and that was it. From then on the boys packed the cars and the girls were in the lounge."

Late Sunday afternoon, however, Dillinger told the Wanatkas that he and his companions would be leaving as soon as Riley returned from St. Paul. When her sister Ruth Voss, paid a visit to see how things were going at the resort, Nan told her about the change in the gangsters' plans. Ruth then drove to the Rhinelander airport to tell her husband and the agents.

About seventy-five customers turned out for the popular Sunday evening dollar dinner at the lodge.[17] Hamilton was at the bar when a husky patron offered him a drink. Red politely refused, saying he did not drink.

"Damn you, you'll drink with me, or I'll pour it down your throat!" the man bellowed.

When he forced Hamilton out of his chair, the gangster's gun almost came out of its holster. Wanatka, hurrying over to defuse the situation, introduced Hamilton as his "good friend, Miller, from Chicago." Meekly, Hamilton told Wanatka that he'd better have a drink because "this man is pretty tough." After agreeing to buy drinks for everyone and a pair of tickets to a local baseball game, the gangster asked if he could leave.

As Henry and Lloyd Voss and a DOI agent headed for Little Bohemia to await the other lawmen, they were flagged down by a car bearing Ruth, her daughter, and her mother, who told them about the gangsters' change in plans. Dillinger's earlier departure meant that Clegg and Purvis would have to raid Little Bohemia immediately, without further preparations. Purvis commandeered five cars from citizens and a local Ford dealer to make the fifty-miles dash to the resort.

Right from the start the raiding party ran into trouble. Two of the cars broke down, and eight agents were forced to endure bitter cold as they stood on the running boards of the other vehicles. Because heavy rains had made the gravel roads almost impassable, the caravan moved very slowly.

As they drew near the resort, at about 8 p.m., the agents left their cars and crept through the dense woods and onto the driveway leading to the lodge. Wearing bulletproof vests, Purvis, Clegg, and four agents were to make a frontal attack, while two other groups of five agents each were to attack the brightly illuminated lodge from the left and right. Soon the right column became trapped in barbed wire, while the other column was delayed when they fell into a drainage ditch. Voss had inadvertently left those features off the map he drew. He had also neglected to mention Wanatka's dogs, whose barking, the agents feared, had warned the outlaws of their presence.

The DOI agents attacked as Dillinger, still waiting for Pat Reilly and Pat Cherrington to return from St. Paul, was playing cards with gang members. They ignored the barking canines.[18]

When three customers left the lodge and climbed into a parked car, the agents thought that they were members of the escaping Dillinger gang. The trio apparently didn't hear Purvis calling for them to stop because of music blaring from the vehicle's radio.

Baszo and Traube, seeing the lawmen, shouted from the porch, "Don't shoot! Those are customers of ours!"

The agents opened fire, however, killing Civilian Conservation Corps worker Eugene Boiseneau. John Morris, the chef at the CCC camp, was struck by four bullets. Mercer gas station attendant John Hoffman was wounded in the arms and managed to flee.

Hearing the gunfire and rushing to their rooms in the lodge, gang members opened fire at the agents from the second-story windows. The two supporting columns of DOI men still had not reached the lodge. After firing for a few seconds, Van Meter, Dillinger, and Hamilton jumped out a back window into a pile of snow and escaped in the moonlight along the shore of Little Star Lake.

Carroll, who had been drinking at the bar, went out a back door on the first floor and attempted to follow them, but the three gangsters were already out of sight.

For his part, Emil Wanatka rushed into the bar and flung open a trapdoor in the floor. Quickly, he, the gangsters' women, Traube, and Baszo clambered through the opening and hid in the cellar. After what seemed like hours but was actually minutes, they heard halting footsteps upstairs and then the voice of wounded CCC chef John Morris, who spoke briefly into the phone before collapsing to the floor.

According to Wanatka, "After Hoffman was shot and Boiseneau was dead, I was in the basement under the telephone when Morris called Alvin Koerner [the local switchboard operator] and said, 'Alvin, I'm at Emil's. Somebody held up the place. Boiseneau's dead and we're shot.'

"When I heard [Morris] fall, I went upstairs. I could hear machine guns spraying, so I went back and asked the girls to lend me a hand so we could drag him to the basement. But the girls said, 'If you want to give him help, you help him. We're staying here.' Which I don't blame them for."[19]

About this time Pat Reilly and Pat Cherrington drove up the driveway to the lodge. Federal agents ordered them to surrender, but Reilly swiftly turned the car around and raced off. Lawmen unleashed a hail of bullets at the vehicle, shattering a window and exploding a tire, but the couple still managed to escape. Reilly was not hit, but Cherrington was cut on the forehead by flying glass. They stopped in Mercer to have the tire replaced before making their way back to St. Paul.

Shortly after Reilly and Cherrington made their getaway, Clegg told his agents at the lodge to cease firing and to make sure the main building was surrounded, since he believed some of the bandits were still inside. Purvis sent agent Jay Newman by car to the Birchwood Lodge, telling him to telephone the federal agent in Rhinelander with details of the raid and to urge the agents coming from that town to hurry to Little Bohemia. Agent W. Carter Baum volunteered to join Newman, and the two soon departed.

Shortly after the sounds of gunfire faded, George LaPorte received a phone call from Alvin Koerner, who quickly told him of the wounded Morris's call from the lodge. LaPorte got in his car and rushed to the CCC camp nearby, where he solicited help from camp physician S. M. Roberts and stationmaster C. J. Christianson. With Dr. Roberts following in the camp ambulance, LaPorte and Christianson headed for the lodge.

Tommy Carroll, unable to catch up with Dillinger, had made it to a field about 500 feet from the lodge when he saw a man approaching. Thinking that it might be Hamilton, Carroll called out, "Is that you, Red?"[20] But when the man—in reality a wounded and very scared John Hoffman—did not respond, Carroll quietly slipped away, finally coming to the main road.

Looking for a car to steal, the gangster walked north until he reached Manitowish Waters, a village a mile above Little Bohemia. There he saw a Packard outside the Northern Lights resort. As Carroll drove off, the owners saw him and ran toward the vehicle but were unable to stop him. As he sped through the night, the outlaw came to a fork in the road and turned right instead of going beyond Mercer to make what would have been an easy escape. Several hours later, realizing he was on a dead-end lumber trail, he abandoned the vehicle and walked through the woods, headed for Chicago.

Dillinger, Van Meter, and Hamilton ran for nearly a mile through the woods until they came to the resort of E. H. Mitchell, an elderly man with gray hair. After Hamilton asked for a drink of water, he entered Mitchell's home and tore out the phone.

"We're not going to hurt you," Dillinger told the startled man. "We're looking for a car."

The gangsters intended to steal Mitchell's truck, but when it wouldn't start they seized a car from Mitchell's employee, Ray Johnson. The bandits made Johnson drive them to Park Falls, Wisconsin, then forced him out of the car and drove away.

Some forty minutes after Clegg called the cease-fire, Wanatka, his employees Traube and Baszo, and the wounded Morris came up from the basement with their hands raised, while the gangsters' women remained downstairs.[21] When Wanatka telephoned Koerner to tell him about Morris's condition, he heard Newman on the party line, making his call from the Birchwood. Newman told Emil that he and his three companions should raise their hands and exit the surrounded lodge, which they did, calling for the federal lawmen to hold their fire. Wanatka told Purvis the outlaws had already escaped from the lodge, leaving behind their girlfriends, but the federal agent remained convinced that the bandits were still inside.

While lawmen continued to search the grounds for the gangsters, Wanatka and the two waiters, without coats and shivering in the cold night air, asked to go inside to get heavier clothing. Over Purvis's objections, LaPorte and Christianson, who had recently arrived with Dr. Roberts, were allowed to take the three men to the Birchwood Lodge to find some coats.

Baby Face Nelson had been in his cabin when the shooting began. Grabbing a machine gun and stepping outside, he spotted Purvis and fired a series of bursts that churned up dirt in front of the special agent. When Purvis returned fire, the bantam bandit retreated toward the lodge. After making a brief foray inside but realizing his comrades had already gone, he made his way to the shore of the lake and ran left, although the other outlaws had gone to the right. Not being in the best of condition, Nelson soon became winded as he stumbled along the lakeshore and soon entered dense woods.

About 10:45 p.m., after about an hour and a half of thrashing through the darkness, Nelson finally emerged from the woods near Manitowish Lake. He spotted the lakeside home of Mr. and Mrs. G. W. Lang, strode through the front door, and forced the startled couple outside to their car, telling them they were going for a ride.

Shortly after the three drove off, the vehicle's headlights stopped working, and Lang, who was driving, was forced to creep along the highway, heading south. As they passed the home of Alvin Koerner, a suspicious Koerner saw the car without headlights and called the Birchwood Lodge, hoping to alert the federal agent who had been there earlier. When the Langs walked up to the front porch and identified themselves, Koerner opened the door and was confronted by a wild-eyed Nelson waving a machine gun. He forced everyone to go inside and sit down.

While Nelson was telling the Koerners he wanted them to drive him out of the area, Wanatka, LaPorte, Traube, Baszo, and Christianson pulled up at Koerner's house in hopes that he could provide them with coats. Christianson remained in the car's back seat, and when the other four entered the house, Nelson took them prisoner as well.[22] When the fugitive asked if he had a car, Koerner told him there was one outside but that it did not belong to him.

"To hell with that, get out there and get in—we're going to take a ride," Nelson ordered.

Nelson took Wanatka and Koerner with him as hostages, leaving behind the other men and Mrs. Koerner, who was relieved not be separated from the couple's two children, who were asleep upstairs. When Koerner tried to talk with him outside, the gangster said, "Get in and shut up. I gotta think." As Wanatka slid behind the wheel, Koerner climbed in the back, where Christianson sat, unnoticed, with LaPorte's rifle near his leg.

As Emil tried to start the car's balky engine, the men noticed another vehicle approaching. Telling his prisoners to keep quiet, Nelson exchanged the .45 he was holding for a machine pistol. The oncoming vehicle, which contained DOI agents Newman and Baum and local constable Carl C. Christensen, pulled up next to the sedan carrying Nelson and his hostages. Rolling down his window, Newman called out, "We're federal officers."

Nelson leaped from the car, jammed the machine pistol through the driver's window, and screamed, "I know you bastards are wearing bulletproof vests, so I'll give it to you high and low!"

Seated three-abreast in the front seat of their coupe, none of the three lawmen was able to draw a weapon. Jerking open the driver's door, Nelson ordered Newman out of the car. When Newman stepped onto the running board, Christensen drew his revolver but was unable to fire a shot before Nelson opened up with the machine pistol. One slug tore into Christensen's elbow, forcing him to drop his gun, and another grazed Newman's forehead, knocking him from the running board.

Baum, holding a machine gun on his lap but unable to use it, was struck in the throat by another round and fell from the car. There is a theory that the agent perhaps could have fired his weapon but was so distraught over the accidental killing of Boiseneau that he did not. Struggling to his feet, Baum tried run away but fell across a fence.

Christensen also tried to make a run for it, but Nelson shot him and he fell to the ground. "I tried to crawl to Baum, who had fallen across the fence. I could still hear him breathing, but he died before anyone got there," Christensen later said, bitterly. "They let us lie there about an hour before anyone dared to come!"

As Wanatka and Koerner ran from their vehicle, Nelson fired at Wanatka but missed. The bantam bandit leaped into the driver's seat of the FBI vehicle and sped away, leaving behind the mortally wounded Baum; Christensen, who had eight bullets in his body; and Newman, who, despite the head wound, emptied his gun at the fleeing car but missed.

A few minutes after Nelson had roared away, he saw another car speeding toward him on the road. It was occupied by Werner Hanni and three other DOI agents from St. Paul, who were hurrying to the Birchwood Lodge. Suspecting the oncoming car was occupied by lawmen, Nelson hit the gas and turned on the vehicle's spotlight, blinding the agents. Hanni, thinking that other lawmen were probably in the speeding vehicle, opted not to give chase and instead drove on to the Birchwood Lodge. Only later did he realize that the driver of the car with the spotlight had been Baby Face Nelson.

When they arrived at the Birchwood, Hanni and the three agents found Ruth Voss bandaging Newman's head wound.

Koerner ran inside his house and telephoned the Mercer police, who in turn called the DOI. Agents did not arrive at Koerner's abode until much later.

Wanatka, seeking help, ran the mile and a half back to Little Bohemia, where federal agents trained their weapons on the panting man who staggered into the lodge's yard.

When Purvis asked him what had happened, Emil gasped, "All your men are dead at Koerner's." Oddly, Purvis asked the lodge owner to spell both his name and the name of the town.

Astounded at the agent's seeming lack of concern, Wanatka yelled, "Did you come for me or Dillinger?"

After considerable argument, Wanatka drove a pair of agents to the Koerner home, arriving a few minutes before Hanni and the other lawmen pulled up. While Wanatka drove Baum back to Little Bohemia, where he was pronounced dead by Dr. Roberts, Hanni returned to the Birchwood, picked up Newman, and drove the agent and constable Christensen to a hospital in Ironwood, Michigan, some forty miles away, to have their wounds treated. Both men survived, as did two others who had been wounded in the night's shootouts and subsequently taken to the same hospital: Johnny Morris and John Hoffman.

Wanatka drove Baum's body to the Ironwood hospital, where it joined the corpse of Eugene Boiseneau in the morgue.

When he returned to Little Bohemia before sunrise, Emil found a small army of federal agents, other lawmen from around the area, and local citizens armed with shotguns and hunting rifles. The federal agents, still convinced that some members of the gang remained inside the lodge, fired tear-gas canisters through the building's windows shortly after sunrise, flushing out from the basement Marie Conforti, Jean Crompton, and Helen Gillis.

During the raid Helen had said, "Goddamn that Dillinger, ever since we hooked up with him we've been having trouble. That fool never wears his glasses and always walks around in public where everybody can see him."[23]

At two o'clock that morning in Washington, DOI Director J. Edgar Hoover, buoyed by early (but erroneous) reports, announced to the media that his agents had surrounded Dillinger. An hour and a half later a report from Mercer led him to believe that a shootout with the Dillinger Gang was imminent. Finally, at 6 a.m., federal agents on the scene admitted that the four gangsters "may" have escaped.[24]

Nelson drove south until his auto quit on him at Squaw Lake, Wisconsin. Abandoning the stolen vehicle, he walked north through the woods, entering the Lac Du Flambeau Reservation, where he stumbled upon the hut of an elderly, full-blooded Chippewa named Ollie Catfish, who had no idea who the gangster was. Threatening Catfish with his machine pistol, Nelson forced the elderly Indian to be his host for three days. Soon, they had consumed all of the food the Catfish had and were forced to eat the only thing left, lard.

At about 6 p.m. on the third day, Nelson and Catfish left the hut and walked about three and a half miles before coming across a postal worker named Adolph Goetz, who was fishing in a lake near the small town of Fifield. Pulling a gun, Nelson asked Goetz for the keys to his car parked nearby and then drove off. By the next dawn the car broke down, and Nelson, posing as a CCC worker, was able to get a farmer to drive him to Marshfield, Wisconsin, for twenty dollars.

During the trip Nelson said, "What are you looking at me for so much? Are you scared? Maybe you think I'm Dillinger?"

Arriving in Marshfield, Nelson brought a 1929 Chevrolet and quickly hit the road for Chicago.

Dillinger, Hamilton, and Van Meter managed to escape the DOI trap and fled toward St. Paul. On Monday, April 23, at 10:30 a.m. as they approached the Spiral Bridge over the Mississippi at Hastings, Minnesota, some twenty miles from St. Paul, the trio was spotted by Deputy Sheriff Norman Dieter and three other lawmen. Van Meter was driving, with Hamilton on the passenger side and Dillinger sitting in the middle.

Ten miles from the bridge the lawmen caught up, and Dieter fired at a rear tire. As Dillinger smashed out the rear window with the butt of his automatic and began shooting, Van Meter wound the car up to its maximum speed. The lawmen returned fire, and one of the dozen bullets that ripped into the car entered Hamilton's back. When Van Meter suddenly turned off onto a dirt road after he had pulled out to a lead of several hundred yards, the officers kept on going. Since it was too dangerous to try to drive into St. Paul, the gangsters headed for Chicago.

Needing a replacement for their bullet-riddled automobile, the bandits seized a car occupied by Roy Francis, his wife, and their infant son. On the road again, the wounded Hamilton asked for a drink, and Dillinger stopped and bought him a soda pop at a gas station. Finally, the gangsters released the captives and drove to Chicago.[25]

Dillinger and Van Meter left Hamilton in a Chicago saloon while they frantically searched for a doctor, but no one, not even Dr. Joseph Moran, the Barker-Karpis Gang's underworld physician, wanted to come to the gangster's aid. The outlaws took the dying Hamilton to a man in Bensenville, Illinois, who referred them to Volney Davis in nearby Aurora. There, Davis's girlfriend, Edna Murray, did what she could to ease Hamilton's suffering, such as cleaning his wound, but gangrene had already set in. Although Dock Barker agreed to try to find a doctor, it was too late, and Hamilton died on the night of April 26.[26]

The raid on Little Bohemia was a disgrace for the DOI. Two men had died and four had been wounded, none of them criminals. Only three women were in custody. No male criminal had been caught or even wounded. Will Rogers wrote, "Well, they had Dillinger surrounded and was all ready to shoot him when he come out, but another bunch of folks come out ahead, so they just shot them instead. Dillinger is going to accidentally get with some innocent bystanders some time, then he will get shot."[27]

Throughout the United States and even the world there was tremendous indignation. Some government officials thought that Hoover should be demoted or even fired if Dillinger was not caught soon. Senator Schall of Minnesota stated that the federal agency "needs fewer politicians and more detectives." The Nazis in Germany thought the incident somehow showed the superiority of their system and the need for their sterilization program. According to British newspapers, Indians on the warpath were hunting Dillinger with bows and arrows.

A petition from a citizens' committee in Mercer, Wisconsin, strongly criticized Purvis for the blunders at Little Bohemia and demanded that he also be fired. Residents of the town accused DOI agents of trying "to hog all the glory." If the DOI had cooperated with local law enforcement and citizens, the Dillinger Gang probably would have been captured at the lodge. A few roadblocks would likely have been enough to trap the gangsters. Adding more fuel to the firestorm of criticism, several Chambers of Commerce passed resolutions of censure, and a grand jury launched an investigation into the reckless killing of Eugene Boiseneau.[28]

33

Curtains for Tommy Carroll

USING JOHN PAUL CHASE TO run such errands as buying food, guns, ammunition, and a bulletproof vest, Nelson stayed at his Chicago hideout for a few days after returning to town. On April 30, 1934, three policemen recognized Nelson, Chase (who they thought was Hamilton), Van Meter, and Harry Fox as they were driving in Bellwood, Indiana, and pursued them. But when the police cut in front of their vehicle and forced the gangsters to stop, Nelson jumped out, pointed a machine gun at the lawmen before they could get a drop on him, and ordered them to get out of their car.

After beating the driver to the ground when he emerged, Nelson told the other two officers to start running. As the men, with their hands still raised, started up the highway, Nelson calmly aimed a machine gun at their backs. The other outlaws begged Nelson not to shoot, telling him it would only make things worse for them. Disappointed, the diminutive gangster lowered his weapon, but then suddenly whirled and peppered the police car with machine-gun fire, completely destroying it and shooting out most of the glass.[1]

During May, Dillinger, Van Meter, and Carroll were hiding in a wooded area near East Chicago, Indiana, sleeping in a small wooden shack and riding about in a closed red truck. Shortly after 11 p.m. on May 24, two East Chicago detectives, Martin O'Brien and Lloyd Mulvihill, left the police station to follow up on a tip they had received about Dillinger's location. Spotting the gangsters in the red truck, the detectives pulled alongside and ordered them to pull over. Van Meter, in the rear of the truck with a machine gun, opened fire before the lawmen could exit their vehicle.

Less than half an hour later, the bodies of the detectives, bearing wounds on their faces and necks, were found in their police car on a lonely and swampy road near Gary.[2]

Police believed Dillinger and Van Meter were in Chicago when they found the car stolen from St. Paul resident Roy Francis in the Windy City. However, speculation abounded, and there were even reports that Dillinger had fled to England by ship.[3]

Many bank robberies were blamed on the Dillinger Gang during the spring of 1934. Van Meter and four other bandits may have robbed the Villa Park Trust and Savings Bank in a Chicago suburb of $6,000 just before noon on April 27. A warrant for his arrest was issued the following day in Chicago. On May 4 three robbers stole $17,000 from the First National Bank in Fostoria, Ohio, wounding Chief of Police Frank Culp and others in the process. Dillinger and Van Meter were identified by witnesses.

Dillinger was also a suspect in the robbery of the Citizens Commercial Bank in Flint, Michigan, of $25,000 on May 18. Three days later Van Meter and another man were accused of robbing a Galion, Ohio, bank of $5,403.40.[4]

On May 3 in St. Paul, Billie Frechette pleaded not guilty to a charge of harboring Dillinger and was held on a bond of $60,000. The trial of Frechette, Dr. Clayton May, and his assistant, nurse Augusta Salt, started in St. Paul on May 15. Eight days later, Billie and Dr. May were each sentenced to two years in federal prison and fined $10,000; Mrs. Salt was acquitted.[5] Helen Gillis, Jean Delaney Crompton, and Marie Conforti were sentenced May 25 in Madison, Wisconsin, to eighteen months on a pair of federal harboring charges, but Judge Patrick Stone suspended the sentences and placed each on a year's probation. The hope was that they would lead police to the Dillinger Gang.[6]

Pat Cherrington lived with Opal Long at the Chateau Hotel in Chicago from May 14 until when the two were arrested by federal agents on June 1. On Decoration Day the former had received a letter from Arthur O'Leary, assistant to Dillinger's lawyer, Louis Piquett, telling of Hamilton's death. Opal was sentenced to serve six months in the Minneapolis Workhouse on June 29, after which she faded into obscurity. On July 6 Pat was sentenced to two years for harboring.[7]

During May and June 1934 Dillinger and Van Meter tried to change their appearance through plastic surgery. On May 28 Dr. Wilhelm Loeser, who was on parole from a federal prison on a drug charge, and Dr. Harold B. Cassidy, the anesthesiologist, gave Dillinger a facelift for which they charged $5,000. The fifty-eight-year-old Loeser, a native of Germany, had received his education there and at Northwestern University. For $35 a day, James Probasco rented his Chicago house to the outlaws for the surgery and convalescent period. The sixty-seven-year-old Probasco, who needed money to buy a tavern, had been arrested many times for receiving stolen property but had never been convicted.[8]

A dimple was removed from Dillinger's chin and a mole was taken from his forehead, as well as two slices from his cheeks near the ears. An attempt was made to change his nose, and the doctor also tried to obliterate the gangster's fingerprints. In the middle of the operation Loeser nearly lost his patient when Dillinger swallowed his tongue and his heart stopped beating. Desperate, Loeser was able to save him by using powerful stimulants and artificial respiration.

Although he still could be recognized, Dillinger was pleased with his new look. He even convinced Van Meter to come to Chicago from his St. Paul hideout to use the services of Dr. Loeser. On June 3 Van Meter went under the knife, but the surgery was a complete failure, for little could be done to change his type of face.[9]

That day Nelson visited the Probasco home. Van Meter, screaming that his face was a "goddamn mess," grabbed a machine gun, while Nelson, who hated Van Meter, sat drinking a bottle of beer and enjoying the spectacle. Finally the doctors were able to pacify Van Meter.[10]

In May, Carroll and Jean spent time with Nelson at Lake Como in Wisconsin. About this time Tommy Carroll met John Henry Seadlund, the kidnapper/slayer of Charles S. Ross. Meanwhile, the DOI searched for Carroll at a lake cottage near Perham, Minnesota, sending in two agents who posed as fishermen looking for a summer cottage.[11]

Now pregnant, Jean Crompton resided with Nelson's wife Helen in Chicago until the night of May 30. Carroll knew of the pregnancy, and later there was a miscarriage or abortion. Jean went for a walk and saw Carroll just a block from her home in a car he had stolen in Chicago on May 25. He picked her up, although the house was under close observation by federal agents. The gangster left Jean at a Chicago hotel and went to Cincinnati to contact the Dillinger Gang.[12] At Little Bohemia, Carroll had had a lot of money, but just a month later, after paying for various services and to keep people from reporting his whereabouts, he was practically broke. Carroll told Pat Reilly that "John was dead," but he meant Hamilton not Dillinger.[13]

On June 4 one of the Michigan City escapees, Joseph Fox, was caught in Chicago and returned to Indiana. Harry Copeland was sentenced to twenty-five years for helping to rob the Greencastle bank on June 27.[14]

Tommy Carroll and Jean Crompton left Chicago on June 6, stopping about 4:30 p.m. at the Evening Star Tourist Camp, some five miles east of Cedar Rapids, Iowa. Using the names Mr. and Mrs. Leonard Murdock of St. Louis, they were quiet and orderly. The couple drove into Cedar Rapids, got something to eat, and later went to a movie. About 10:50 p.m. they returned to the tourist camp.

Carroll's end came on June 7, 1934. The gangster and his girlfriend left the camp about 10:30 that morning to drive to Minneapolis to visit Jean's mother. When they stopped at a service station near Waterloo, Iowa, a gas station attendant greasing Carroll's sedan saw three different license plates on the rear seat. He called the police and gave descriptions of the couple and the car. Postal inspectors also claimed that the attendant had recognized Carroll from post office wanted posters. For an hour detectives Emil Steffen and Paul E. Walker drove through the town searching for the couple. When the detectives returned to the police station, they spotted Carroll's car parked across the street.

Meanwhile, Carroll and Jean had decided to go to a show, but when they left a beer parlor and returned to their car about 1:45 p.m., the detectives were waiting for them. Jean asked Carroll if she could act as a decoy by going to the vehicle and finding out if the men standing near it were lawmen. However, according to a DOI report, "Carroll would not permit her to go alone, and stated that, if there were any danger, he wanted to share it with her."[15] The gangster walked to the car and as he started to get in, Walker placed a hand on his shoulder and said, "We've police officers, and want to have a little talk with you."

"The hell you are," snapped Carroll, reaching into his side coat pocket for his .38 automatic Colt pistol. Not attempting to draw his own gun, Walker slammed a brawny left fist into the gangster's mouth. Carroll dropped his gun but picked it up as he attempted to regain his balance and fire. Walker pulled out his weapon and shot the gangster beneath the armpit. To stop Jean from getting into the car, Steffen pushed her to the sidewalk, giving Carroll the opportunity to flee into an alley. Walker and Steffen chased after the outlaw and loosed a volley of shots at him. Carroll crumpled to the ground, mortally wounded, with four bullets lodged in his left shoulder, chest, and spine.

Steffen later said, "Walker and I covered the car and waited some time before this fellow and a girl showed up. We stepped up and identified ourselves. He tried to reach for a gun.

"Walker jumped for him and grappled with him. That gave a chance to draw my gun. I plugged him at least once—I know I fired four shots—and the guy made a break.

"By that time Walker had a chance to get out his gun, and he opened up as the man tried to get away."

In Carroll's car lawmen found an automatic rifle with 300 rounds of ammunition, a complete doctor's first-aid kit, and car license plates from Illinois, Missouri, and Minnesota. The gangster was quick to admit his identity as he was rushed to the St. Francis Hospital. His first words to lawmen were, "Take care of the little girl. She doesn't know what it's all about. I've got seven hundred dollars on me. Be sure she gets it." But only $500 in twenty-dollar bills was found, which Carroll insisted was "legitimate."

When Sheriff H. T. Wagner came to the hospital room he was wearing a bulletproof vest.

"What's the matter, Sheriff, are you afraid of me?" the dying gangster asked.

After asking for and getting a drink of whiskey, Carroll mentioned that he had some insurance. The sheriff asked him who the beneficiary was, so that person could be notified. Carroll, who cursed the officers and newspapermen, replied, "Don't lie to me! You won't get me to squeal."

DOI agent O. C. Dewry questioned the gangster for forty-five minutes. In a state of semi-delirium Carroll muttered that he "hid him" when Dewry asked if he had buried "John."

The Rev. H. A. Holthaus, chaplain at the Catholic hospital, administered extreme unction to the dying man at his request. Refusing to give lawmen any information about his criminal pals up to the last cursing moment of his life, Carroll died at 6:55 p.m. Carroll was identified through fingerprints.[16] The ace criminal's body was viewed by about 2,000 persons that night and the next day at the O'Keefe & Towne morgue.[17]

Members of the Dillinger Gang were believed to be still in the area, and several DOI agents from St. Paul came to Waterloo to question Jean, who denied that the couple had any companions in Waterloo. In jail the pretty, well-dressed, soft-spoken woman mourned the death of her lover. Dressed in a dark brown skirt with a red and white striped blouse, Jean admitted that she had dyed her hair to be a brunette instead of a blonde since the Little Bohemia raid. She told agents that she "loved Tommy and didn't know he was in the rackets." Jean said she never saw John Dillinger, did not know that Carroll was armed when officers approached their car, and that he had an automatic rifle or ammunition in the vehicle.

"He didn't try to shoot," she said. "He could have shot that fellow if he wanted to."

According to Jean, she and Carroll had been staying at a tourist camp, even though she was on parole and had been forbidden to associate with the gangster. "I loved him and I wanted to be with him again," she explained. Jean claimed she had married Carroll two weeks earlier in a "little town in Michigan" and that they were on their honeymoon. She showed the agents a narrow, white gold band on her left hand.

After providing little information, Jean demanded that Sheriff Wagner let her seen her "husband." When the sheriff haltingly admitted that Carroll was dead, she broke down and soon fainted. So distraught was the woman that she attempted to commit suicide by slashing her wrists with a broken jar. After that, she was kept under continual surveillance by matrons, and a special guard was placed around the jail.

Early the next morning, surrounded by seven officers, the violently weeping woman walked four blocks to the funeral home to see her lover's body. "I knew he was in the rackets, but I loved him," she explained to DOI agents. "I would follow him anywhere. I was in love with him. That was all that mattered to me. Lovers don't talk about that kind of thing."

Jean was arrested for parole violation and returned to Madison. On June 11 Judge Stone sentenced her to a year and a day in the federal women's reformatory at Alderson, West Virginia.[18]

That same day, Carroll's body was taken to St. Paul, where he was buried at Oakland Cemetery. His widow, Viola, and brother Charles each wanted to be the sole heir to his estate.[19]

The *St. Paul Daily News* gave this account of the outlaw's funeral:

Anything But Romantic

Tommy Carroll, St. Paul's own gunman, was buried Monday.

But the funeral was anything but a swanky affair.

The body in a plain coffin was taken out of a mortuary chapel into an alley after a mortician had pronounced a few words of prayer.

Some of the pallbearers were not any too anxious to be seen by the federal agents and police who were present out of official curiosity.

A brother and a woman who insists she is the widow were the principal mourners.

Altogether the funeral was a restrained, furtive and hurried affair in keeping with the life of the deceased.

Whether or not from lack of funds, the florid ostentation with which gangland a few years back marked such passing events was entirely absent.

And with all due respect to the principle of Christian charity, it was just the kind of a funeral Carroll deserved—and the public needs—to end the false glamour in which so many underworld characters have been invested.

Anyone still cherishing the romantic vision of a life of dashing, daring luxury with plenty of wine, women and song as led by these modern bandits would have been quickly disillusioned by the Carroll obsequies.[20]

U.S. Attorney General Homer Cummings wrote in a June 23 press release: "I desire especially to point to the valor exhibited by Paul Walker and Emil Steffen, two police officers of Waterloo, Iowa, in their encounter with the notorious Tommy Carroll."[21] *Startling Detective Adventures* magazine called Carroll a "onetime taxi driver who shot himself into the big leagues as Dillinger's ace gunman, but finally was struck out by the great No Hit–No Run Pitcher," and predicted that "the message of blood spells the beginning of the end for John Dillinger and his mob!"[22]

Dillinger, still recuperating from plastic surgery at Probasco's home in Chicago, was very upset when he heard of Carroll's death and thought he was a jinx to all his friends. In a severe depression, he sat for hours without saying anything.[23]

Public Enemy Number One

DESPITE THE INTENSE NATIONWIDE MANHUNT for John Dillinger and his gang, the outlaw visited reporter Tubby Toms at his home in Indianapolis in mid-June. Pulling his car to the curb in front of the house, Dillinger told the reporter, "Get in. I want to talk to you."

Apparently, Dillinger wanted to ask Toms about a pardon from the governor but never quite got around to it. The gangster asked Toms to delay reporting the visit to the authorities, and half an hour later Toms called Captain Matt Leach.[1]

On June 13 in Chicago, Homer Van Meter was reunited with his girlfriend Marie Conforti. The bandit prevailed upon Angeline Digorio (alias Bobby Harland) to go to Marie's residence and bring her to Van Meter's car, which was parked nearby. Although two DOI agents were stalking Marie and another agent was watching Digorio's house, the rendezvous was not detected and the couple quickly fled to the home of William Finerty in Calumet City, Illinois. Marie's foster mother, a Mrs. Costello, received a letter saying that Marie might return for her clothes.[2]

About ten days later the gangster told Marie he was going to kill her. He said Nelson had told him he had learned through his brother-in-law Bob Fitzsimmons that Marie had visited the Fitzsimmonses after her release from custody in Madison, Wisconsin, had asked too many questions, and had been "running around" with a federal agent. Nelson was angry with Van Meter because he would not "ditch" Marie and also thought that Marie had talked to government agents.

Van Meter, however, was satisfied with her story that she had visited the Fitzsimmons home only to get an address in St. Paul where she could pick up her clothes. She also denied that she had been seeing any federal agent. Never friendly, Nelson and Van Meter stopped trusting each other and no longer passed along the addresses where they were living. The bantam gangster also told Van Meter that he had paid a St. Paul lawyer named Newman $1,500 to represent Marie, who insisted the lawyer had done nothing for her. When Van Meter refused to pay, the gangsters had an argument.[3]

In a speech on June 22, 1934, U.S. Attorney General Homer S. Cummings declared John Herbert Dillinger to be America's Public Enemy Number One, a dubious honorific the media had unofficially bestowed upon the outlaw after his spectacular breakout from the Crown Point jail. It would be the first and last time the Justice Department, the DOI, or the agency's successors would rank their most-wanted criminals by number.

The original public enemies list was devised by the Chicago Crime Commission and published on April 24, 1930. It listed Chicago crime czar Al Capone as the nation's most nefarious hoodlum. The Federal Bureau of Investigation, which succeeded the DOI on July 1, 1935, released its first Most Wanted list in 1950 but did not rank the criminals listed therein by number.

The day that Dillinger was acknowledged as the nation's premier badman also marked the outlaw's thirty-first birthday. That same day Audrey Hancock put a notice in the classified section of an Indianapolis newspaper which read: "Birthday greetings to my darling brother, John Dillinger, on his thirty-first birthday. Wherever he may be, I hope he reads this message." The next day, June 23, the Justice Department placed a $10,000 reward on Dillinger and a $5,000 reward on Baby Face Nelson and issued shoot-to-kill orders on both men. In addition, the states of Michigan, Ohio, Indiana, Illinois, and Minnesota each offered rewards of $1,000 for Dillinger.[4]

His great skill in avoiding capture was reported in the press, which frequently compared him to famous outlaws from the Wild West era. The *New York Times* wrote that the crimes of Dillinger were "true to the old frontier types," such as Black Bart and Jesse James. According to crime writer Jay R. Nash, "John Herbert Dillinger is America's classic bank robber. No other criminal ever approached his exploits and reputation." The *Chicago Tribune* opined that Dillinger "is today what Dick Turpin, the English highwayman, and Jesse James, the American road agent, were to the public of their day."[5] In the words of that newspaper:

> No other criminal in American history ever so captured the imagination of the public. His insouciance, his cynical attitude, his put-on good humor when bullets did not serve the immediate purpose he had in mind, were as much a part of the legend of this super criminal as his uncanny ability to shoot his way out of traps or his unfaltering courage in battle.[6]

According to one writer:

> Hero worship of glamorous criminals is nothing new. The larcenous Robin Hood and the homicidal Billy the Kid are minor national heroes. [During the Depression] the supply of persons properly qualified for our veneration does not equal the demand. In this sweet land of superlatives we insist on having super-criminals, and they exist only in detective stories.[7]
>
> In much the same way that a journeyman prizefighter like Tom Heeney is "built up" as a logical contender for the heavyweight championship, our super-criminal is fashioned by newspaper ballyhoo from the ordinary stickup men or the gangster. There must of course be some basis for his reputation, at least one gaudy crime or sensational prison break. But once he has his reputation, he need never do anything more to justify it. Innumerable crimes of which he is entirely innocent will be credited to him until he is regarded as a local or even a national menace.[8]

Lawmen often exploited these "super criminals." Unsolved crimes could be blamed on them, and if their apprehension was not immediate, it could often be attributed to the criminals' ruthlessness rather than police incompetence. Glory would go to the federal "G-Men" or other law enforcement officials who killed or captured them. The regional or national crime menace was used to justify bigger police budgets and increased powers for law enforcement.[9]

There was tremendous public interest in the national "war on crime," as J. Edgar Hoover termed it, especially the hunt for Dillinger. Harold Rissmiller wrote to President Franklin Roosevelt, "If you can see that my family is supplied with food, clothing, and shelter, I will get him," adding that he wanted the arrangement to be "a secret between you and I alone."[10]

The rising tide of crime caused many Americans to want security and safety at the cost of civil liberties. Some even wanted the federal government to take over local and state police agencies. One Jesse Kennedy thought that federal police could join with "each sheriff's force . . . to visit every house in his jurisdiction . . . search every building . . . patrol the highways for a day and scrutinize and question men traveling out of the zone agreed upon."[11]

With the arrival of summer, Dillinger seemed to have vanished into thin air, although the massive manhunt was still underway and police were receiving hundreds of false reports on his whereabouts. On June 27 Pat Reilly, who claimed to have heard that the outlaw was dead, was arrested by DOI agents in St. Paul on a charge of harboring Dillinger.[12]

About that same time, Dillinger received a letter from Harry Pierpont that had been smuggled out of the Ohio State Penitentiary, asking him and the gang to free him from prison. The letter concluded: "If you can't make it, Johnnie, I'll see you in hell. [signed] Harry."[13] While he may have wanted to help his old friend, all Dillinger could do was provide money to secure legal aid for Pierpont's mother.

On the hot, bright morning of June 30, four members of the Dillinger Gang and Pretty Boy Floyd committed what would be the gang's last bank robbery. At 11:30 a.m., Dillinger, Floyd, and Jack Perkins entered the Merchants National Bank in South Bend, Indiana, while Baby Face Nelson and Homer Van Meter stood guard outside. After Dillinger announced the bandits' intentions, Floyd fired a machine-gun burst into the bank's ceiling to convince the stunned customers to lie on the floor. When local policeman Howard Wagner hurried to the bank to investigate the gunfire, Van Meter fatally shot him.

As Dillinger and Perkins loaded two pillowcases with cash from the teller cages, Nelson was having a terrible time outside. Jewelry store owner Harry Berg, hearing the commotion and seeing frightened people running down the street, retrieved his .22 pistol and fired two shots at Nelson, one of them striking the outlaw's bulletproof vest. Spun around by the bullet's impact, the angry Nelson loosed a volley of machine-gun fire at his assailant, but Berg had prudently ducked back inside his store.

Nelson's barrage shattered the store's front window, and a ricocheting slug hit customer Jake Soloman in the leg. Samuel Toth, who was sitting in his automobile across the street, was struck in the head by a stray bullet. Joseph Pawlowski, a sixteen-year-old student, jumped on Nelson's back, hoping to subdue him, and as the two spun around and around, Nelson's machine gun spat out a hail of bullets. At last, the diminutive gangster threw off his tormentor and fired at him. The boy fell through a store window, shattering the glass, and fainted after a bullet passed through the palm of his hand.

As police arrived on the scene, Van Meter held them at bay with his rifle while grabbing several pedestrians and customers from a nearby store to use as human shields. Dillinger, Perkins, and Floyd also took hostages before exiting the bank with less than $30,000.

The lawmen couldn't get a clean shot at Dillinger, but a local detective began firing at Nelson, who squeezed off a long burst in return. As more police arrived, the firefight intensified, with outlaws and officers shooting around the hostages as targets presented themselves. When their human shields broke away and dove for cover, the bandits raced for their getaway car amid a hail of bullets.

Reaching the vehicle, Van Meter was trying to slide behind the wheel when a slug gouged a deep furrow along the right side of his head, nearly knocking him unconscious. Nelson pushed the wounded bandit out of the way and squirmed into the driver's seat as the other outlaws piled into the vehicle, lead flying in all directions. Nelson roared through downtown South Bend, outdistancing a pair of pursuing police cars by the time he had reached the town limits. A motorcycle officer took up the chase but his engine blew as he struggled to keep up with the hurtling getaway car.

Near Knox, Indiana, the gang's car had a flat tire. When the bandits got to Goodland, Indiana, several hours after the holdup, they abandoned their bullet-riddled auto and left the area in a car driven by John Paul Chase. Four farm boys saw the exchange and called the police.

In the final tally, six South Bend citizens had been shot and a policeman killed, Van Meter had sustained a serious but not fatal head wound, and Floyd and Perkins had received minor leg wounds. Dillinger and Nelson emerged virtually without a scratch. No one was happy with the score, as Van Meter had told the bandits the bank would have at least $100,000 in its vault. Each bandit's cut amounted to just $4,800.

Floyd left the gang before the car swap at Goodland, which caused a good deal of resentment among the other outlaws. The gang split up, with Dillinger returning to Chicago, where he took Van Meter to James Probasco's home to have the lanky outlaw's head wound treated; Van Meter then headed for St. Paul. Perkins also returned to Chicago; Floyd is believed to have gone to Buffalo, New York; Chase to Gary, Indiana, where he had a girlfriend; and Nelson and Helen went to a hideout in Barrington, Illinois.[14]

The Lady
in Orange

O N JULY 4, 1934, THE East Chicago underworld provided Dillinger with a hideout at the Chicago apartment of Anna Sage, a woman with a record of running houses of prostitution. The forty-two-year-old woman with a strong foreign accent had been born Ana Cumpanas in Romania, a country she had left fifteen years earlier. She started a bawdyhouse in Gary, Indiana, where she was known as Katie from the Kostur Hotel, and then opened another in East Chicago. Despite of being convicted twice for "operating a disorderly house," Sage was able to continue her business because Indiana's governor, Harry Leslie, had pardoned her both times. But the next governor, Paul McNutt, refused to pardon a third conviction, and now the Immigration Bureau wanted to deport her as an undesirable alien.

In mid-June Sage introduced Dillinger, who was using the alias Jimmie Lawrence and pretending to be a Board of Trade clerk, to Polly Hamilton, a twenty-six-year-old redheaded waitress, whom he often took to nightclubs and the movies. The five-foot-three, blue-eyed, 120-pound Polly also worked as a prostitute, and her co-workers joked that her new boyfriend looked liked Dillinger. Polly, divorced from a Gary policeman, saw the outlaw almost every day, except for a few short trips out of town. She soon moved into Sage's apartment with Dillinger.[1]

"I was crazy about him. He had a marvelous personality," she would say later. "He really *couldn't* have been kind and good and do the things he did, but he was kind and good to me. He had very good innate intelligence and was interested in what was going on—and I don't just mean cops and robbers, but daily events.

"We went out a lot. He was crazy about movies, and we went to nightclubs. He looked like an average businessman type, and always had plenty of money. That's when I first started to drink. . . . Anna used to make us Romanian coffee, and later told me, 'I knew who he was right away.'

"We were at the Grand Terrace one night, and some people kept looking and looking at him. You never saw anyone call for a bill as fast as he did. I don't think he even waited for his change. We took a cab to the Loop, then got another cab and went to the Chez Paree.

"He had a low voice, rather pleasing, and was a terrific card player. . . . We played pinochle and regular rummy. Penny-ante stuff, a nickel limit. One time I wouldn't pay my card bill, and he started twisting my arm.

"Dillinger was short and stocky and very solid. He was broad-shouldered and had a fascinating smile, especially when he was playing a joke . . . He was a good dresser, clean and neat . . .

"There was one song Dillinger was crazy about, from a picture we saw with Joan Crawford at the Marbro: 'All I do is dream of you the whole night through . . .' He used to sing it and sing it to me. Did he have a good voice? At least he could carry a tune.

"It was the Depression and I was broke. I got a thrill going around in cabs. We cabbed everywhere. Twice he gave me money so my girlfriend and I could go to the World's Fair. . . . I remember I said I couldn't go to the beach because I didn't have a decent bathing suit. He . . . handed me forty dollars.

"One time he said he had to go to Ohio. He was gone four or five days once, another three or four . . .

"We had a lot of fun . . ."[2]

One time Dillinger, Polly, Van Meter, and Marie Conforti visited the World's Fair,[3] and Polly also got money from Dillinger to get her teeth fixed. The couple liked to give each other presents, such as rings. Polly later claimed that she never knew Dillinger's true identity.

Sage's son, Steve Chiolak, had no idea that the man staying at his mother's place was Public Enemy Number One. To him and his girlfriend, the boarder was "Jimmie Lawrence." Chiolak first saw Dillinger in late June and would see Dillinger at his mother's apartment three times. He went to a drinking party and saw a couple movies with his girlfriend, Dillinger, and Polly, including *Viva Villa* with Wallace Beery at the Grand and *You're Telling Me* with W. C. Fields at the Marbro, both times attending the 8 p.m. show, "just like real people," according to Chiolak. Dillinger always paid the bill, according to Chiolak, who was unemployed at the time. They also went to the nightclub Stables, where Dillinger talked about the show and drank only mild gin fizzes.

According to Chiolak, "I never saw any great amount of money on him. If he was the man they said he was, he was an all-around fellow. He didn't act tough, and he didn't talk rough.

"I didn't even ask him where he worked. My girlfriend asked him if he lived in the city and he said, 'Yes, up north.' She said, 'Working?' and he said, 'Yes, at the Board of Trade.' It was like talking about the weather."[4]

In the neighborhood Dillinger bought an $8.95 striped white shirt at the Ward Mitchell Company, ate strawberry sundaes at a local ice cream parlor, dined at the Seminary Restaurant, placed bets with a bookmaker located upstairs from the Biograph Theater, and got his hair cut at the Biograph Barber Shop. One time a barber there called police to report that he had just cut Dillinger's hair, but he was told he had called the wrong police station.

Continuing to mock the law, Dillinger even went inside a police station and asked to see a nonexistent girl he said had been in prison with Anna Sage. When he attended a Chicago Cubs game at Wrigley Field, Dillinger saw his lawyer Louis Piquett standing next to a policeman and called out, "Hello, Counselor," then quietly left.

The gangster may have decided to leave Chicago and, according to some historians, made arrangements to flee with an elderly couple to Mexico on Monday morning, July 23. He was to pay them $10,000, almost all the money he had.[5] There were also reports that Dillinger was planning to rob a mail train.[6]

On July 9 Fat Charley Makley and Harry Pierpont, awaiting execution at the Ohio State Penitentiary in Columbus, talked to newsmen. "We have heard nothing from Dillinger since they kidnapped him out of the Tucson jail and took him to Indiana," he told reporters. "They say Dillinger is sending me fifteen thousand dollars. I wish he'd send me a few fins right now so I could buy cigarettes."

Both men denied rumors that Dillinger was robbing banks to raise money for their appeal. They also said they had not killed Sheriff Sarber while springing the outlaw from the Lima jail, that Indiana police officers knew who had, and that Dillinger had not provided the guns for the Michigan City breakout.

"They [the authorities] know, too, why Dillinger got loose from the escape-proof Crown Point jail with a wooden gun, just fifteen minutes before he was to make a deposition in our case," Pierpont said. "He was to tell who delivered him. I can tell you it was not us.

"I wish Dillinger all the luck in the world. We don't expect any help out of him."[7]

Early on the morning of July 16, Illinois state troopers Fred McAllister and Gilbert Cross, checking for stranded motorists along a rural road northwest of Chicago, noticed three late-model vehicles parked in a schoolyard. Seeing a woman in one of the cars, they stopped to investigate. The woman was Helen Gillis, and the cars belonged to members of the Dillinger Gang, who were meeting to discuss a future heist.

Stepping out of his patrol car, McAllister called out to the woman, "What's the trouble there?"

"No trouble at all," purred Baby Face Nelson, popping out from the shadows behind the cars where he had been hiding. The gangster aimed a machine-gun pistol at the lawmen and loosed a fierce volley of .45 slugs. McAllister was shot in the right shoulder, and Cross was hit six times, including twice near the heart. Despite their wounds, the troopers managed to crawl into weeds alongside the roadway as the gangsters fled in their cars.

Although doctors gave Cross little chance of survival, he and McAllister both completely recovered from their wounds.[8]

Four days after the shootings, on July 20, two East Chicago police officers, Detective Sergeant Martin Zarkovich, a close friend of Anna Sage, and Captain Timothy A. O'Neill, visited Chicago Police Captain John Stege. The pair told the Dillinger Squad chief that they could set up the outlaw through Sage. Their only condition was that Dillinger be killed outright and not be given a chance to surrender. Stege refused and kicked them out of his office. "I'd even give John Dillinger a chance to surrender," he said.

Zarkovich and O'Neill telephoned DOI Special Agent in Charge Melvin Purvis the next afternoon to tell him they knew where Dillinger was. Arrangements were made to meet Purvis and Inspector Samuel Cowley at 6 p.m. in Cowley's room at the Great Northern Hotel. The policemen told the federal agents all about Anna, who wanted to meet privately with Purvis. They claimed they had observed Dillinger when he went to the Biograph Theater. Director Hoover approved the meeting with the informers in a telephone call, and with the help of Anna Sage, Purvis decided to lay a trap for Dillinger.

Around 9 p.m. Zarkovich and Purvis drove to the rendezvous with Sage near Children's Memorial Hospital. Cowley and O'Neill followed in another car. Thirty minutes later Sage arrived and got into Purvis's car. They drove to an isolated spot on the shore of Lake Michigan. Anna told Purvis she had not known who Dillinger was until she saw his picture in a newspaper, adding that when she pointed out the photo to the gangster, he had admitted his true identity.

Sage was facing deportation to her native Romania and wanted the DOI to intercede on her behalf. Purvis agreed to do what he could and said she would receive a big reward if she would help the agency apprehend the criminal. She agreed to betray Dillinger and told Purvis she and the outlaw would probably go to the movies at the Marbro Theater the next day, Sunday, July 21.

In a telephone conversation with Cowley, Hoover told the inspector to take Dillinger alive if possible. He ordered that the agents assigned to the strike force be armed only with pistols, and that they should take out their weapons only if "absolutely necessary." Cowley and his assistant, Virgil Peterson, immediately went to the Marbro to set up the ambush.[9]

In a meeting at the DOI's Chicago office on Sunday morning Inspector Cowley told the lawmen attending that Dillinger might be armed when he emerged from the theater. He rejected a suggestion from an East Chicago police officer that a pistol be "planted" on Dillinger if he was not.[10]

On the very hot evening of July 22 (the temperature had reached 108 degrees at the municipal airport during the day before) Dillinger decided to take his girlfriend Polly Hamilton and Anna Sage to an air-conditioned movie house to cool off. Steve Chiolak and his girlfriend came by the apartment, but Sage soon got rid of them. Dillinger narrowed the choices to the Biograph and the Marbro, and about 5:30 Sage called Purvis to tell him they would be going to the evening show at one of the two theaters.

Purvis went to the Biograph with one of his men and kept watch on the entrance from a car parked nearby. Every once in a while he would go into a nearby tavern to telephone Samuel Cowley at the DOI's Chicago field office. About 8:30 Purvis and his partner saw Dillinger, wearing a striped shirt and gray trousers, and two women enter the Biograph, where *Manhattan Melodrama*, a gangster film starring Clark Gable, was playing. As soon as they were inside, Purvis rushed to call Cowley, who immediately headed for the scene. The men waiting at the Marbro—Sergeant Walter Conrey of the East Chicago police and a DOI agent—were ordered to go to the Biograph.

As reinforcements began to arrive, Purvis entered the theater but found it too crowded to attempt to arrest Dillinger inside. Cowley arrived and kept Director Hoover, in his library at home, abreast of the situation by telephone. Soon sixteen federal agents and five East Chicago policemen went to positions assigned by Cowley and surrounded the theater. Interestingly, the Chicago police had not been notified of the operation to apprehend Public Enemy Number One. Just before the movie was to end a Chicago police car containing two officers pulled up outside, responding to a call from theater employees who thought the large number of men outside might be criminals planning to rob the theater or its patrons. They quickly departed after a federal agent showed his identification.

At about 10:40 p.m., an unconcerned Dillinger, Polly, and Anna Sage—attired in an orange dress that appeared red under the marquee lights, leading to her designation as the "Lady in Red" in accounts of the event—exited the theater and turned left toward Anna's apartment.

"Boy, wasn't that a great show!" Dillinger remarked to his companions.

As they passed the doorway of the Goetz Country Club, a tavern, Dillinger saw a man standing there but paid no attention to him. It was Purvis, who, as the trio reached the National Tea Company store, tried to light a cigar to signal the DOI agents to move in. Although Purvis was so nervous that he was unable to strike the match, the agents nonetheless caught his signal.[11]

As Mrs. Sage lagged behind, Polly saw men with guns and shoved her elbow into Dillinger's ribs, alerting him to their presence. According to the official DOI report, Purvis called out to the gangster and told him to give up; however, several eyewitnesses said no warning was given. Purvis, in his account just afterward, did not say he had called out to

Dillinger, but he later insisted he had said, "Stick 'em up, Johnny, we have you surrounded."[12]

Dillinger bolted toward a nearby alley, allegedly reaching into his suit for a gun. Agents Herman E. Hollis, Clarence O. Hurt, and Charles B. Winstead fired five shots at the fleeing outlaw, striking him three times and also wounding two women standing nearby. One bullet struck Dillinger in the left side, one grazed his face, and another went into his back as he doubled over, exiting from his right eye. Dillinger fell to the ground and died in the alley. Agent Winstead is believed to have fired the fatal shot.

At 10:51 p.m. Dillinger was pronounced dead at the Alexian Brothers Hospital. The contents of his pockets included a mere $7.70 in cash, two keys, a handkerchief, a magazine clipping, and a pocket watch containing a photograph of Polly Hamilton.[13] Many thought it odd that so little money was found, since Dillinger was often known to carry thousands of dollars in a money belt. Some believe that Martin Zarkovich stole Dillinger's "getaway stash."[14]

Purvis took Dillinger's gun from his hand in the alley and sent it to Hoover, who later gave it to a Hollywood celebrity as a souvenir.

In the media frenzy that followed the slaying, several witnesses stepped forward to give their accounts of Dillinger's demise.

Edgar l'Allemand, a mechanic, who had a good view of the event, said, "I glanced across the street as I stood there. Everything seemed calm and peaceful. There were not many people around and very little traffic. I had a clear, unobstructed view of the sidewalk in front of the theater on the opposite side.

"Suddenly, I saw a tall man fire two shots in quick succession. He seemed to be standing almost beside the man who was shot. The wounded man fell to the alley without uttering a sound."

Mrs. Ester Gousinow, sitting in her second-floor parlor, claimed she saw the whole thing:

"I saw a young man walk out of the theater, accompanied by two girls. They were only about ten feet from the alley, and I was looking right down on them when I saw three men walk up behind them. I heard two shots—there may have been more—and the man with the two girls fell to the sidewalk. I thought first that it was a holdup and that the victim was killed. Then I thought of Dillinger, and because it appeared to me that the three men shot without giving a warning, I thought immediately that the victim was Dillinger.

"I sent my brother-in-law running downstairs, and he called to me in a few minutes that the man who had been shot had been carrying a gun."[15]

As word of the killing spread, a huge crowd gathered around the Biograph. Several women, some of them crying, dipped their handkerchiefs in the blood of Public Enemy Number One. On a nearby alley wall someone scribed:

> *Stranger, stop and wish me well,*
> *Just say a prayer for my soul in Hell,*
> *I was a good fellow, most people said,*
> *Betrayed by a woman all dressed in red.*[16]

The death of the notorious outlaw, who was hailed as an anti-establishment hero by many and reviled by others, created almost as big a stir nationally as it did locally. So curious were the residents of Chicago to see the celebrity criminal that almost 15,000 people viewed Dillinger's body at the morgue.[17]

Three days after his death, Dillinger was buried in the Crown Hill Cemetery at Indianapolis. His father told reporters, "They shot him down in cold blood. I don't approve of shooting a fellow down in cold blood. He was surrounded by fifteen men, and that ain't fair. I'd rather have him shot than captured, though, and John would rather have had it that way."

Lawmen who participated in the operation had their stories to tell, too. A DOI agent told Chicago plainclothesman Frank Slattery he was "lucky to be alive."

"When we got the signal, you were close to Dillinger," the agent said. "You looked like Dillinger, and I was about to shoot you when the other fellows let loose and killed the right man."[18]

Another lawman in danger of being shot because of his resemblance to the bandit was agent Thomas Connor. Like the gangster, he wore a white suit and straw hat and was a man of medium height and build, with a pronounced cleft chin.[19]

When Makley and Pierpont heard the news of Dillinger's death, both expressed sorrow. Always the comedian, Makley told one interviewer, "Why, I would even be sorry if they bumped *you* off. . . . Yes, he was the kind of guy anyone would have been glad to have for a brother."[20]

Pierpont told reporters, "They got John. I'd be willing to trade places with him tonight."[21]

Dillinger's demise gave rise to countless rumors, many of which have attained legend status over the years, and most of which have been disproved by historians. Among the more popular are claims that the man killed outside the Biograph was not Dillinger but a look-alike, and that the outlaw had hidden $200,000 in a suitcase near Little Bohemia.[22] He was even accused of being a Nazi party member.[23] Some accounts say Dillinger had such a large penis that it was preserved and sent to the Smithsonian.[24]

There was much criticism of the DOI over the manner of Dillinger's death. British newspapers voiced their displeasure over what they thought was an unnecessary homicide without arrest or trial.[25] In November 1937 Inspector Dan O'Neill of the San Francisco Police Department's Identification Bureau, speaking to the Railway Detectives Association, said he believed Dillinger had been "murdered" by the G-Men, who had "put out hooey" about his death. "I don't mean to rap the federals, I'm just telling the truth," he told the audience, which included the head of the DOI's San Francisco filed office, N. J. L. Pieper.[26]

But many believed that Dillinger, who had killed one law enforcement officer, deserved what he got. As one newspaper editorial stated, "Why not shoot Dillinger? . . . Honestly, wouldn't it be more satisfactory to plug Mr. Dillinger with a volley of lead than to capture him and bring him to trial?"[27]

Citizens wrote to President Roosevelt that Dillinger's crimes were so dangerous that he should have been be shot on sight. An Indianapolis resident wrote that Dillinger's terror spree was "the worst crime the state of Indiana has ever suffered," adding that, "the women who were with them even laugh and joke about how much fun they have had." He continued that the president should use his "wonderful power and influence, so [they can] be brought to their justice—death."[28]

The End of the Dillinger Gang

WO DAYS AFTER DILLINGER'S DEATH, Dr. Wilhelm Loeser was arrested by federal agents in Oak Park, Illinois. Three days later, James Probasco, owner of the house in which Dillinger had undergone plastic surgery, allegedly committed suicide by jumping from a nineteenth-floor window of the FBI office in Chicago's Bankers Building. It was rumored that he fell to his death while being dangled out the window during interrogation.[1]

Homer Van Meter and Marie Conforti heard about Dillinger's slaying on the radio and sought hideouts in Minnesota. His brother Harry said at the time that he expected Homer to meet the same fate. At first the couple hid at Leech Lake Log Cabin Camp on Route 34 near Walker, Minnesota. Later, Van Meter had secret meetings with criminals in St. Paul at Rice Street bars and bowling alleys. In August, *Liberty* magazine offered a $1,000 reward for information leading to his arrest.

On August 3 in St. Paul, Van Meter met mobster Frank Kirwin, who recommended Bear Island, noted for its great fishing, as a hideout. From August 6 to August 14, Van Meter and Marie, posing as Henry and Ruth Adams, hid at LeClaire's Resort on Leech Lake near what is today

213

Longville, Minnesota. While there, he enjoyed fishing, while Marie went swimming, and both ate a lot of spaghetti. Federal agents suspected that Van Meter was hiding at a cottage on one of the lakes in the area, but the underworld had so many contacts there that his hideout was impossible to find. To make things worse for his pursuers, many St. Paul gangsters had gone into deep hiding to avoid questioning by the police.[2]

That month the DOI also tried to get information about Van Meter by questioning Pierpont's family, who contacted lawyer Louis Piquett. They told the FBI that Piquett wanted Van Meter to help finance his lime kiln business.[3]

After leaving LeClaire's Resort on August 14, Van Meter and Marie went to the Birches Camp Resort near Grand Rapids and later the Green Gables Tourist Camp outside Minneapolis. Van Meter finally returned to Minneapolis on August 23, but when the outlaw began talking too much about future bank robberies and drawing unwanted attention to St. Paul's criminal-protection system, the local underworld leaked information about his whereabouts to the authorities.

As Pat Reilly told federal agents, "Van Meter returned to St. Paul and consequently brought heat on the underworld here. . . . He was advised by the underworld that if he did not keep under cover, he would cause trouble to the remaining members of the underworld. However . . . Van Meter was not the type that would stay under cover, and his constant appearance on the streets in St. Paul angered the underworld."

According to some accounts, Van Meter went to see mob banker Dutch Sawyer to retrieve $9,000 that Schultz was holding for him. He also wanted his cut of the $49,500 stolen from the Security National Bank of Sioux Falls. Sawyer allegedly kept the cash and told the police where they could find the gangster.

Another researcher claims that bank robbers Tommy Gannon and Jack Peifer tipped police to Van Meter's location. Under this scenario, Peifer and members of the St. Paul Police Department divided up Van Meter's bank loot, while Gannon was given Van Meter's guns as a reward.

On August 23 Van Meter was scheduled to meet Frank Kirwin, with whom he was furious for stealing money from him, and Jack Peifer at the Hollyhocks Club. That afternoon at 5:12 p.m. Van Meter, wearing a blue serge suit, a blue tie with white dots, a straw hat, an expensive gold Bulova watch, and a fake mustache, stepped out of a car driven by either Kirwin or Gannon in front of St. Paul Motors, an auto dealership near the intersection of University and Marion. Under his arm was a brown zippered bag containing $6,000. In his money belt was $2,000, and in his pockets was $923.

The driver had set up Van Meter and was part of a plot to eliminate the outlaw and the trouble he was causing for the city's underworld-police relationship. At 12:20 p.m. that day, St. Paul Police Detective Tom Brown had visited the dealership's manager and had told him that a man wanted by the police would arrive later that afternoon to buy an automobile. Brown gave him a description of Van Meter.

As Kirwin or Gannon drove away, Van Meter was suddenly confronted by four men—Brown and Police Chief Frank Cullin, armed with a pair of sawed-off shotguns, and two other officers, each carrying a machine gun—who shouted for the bandit to surrender. Van Meter ran toward an alley, firing two shots over his shoulder from a .38-caliber Colt automatic.

An eyewitness later stated that Van Meter "either got rattled or didn't know the neighborhood when he turned into that alley, because it's a blind alley. If he had turned right, he might have got away."

Brown fired a blast from his shotgun, the force of the buckshot knocking Van Meter off his feet. The outlaw attempted to raise his revolver to fire another shot but was struck by a machine-gun burst that nearly severed his arm. The officers unleashed a storm of lead, and by 5:30 Van Meter, with some two dozen buckshot pellets and a single machine-gun slug lodged in his body, and his face a lumpy mess as a result of plastic surgery, lay slumped against a garage wall. A pistol lay ten feet away.

A large crowd soon gathered, and many of the curious pushed to get close to the slain hoodlum. As the body was taken away, a woman fainted when a newspaperman pretending to be the dead Van Meter for a photo stood up.

J. Edgar Hoover was furious that the St. Paul police had not notified him about Van Meter's presence until after the outlaw had been killed. "Our St. Paul office has shown an utter lack of aggressiveness," he fumed. In fact, local lawmen told several lies to federal agents, among them, that the police had only learned of Van Meter's location five or ten minutes before the ambush. DOI officials were outraged when they later learned from the manager of the auto dealership that the business had been under surveillance for as long as ten days.

Newspapers falsely reported that Van Meter had been turned in by a girlfriend. Opal Long apparently believed the stories. Reflecting on her dead friend, she said, "Van was afraid of women—I mean he figured that most of them couldn't be trusted. And I guess he was right. If he had just stuck to that idea, maybe he wouldn't have got killed the way he did."[4] Most of the $8,000 that Van Meter was said to have had on him was gone when federal agents examined his body at the morgue. However, they did find $1,394 that had been overlooked by the St. Paul police, who claimed they had found only $450. Members of the Barker-Karpis Gang later told the DOI they did not give Detective Brown $5,000 they owed him from the Bremer ransom as punishment for killing Van Meter.[5]

The *St. Paul Pioneer Press* hailed the killing of Van Meter as "a first class serving of notice on the country at large and on the underworld in particular that St. Paul is really cleaning house and no longer deserves the evil reputation it acquired as a friendly harbor for gangsters."[6]

Van Meter was buried August 28, 1934, at Lindenwood Cemetery in Fort Wayne, Indiana. Since Van Meter lacked the charisma of many other well-known Depression desperados, only his immediate family and a large contingent of police were on hand for the funeral. His brother Harry, who was seriously ill with diabetes, could not attend, and his sister Helen had no interest in going. The bandit left property valued at about $1,000 and had $500 in a Citizens Trust Company receivership.

According to the *Fort Wayne Journal-Gazette*, "Van Meter was the unheralded leader of the [Dillinger] mob, the cunning gunman who did the thinking for the mob. He was not the sensational and spectacular criminal but the tricky, treacherous bandit."[7]

Marie Conforti was soon captured, and a DOI raid on a Leech Lake resort on September 7 netted three Van Meter associates: housekeeper Marie McCarthy, handyman Frank Kirwin, and caretaker William Gray.

On October 9 Tommy Gannon was sentenced to serve a six-month sentence in the Ramsey County Jail for harboring Van Meter.[8] On December 22 Kirwin was sentenced to two years and a $10,000 fine; Gray to eighteen months and a $5,000 fine; and McCarthy to a year and a day for harboring Van Meter.[9]

On September 22, 1934, mimicking Dillinger's breakout from the Crown Point jail, Harry Pierpont and Charley Makley attempted to escape from the death house at the Ohio State Penitentiary using fake guns. The bogus weapons, fashioned to look like a .32-caliber revolver and an automatic pistol, looked real from a short distance. Made of soap and such odds and ends as toothpaste tubes and paper clips and covered with shoe polish, they had required weeks of careful preparation, yet they were not uncovered by prison guards who were supposed to search each death cell daily. The condemned men, who had boasted they would not die in the electric chair, were kept under constant surveillance.

When a guard named Slagle carried Pierpont's breakfast to him about 10:30 that morning, Pierpont, lying on his cot, complained that he was ill. As Slagle turned to leave the cell, Pierpont leaped up, slugged the guard, and demanded his keys. Drawing his "gun," Pierpont backed Slagle into a corner. When the guard refused to hand over the keys, Pierpont hit him again and took them. Makley drew his "gun" at the same time and threatened a guard named Pharr stationed outside Makley's cell. Using Slagle's keys, Pierpont freed Makley, Russell Clark, and the six other prisoners on death row.

Pierpont, Makley, and Clark broke apart a wooden table. Then, using the two guards as shields, Pierpont and Makley rushed down the main corridor to a locked steel door leading to a special guard room between death row and cell block "L" and banged on it with pieces of the wooden table. When guard J. T. Jones looked through a peephole in the door and saw what was transpiring, he grabbed a rifle, shouted for aid, and pushed a warning buzzer to alert other guards. Even if the convicts had gotten through the guard-room door, there were still four more steel doors separating them from the outside.

Warden Preston Thomas was holding a press conference concerning accused Lindbergh baby kidnapper Bruno Hauptmann when Jones's alarm sounded. When a warning gong went off in the guard room, an emergency squad jumped to their feet, grabbed their riot guns, and raced toward death row. As Warden Thomas shouted orders, guards in the prison yard began forcing inmates back into their cells. City police were summoned and surrounded the prison.

When the prison's riot squad arrived at the cellblock door and a guard opened it, Makley pointed his "weapon" at the offices and yelled, "Stand back!" Two squad members opened up with their riot guns, one firing eight shots and the other four. A ricochet slightly wounded a guard named Whetstone, who had blood dripping from his fingertips.

Both Makley and Pierpont went down with the first volley. Shot in the spine, head, and shoulder, Makley died an hour later in the prison hospital. A bullet passed through Pierpont's abdomen and lodged in the soft tissue beneath his kidney. Bullets also struck him near the base of his spine and in his back, and one shot creased his scalp. None was fatal. After the shootings, the other death row convicts were herded into their cells.[10]

The next day Pierpont, who had not eaten anything in two days and maintained a stoic calm while being treated for his wounds, refused food for most of the day. Prison physician Dr. George W. Kell said, "I ordered a bowl of noodle soup sent in to him after I left, but I don't know if he ate it or not. He told me he didn't want any food." Later Pierpont ate milk and toast. Doctors thought his condition was not serious, although he was running a slight fever and had some slight paralysis in his legs. He was able to stand and take short walks back and forth across his death-row cell.

Pierpont and Clark were questioned at an inquest held to look into the escape attempt. Clark said he was unaware of the escape plan until Pierpont unlocked his cell door.[11] A few days after the outlaws' bid for freedom, Pierpont told Mary Kinder, "We thought we'd do some good, but we didn't."[12] Silent and sullen, Pierpont awaited his execution. He was given magazines but refused to read them. On October 6 Warden Thomas doubled the guard force and even assigned a personal guard to the recuperating outlaw. He had officers check the license plates of all out-of-state cars seen in the prison's vicinity.[13]

When Pierpont's parents visited him on Saturday, October 13, he told them not to make any more attempts to obtain intercession from Governor White. On Tuesday morning Pierpont also spent time talking with his parents through the steel mesh partition in "L" block. "I want to die," Pierpont sobbed.

Later that day, the outlaw requested a quiet funeral, made a public gesture of acceptance of his Catholic faith, and got the prison chaplain to give him the Last Sacraments. Mary Kinder also tried to visit him briefly that day, but the warden denied her request. Pierpont wrote a letter to his attorney Jessie Levy during his last hours, thanking her for her efforts on his behalf. During his last supper he nibbled at a chicken dinner, then pushed the dishes aside. Governor White denied an eleventh-hour plea by Pierpont's parents, saying, "I see no justifiable reason to extend clemency."

Pierpont's sudden execution on Wednesday, October 17, was ordered by Warden Thomas to prevent any attempt by the remnants of the Dillinger Gang to free the outlaw. The condemned man knelt and read a prayer a few minutes before guards took him on his final walk. On the way to the death room he passed the cell of Russell Clark, but the warden refused to let the two meet even for a handshake. By some accounts, the wounded gangster walked without assistance (others say he was carried to the death room), kissed a crucifix, and handed it to a Catholic priest.

Dressed in a blue serge prison suit, a light blue dress shirt but no necktie, and with his coat unbuttoned, Pierpont came face to face with the electric chair at midnight. There was a slight, sardonic smile on the gangster's face as he seated himself in the chair. His eyes, however, were bloodshot, showing the effects of numerous crying spells over the past few days. After a current of 2,000 volts was passed through his body, he was pronounced dead at 12:14 a.m.[14]

His body was taken to a small house that adjoined a filling station and tourist camp operated by his parents on U.S. Highway 31, eight miles south of South Bend, Indiana.[15] Family and friends were allowed to view the body, and a private funeral service was conducted at 10 a.m. on October 20 at the home by a Catholic priest. Afterward, Pierpont's body was taken to the Holy Cross Cemetery in Indianapolis and buried in the family plot beside his sister Fern. At the graveside service were his parents, his brother Fred, Mary Kinder, an uncle, and other friends and relatives.[16]

37

Bye-bye Baby Face

BABY FACE NELSON DID NOT feel remorse over Dillinger's death, nor did he fear the intense manhunt under way for himself, but he knew his death was inevitable and liked being the nation's new Public Enemy Number One. Only Pretty Boy Floyd offered any competition for that dubious honor. Feeling the West Coast would be safer for him, Nelson drove there with wife Helen and John Paul Chase. As a cover, they also brought along Jack Perkins and his wife, Grace; their son; and Chase's lieutenant, Fatso Negri.

The group drove throughout Northern California, then headed back east at a leisurely pace, driving through Nevada, the Rocky Mountains, Colorado, Nebraska, and Iowa, before pulling into the Chicago area on September 1. Two days later, on Labor Day, Nelson and Helen and Chase and girlfriend Sally Bachman drove to Lake Geneva, Wisconsin, to see Hobart Hermansen, owner of the Lake Como Inn, and arrange to use the inn as a hideout during November.

On September 10 Chase and Sally boarded a train for New York, and Baby Face, Helen, and Fatso Negri hit the road for Reno, arriving nine days later. While there, Nelson looked up his friend Frank Cochran, a garage owner and airplane pilot, who made repairs to Nelson's car. On September 26, the trio checked into a tourist camp in Fallon, Nevada, some sixty miles from Reno, and spent evenings clandestinely socializing with Cochran and his wife.

A couple of days later they drove to Tobe Williams's underworld hospital in Vallejo, California, and retrieved $1,000 of a sizable cache of cash Nelson had earlier left in the administrator's keeping. Returning to the Reno area, the three stayed in tourist camps, again visiting the Cochrans at night.

On October 9 Chase arrived in Reno and stopped by Cochran's garage to have his auto serviced, then checked into a local hotel and attempted to contact Nelson. The DOI had been tracking Chase across the country, and when his car was spotted in Reno, a contingent of nearly a dozen federal agents was dispatched to the city and arrived on the morning of October 10.

Local police had traced Chase's car to the Air Service Garage, and the federal strike force quickly went there to search the vehicle and talk to the garage owner. Cochran said he had never seen the driver before he pulled into the garage and, when shown a photograph of Chase, said the driver didn't look like the man in the picture. Agents also showed him photos of Nelson, Perkins, and Negri, but Cochran said he didn't recognize them either.

Believing Cochran to be an upright citizen, the lawmen sought his help is setting a trap for the driver when he returned to pick up his car. At his first opportunity, Cochran phoned Chase at the hotel and warned him of the trap and the large group of G-Men who were in town to spring it.

When Nelson, Helen, and Negri turned up at Cochran's house late that afternoon, the garage owner warned them away and told them he would take Chase to a spot several miles from town in a few hours to meet Nelson. During the meeting, Cochran told the outlaws all about the federal agents' plans and agreed to meet them again the next night.

Cochran kept his word and the next evening gave the bandits the license numbers of the agents' cars and the address where they were staying. They met again a few times over the following week and the bandits became alarmed when it became apparent the G-Men were beginning to check the local tourist camps for signs of their quarry.

On October 24 the outlaws left Reno, driving first to Las Vegas so Chase could buy another car, then turning east. After leaving Negri in Colorado to wait on one of their cars, which had broken down, Nelson, Helen, and Chase headed for Chicago, arriving in the area about November 1. They hid out at different hotels in small towns outside the city by night and drove along the region's rural roads by day. They were pulled over for speeding in a small Illinois town during November, but the officers didn't search the vehicle and thus did not find the group's weapons stashed in the back seat. Nelson went to the police station and paid the $5 fine without being recognized by officers on duty.

There were reports that Nelson and his gang were planning to rob a messenger service for a major department store in Chicago's Loop during the Christmas season. The holdup was supposed to take place the week after Thanksgiving and, if successful, could have netted a full day's sales receipts, perhaps as much as $150,000 or more.[1]

On November 27, two days before Thanksgiving, Nelson, Helen, and Chase drove to Lake Geneva to spend a few days at Hobart Hermansen's Lake Como Inn. As the bandits' car pulled up to the house, Nelson noticed a stranger on the porch and warily asked him if Hermansen was home. When the man said the resort owner would be back later, Nelson backed up the car and quickly drove away.

Nelson surmised that the stranger was a federal agent, and he was right. The man was part of a detail sent to stake out the inn earlier that month, working on information provided by Chase's girlfriend Sally Bachman.[2] Sally had been arrested by federal agents when she returned to San Francisco in early October and, after weeks of questioning, had finally told them what she knew about Nelson, including their trip to Lake Geneva to arrange for a place to lay low in November. Later, she was flown to Chicago and driven to Wisconsin to help agents identify the inn, and in early November, G-Men interviewed Hermansen, who reluctantly agreed to allow the stakeout team to stay in his home.

On the day Nelson arrived at the Como Inn, Special Agent James Metcalf was the stranger Nelson talked with; upstairs, armed with a high-powered rifle equipped with a hunting scope, was Special Agent Charles Winstead, the man believed to have fired the fatal shot into Dillinger. Their partner, Special Agent C. E. McRae, had driven their car into town to buy groceries.

Metcalf immediately called Inspector Samuel Cowley at the DOI's Chicago office with a description of Nelson's black Ford sedan and gave him the license number: Illinois plate number 639-578. Cowley quickly sent two special agents, William Ryan and Thomas M. McDade, by car from Chicago to Lake Geneva, and half an hour later the inspector and three more agents left in two government vehicles for Wisconsin.

Shortly after 3:30 p.m., as Ryan and McDade were driving just north of Fox River Grove, Illinois, they saw a black Ford approaching from the opposite direction. As they passed, McDade noticed the Ford's license plate and Ryan observed two men and a woman inside. Nelson, noticing the men staring at the car as he sped past, became suspicious, and when he saw one of the agents trying hard to get a good look at him, and the government car begin to turn around, he knew for sure. "That guy in that car—he was a Fed, I'm sure of it. And we're going to take another look," he said as he pulled the Ford into a U-turn.

As the two cars again approached each other, both agents read the license plate number. Deciding to force the issue, Nelson quickly spun his vehicle around and began to pursue the lawmen. Chase and Helen were seated in the back, and after ordering Helen to duck, Chase picked up an automatic rifle from the floorboard. As Nelson gained on the G-Men's car, Chase opened fire through the Ford's windshield. The agents returned fire. Chase's shots were ineffective, but at least one of the lawmen's rounds hit the engine of Nelson's Ford. The agents continued into the town of Barrington, stopping when Ryan spun the car around after failing to negotiate a turn. Both men jumped out of the vehicle and took up defensive positions, but the gangster's car never arrived.

"They hit something; the car has quit on me," Nelson cursed as his Ford slowed and began spewing smoke and steam. Meanwhile, Cowley and Special Agent Herman E. Hollis, en route to Lake Geneva and traveling in the opposite direction, saw the gangsters and government men exchanging gunfire, and quickly turned around to follow them. As they pulled up behind Nelson's vehicle, Chase began firing out the rear window at them.

As the gangsters entered Barrington, their Ford obviously failing, Nelson whipped the car onto a gravel road leading to the North Side Park where it lurched to a stop. Hollis and Cowley, surprised by the maneuver, overshot the gravel road and squealed to a stop about fifty yards beyond Nelson's smoking Ford.

Nelson yelled at his companions to get out, then screamed at Helen to take cover. She hurried across a plowed field, dropping to the ground and covering her head with her hands as shooting began. As Nelson and Chase took up defensive positions behind the Ford, Chase opened up with the rifle, slugs pounding the government vehicle. Cowley, armed with a machine gun, and Hollis, carrying a shotgun, rolled out the passenger-side door and sought cover. Cowley jumped into a roadside ditch by the rear of the car, while Hollis crouched by the front bumper.

A fierce gun battle ensued, with Cowley and Nelson blasting away with machine guns, Hollis firing his shotgun, and Chase returning fire with the automatic rifle. A minute into the firefight, Nelson doubled over and grasped his left side, then moved behind the car and swapped weapons with Chase. When Chase had emptied the machine gun, Nelson took back the weapon, slammed in a fresh drum of ammunition and began firing at the G-Men.

According to some accounts, the outlaw stepped from behind the vehicle and, like Jimmy Cagney in a gangster movie, as one observer later put it, declared, "I'm going down there and get those sons of bitches!" and advanced toward the lawmen. Other historians claim Nelson's machine gun jammed and that the outlaw grabbed another automatic rifle from the disabled Ford and began blasting away at the agents.

Heading straight for his adversaries, Nelson exchanged several shots with the lawmen before staggering as slugs tore into his legs. The bantam bandit and Cowley continued to fire long bursts at each other, until Cowley pitched forward on his face, mortally wounded.

His shotgun empty, Hollis threw the weapon aside and pulled a pistol while making a mad rush for the ditch. As he neared the spot where Cowley had fallen, he spun around and tumbled to the ground, dead from a bullet in the head.

As more than thirty people looked on from the lots of three gas stations that lined the road nearby, Nelson turned to Chase and yelled, "Get Helen, and let's get the hell out of here!"

As the three piled into the DOI vehicle to make their escape, Chase thought of weapons left in their disabled Ford and went back to get them. He returned and slipped behind the wheel, started the engine and rapidly drove away.

An eyewitness at one of the gasoline stations, State Patrolman William Gallagher, later stated, "The cars stopped on the northwest highway about five hundred feet west of State Route 63. I sensed that it was a case of police authorities after hoodlums of some sort.

"As the agents advanced with drawn guns, instinctively I pulled out my rifle. When the shooting started, I started firing at the desperados. There were about fifteen people getting in my line of fire, and I had to stop. The people in the other machine got out, too, swinging a machine gun, its muzzle flaring lead. Then, with the agents lying on the ground, they jumped into a machine and roared away."

While being taken to a hospital in Elgin, Illinois, the dying but fully conscious Cowley repeatedly insisted on talking to Melvin Purvis, who had not been told of the gangsters' sighting in Lake Geneva. "Did you get Purvis? I must talk to Purvis before I die," he gasped as doctors began to give him ether for an emergency operation.

When Purvis, who finally had been alerted to the situation, arrived at the hospital, Cowley was undergoing surgery. Cowley was unable to talk clearly the three times he regained consciousness following the operation, and at 2:40 a.m. the following morning he died.[3]

"If it's the last thing I do, I'll get Baby Face Nelson—dead or alive," Purvis told a reporter. "Nelson ought to know he hasn't a chance at eventual escape. . . . We aren't particular whether we get him alive or dead."

Hoover, believing that Purvis was seeking too much publicity and thus stealing the FBI director's limelight, was outraged.[4]

By the time Purvis made his statements to the press, Baby Face Nelson was already dead. The slug from Cowley's machine gun that had caused the outlaw to double over during the firefight had torn through his liver, stomach, and pancreas.[5] His movie-like standoff with Cowley had been his last blaze of glory, and by the time he got into the government car to leave the scene, he was bleeding heavily. There were also eight slugs from Hollis's shotgun lodged in his legs and thighs.

Chase rapidly drove toward Wilmette, Illinois, where the outlaws tried to get help from Father Phillip W. Coughlan. The priest refused to take the dying bandit into his sister's home but offered to lead the group to a safe haven. As they followed the priest's car, Nelson, fearing Coughlan was leading them into another trap, became suspicious and told Chase to turn off. He then guided his partner through several residential streets, eventually stopping behind a small house on Walnut Street in the town of Winnetka.

With help from a man inside the house, Chase carried Nelson into a bedroom, where Helen cleaned and dressed her husband's wounds. Later, as Nelson continued to fade, Chase left to dispose of the bullet-riddled government car. Unfamiliar with the area, he became lost, ran out of gas, and, suspecting that his friend would soon be dead, eventually was able to board a train for Chicago.

At 7:35 p.m. Lester Gillis, known as Baby Face Nelson, America's Public Enemy Number one, expired in Helen's arms.

At 7:55 the next morning, undertaker Phillip Sadowski in Niles Center (now Skokie) received a call from a woman who told him that the body of a man named Lester Gillis could be picked up at Lincoln and Harms Avenue. Although the undertaker asked for more information, the caller hung up.

When Sadowski told Chief of Police Axel C. Stollberg about the mysterious call, Stollberg exclaimed, "My God, man, don't you know who that is? That's Baby Face Nelson!"

Stollberg called the DOI, and twelve agents were sent to where Nelson's body was supposed to be, some fifteen miles from the site of the gunfight near Barrington. Although there was no body, the agents found a pile of bloody clothing, an empty money belt, and a laundry bag stamped with the name of the Pratt Lane Hotel in Chicago.

After a slow and meticulous search in an ever-widening circle that extended almost two and a half miles, law enforcement officials discovered a body with twisted arms and legs, a contorted cherubic face, and a blonde moustache lying in a drainage ditch. The torso was wrapped in a blood-soaked blanket that covered a gaping wound on the left side. The body was taken to a local undertaker, where DOI agents took fingerprints and confirmed that it was in fact Nelson.

That evening the body was moved to the Cook County Morgue, where some 2,000 people viewed the remains, a far cry from the 15,000 who had seen Dillinger's body there.

The government car was found the next day in a muddy ditch on a Winnetka side street.

Among the barrage of media coverage regarding Nelson's demise, some newspapers declared Helen Gillis to be the nation's first female public enemy while others touted her as the new Public Enemy Number One. Others trumpeted that the federal government had told its agents to shoot her on sight. DOI spokesmen insisted the order issued by Director Hoover had only meant that they would not withhold fire because she was a woman.

Helen turned herself in to federal agents two days after her husband's death when her father, Vincent Wawrzyniak, went on the radio to ask his daughter to surrender before she was killed. According to author William J. Helmer, Helen went to the Chicago home of Nelson's brother-in-law Bob Fitzsimmons, who made arrangements for her to surrender to DOI agents in downtown Chicago. She spent the next five days undergoing questioning at the agency's Chicago field office and was not allowed to attend her husband's funeral. On December 6 Helen was taken to Madison, Wisconsin, where the next day her two-year probation was revoked and she was sentenced to serve a year and a day in the federal women's correctional facility at Milan, Michigan.

On December 1 more than 200 people turned out for a brief funeral service at the Sadowski mortuary for Lester Gillis, alias Baby Face Nelson. Six unidentified men serving as pallbearers loaded the casket bearing his body into a hearse for the drive to St. Joseph's Cemetery in River Grove, Illinois, where Nelson was interred later that day.[6]

Among the forty or so mourners were his mother, Mary Gillis, and sister, Julie Fitzsimmons, and her husband, Bob. Also on hand were several reporters and cameramen, and at least one federal agent who had been instructed to watch for criminals.

Meanwhile, upon his return to Chicago, Chase had gone into hiding at a downtown hotel. He felt reasonably safe because newspapers were reporting that Nelson's male companion in the Barrington shootout were most likely the already dead John Hamilton, Tommy Touhy, or Alvin Karpis. After a few days he replied to a newspaper ad and got a job ferrying a car to Seattle. Using the name Elmer Rockwood, he had no problem obtaining a chauffeur's license and had his photograph taken at a police station before leaving Chicago. Still feeling safe, he went to Butte, Montana, to retrieve $2,000 from a safety-deposit box there. But when he called the friend who had rented the box for him, he was told to get out town fast because federal agents had it under surveillance.

Although he now knew the DOI was looking for him, Chase, on December 26, his thirty-third birthday, went to the California State Fish Hatchery in Mount Shasta, where he had once worked, to borrow money. The next day federal agents, having received a tip from the hatchery foreman that the outlaw was staying in town, quietly took the outlaw into custody without firing a shot. Chase was later tried and found guilty of the murder of Inspector Sam Cowley. He was sentenced to life imprisonment at the new federal prison called Alcatraz.[7]

Other friends of Nelson also stood trial over the next several months. Thomas C. Cohen, alias Tobe Williams, received a prison sentence of eighteen months and was fined $5,000 for harboring Baby Face. Henry O. "Tex" Hall and Frank Cochran were also convicted of harboring Nelson, and each was fined $2,000 and sentenced to a year and a day in a federal penitentiary. For conspiracy in the Nelson case, Anthony Moreno, a San Francisco bartender, received six months in jail.

Bye-bye Baby Face

On April 5, 1935, federal Judge Walter C. Lindley in San Francisco commented about the four men, "No man can consider himself decent who aids and gives shelter or comfort to help the fugitive from justice, the gunman, the gangster, the spume of humanity!"[8]

Many reports circulated in the underworld regarding John Hamilton's death. DOI Inspector Cowley had thought the outlaw was very much alive, and Hamilton was a suspect in the South Bend bank robbery. There was even a report that he had kidnapped the Lindbergh baby. He was also accused of stealing $5.[9] The FBI had tried to get to Hamilton and Van Meter by using the Pierpont family, who allegedly could get in contact with them.[10] Hamilton was a candidate for Public Enemy Number One, and *Liberty* magazine offered a $1,000 reward for his capture.[11]

However, Hamilton's badly decomposed body was found by federal agents in Oswego, Illinois, on August 28, 1935. A prison dentist confirmed the body was that of the gangster. His right hand with the telltale missing fingers had been cut off, and to further prevent identification lye had been poured on the corpse. A horseshoe was found on top of the body, apparently a sentimental gesture by person or persons unknown. The outlaw was buried on August 30 at Oswego's small city cemetery.[12]

A nephew, Bruce Hamilton Jr., believes that Hamilton died long after he was reported killed. Hamilton claims he met his uncle John in a small Canadian town during a childhood trip.[13]

Epilogue

WITH THE DEMISE OF THE Dillinger Gang and other Depression-era outlaws, J. Edgar Hoover became "Public Hero Number One"—at least according to one pulp magazine. His DOI would be designated the Federal Bureau of Investigation on July 1, 1935, and would develop into America's premier federal law enforcement agency.[1]

On May 23, 1934, Clyde Barrow and Bonnie Parker were ambushed and killed near Gibsland, Louisiana. Pretty Boy Floyd met his end on October 22, 1934, on a farm near East Liverpool, Ohio.

The Barker-Karpis Gang began to fall apart in early 1935. On the night of January 8 Arthur "Dock" Barker was arrested while taking a walk near his Chicago apartment. "This is a helluva time to be caught without a gun," he lamented.

Later that night two other members of the Barker-Karpis Gang were trapped by federal agents. One surrendered, but the other, Russell Gibson, was slain when he tried to shoot his way to freedom. On January 16, 1935, Hoover's agents attacked the hideout of Arizona Clark Barker— better known as "Kate" or "Ma"—and her son Fred near Oklawaha, Florida, and after a one-sided, four-hour gunfight, Fred and Ma were dead.

At least one U.S. Senator attacked Hoover for not catching new Public Enemy No. 1 Alvin Karpis and for never making an arrest himself. The public enemy period ended when Hoover and his agents arrested Alvin Karpis in New Orleans on May 1, 1936.[2]

However, of all of the major public enemies, the popular culture considered John Dillinger and his gang to be the most interesting. Hoover said at the Attorney General's Conference on Crime in December 1934:

> John Dillinger, the flag-bearer of lawlessness, is dead, killed by federal bullets. Pretty Boy Floyd, who for years laughed at the law, lies in his grave, dead of gunshot wounds inflicted in open battle by our special agents. The career of Baby Face Nelson is over: he died of seventeen bullet wounds, while two of the finest men I ever knew gave their own clean lives that they might serve society by ending his filthy one. Wilbur Underhill no longer carries the name of the "Tri-State Terror." He too is gone, as well as such men as Homer Van Meter, Tommy Carroll, and others. That is progress.[3]

In the anteroom outside Hoover's office, the director placed in display cases items related to Dillinger, which symbolized the greatest glory of the federal agency. In 1938 a commentator wrote, "A tourist is dull-witted indeed if he fails to comprehend, as he gapes at the display cases, that he is looking upon the rude implements and superstitious talismans of a barbarous race that is slowly perishing under the relentless impact of a superior one."[4]

Especially impressive was Dillinger's death mask and the items around it:

- the straw hat he was wearing;
- a wrinkled snapshot of a girl which was fished from his trousers pocket;
- the silver-rimmed glasses he was wearing to heighten his disguise, one of the lens rims snapped by a bullet;
- a La Corona-Belvedere cigar he was carrying in his shirt pocket that summer night, still banded and wrapped in cellophane.

There is an almost unholy shriek of triumph in these stark, simple objects.[5]

Epilogue

As a tangible symbol of the success of the government's "war on crime," Hoover and Attorney General Homer Cummings wanted an "escape-proof" American version of Devil's Island. They chose Alcatraz Island, located in the middle of San Francisco Bay, which had been a military fortification and army prison. Surrounded by a mile or more of cold, fast-flowing, shark-infested water, the island was transferred from the aegis of the War Department to the Justice Department on October 12, 1933. Incorrigible and infamous criminals hated to be sent to "the Rock," as it came to be known. Ultimately, however, Alcatraz was a failure. After many escape attempts, and partly because of deteriorating buildings, the prison was closed in 1963. By 1973 it had become a tourist attraction.[6]

For a long forty-eight years Hoover would reign as FBI director. The files he kept on famous and powerful people made it impossible to force him out. But by the time of his death in 1972, his image was already under attack. His violation of citizens' civil liberties caused further decline, as did his lack of attention to nationally organized crime until the 1960s.[7]

According to a former assistant to FBI Director William C. Sullivan:

> Hoover had a thing about Dillinger. If he were alive today and you went in to see him, he'd tell you about Dillinger. The older he got, the more he talked about Dillinger, Ma Barker, Karpis, and all those old cases of the thirties. He would talk on and on about this stuff, which I guess is understandable and is no criticism, but that's the way it was. He'd go on in great detail, over and over the same stuff, and one of our liaison men, who would take visitors in to meet Hoover, told me, "Jeez, I wake up at night reciting what Hoover has said, because he says the same things over and over and over again."[8]

Hoover's rival in public esteem, Melvin Purvis, went downhill after the Pretty Boy Floyd killing. Hoover could not tolerate anyone who got more press than he did, and Purvis's acting like a personal avenger when Nelson killed Cowley and Hollis on November 27 only increased the director's wrath. Purvis had gone to the dying Cowley's bedside and swore to him that he would personally bring Nelson down. This was too much for Hoover, who removed Purvis from any important work and made him go on useless inspection tours that kept him out of the headlines.

Purvis was too popular to fire summarily, so Hoover made unreasonable demands on the agent, forced him to make excessive office inspections, and criticized him unmercifully to get rid of him. Purvis even had to defend himself against the ridiculous rumor that he had drunkenly waved a gun around at a party. Finally, Purvis could take no more and resigned on July 10, 1935, citing personal reasons. Many thought he had resigned to protest the agency's refusal to prevent the deportation of Anna Sage.

Purvis's efforts to earn a living were hindered by Hoover, who prevented him from getting any job related to law enforcement. Instead, Purvis went into advertising, promoting such things as razor blades and Dodge automobiles. He also was involved with the "Melvin Purvis Junior G-Men" club for Post Toasties breakfast cereal.

Things got worse with the publication of Purvis's book *American Agent* in 1936, which did not mention Hoover by name, although it highly praised the FBI. In turn, Hoover, in his 1938 book *Persons in Hiding*, ignored Purvis completely and gave Samuel Cowley the credit for his accomplishments in the agency. Purvis was even eliminated from the official FBI map showing Dillinger's killing in front of the Biograph Theater. Although Purvis was listed among those at the Biograph in the 1950s book *The FBI Story* by Don Whitehead, he was not mentioned in the book's index.

For twenty-five years Purvis unsuccessfully tried to make up with Hoover, but Hoover sabotaged his efforts. Purvis's attempts to work as a lawyer, newspaperman, and radio station owner were mostly unsuccessful, and he developed serious health problems. Purvis committed suicide on February 29, 1960, by shooting himself with the same Colt .45 automatic he had been given by his fellow agents when he left the FBI. His family was deeply upset that Hoover ignored his death.

Things also did not go well for Anna Sage. In 1936, after being deported, Romanian authorities refused to let her perform for a vaudeville company. Criminals also tried to extort money from her when she opened a restaurant and night club in the town of Timosuara. Desperate, she changed her name and traveled throughout Europe in an effort to avoid troublemakers.

She went to the extreme of having plastic surgery in Budapest that made her look like a victim of a tropical disease called chafar by disfiguring her face with scars, so that she could enter a private sanitarium near Cairo. Finally, in July 1939, reporters found her there living in seclusion, but she was essentially ignored by the media during World War II and she died of a "liver ailment" on April 25, 1947, in Romania.

Epilogue

After Billie Frechette finished her harboring sentence in 1936, she toured with Dillinger's father in a crime-does-not-pay carnival show. She married, divorced, and remarried. Billie succumbed to cancer on January 13, 1969, in Shawano, Wisconsin, at the age of sixty-one.

Polly Hamilton first went into hiding but later lived a normal and quiet life. Using such names as Kay Sullivan and Kay Donahue, she was a waitress in Chicago and married William Black, a Chicago salesman. She died as Edythe Black in Chicago on February 19, 1969.

After Opal Long finished her harboring sentence, she slipped into obscurity and also died in Chicago in 1969.

Her sister Pat Cherrington was released from the U.S. Detention Farm at Milan, Michigan, on July 27, 1936. She also toured in a crime-does-not-pay show, then worked as a waitress, tavern hostess, and dice girl on North Clark Street in Chicago. She continued to maintain ties with the underworld, and in 1938 she and two men were accused of trying to cheat a pool player out of $9,000. For the rest of her life she lived a meager existence in rooming houses. Harry Copeland sent her love letters from prison, saying he thought he would be out by November 1949. An employee found her dead in her room at the Burton Hotel in Chicago on May 3, 1949. She had only $2.16 in her possession.[9]

Harry Copeland was released from prison on November 24, 1949. He died December 7, 1963, when he was run over by a car.[10]

An indictment was returned on June 6, 1934, against Anna Steve for harboring Dillinger and Red Hamilton.[11] On June 7, 1935, Anna and her son Charles Campbell went to trial. She was found guilty and sentenced to four months imprisonment. Campbell was found not guilty.[12]

Helen Gillis returned to Chicago after her release from the federal prison in Milan, Michigan, on December 13, 1936. Working under her real name, Helen Nelson, she spent the rest of her life in Chicago with her son, Roland, avoiding any kind of recognition. She died in 1987 and was buried near Chicago.[13]

Edgar Singleton, "John Dillinger's first partner in crime," was run over and killed by a train in 1937. The drunken Singleton had fallen asleep on a railroad track.[14]

After his capture in California in December 1934, John Paul Chase was flown back to Chicago, where his trial for murdering DOI Inspector Sam Cowley began on March 18, 1935. He was the first criminal to be tried under a new federal law that made it illegal to kill a federal agent while in the performance of his duties. Chase was found guilty one week later and was sentenced to life imprisonment at Alcatraz. He became eligible for parole on October 17, 1955, when a district judge in Chicago dismissed the indictment charging him with the murder of

Agent Herman Hollis because he had never been tried for the crime. He was released from prison on October 31, 1966, and died seven years later in Palo Alto, California.[15]

After Ed Shouse was released from prison on September 9, 1946, his fortunes declined.[16] He was arrested in Spokane, Washington, on a vagrancy charge on February 26, 1952, and in Minneapolis on March 18, 1955, for refusing to pay for a meal.[17] Shouse died in Chicago on September 13, 1959.[18]

Leslie Homer, who had helped Dillinger rob a Racine, Wisconsin, bank in November 1933, was sentenced to serve twenty-eight years at the Waupun Prison in Wisconsin. On April 18, 1936, Homer led five convicts armed with hatchets, knives, and bars in a failed escape attempt. Afterward, Homer became a model prisoner and even became editor of the prison magazine.[19] In 1943 he was released on parole.[20]

Richard Pyes, an associate of Thomas Carroll, was not apprehended until March 12, 1942, when he was arrested in Los Angeles. He was sentenced to four years for post office burglary in St. Paul on May 14, 1942. Another associate, William Louis Schepers, received a presidential pardon on November 19, 1942.[21]

Dillinger's lawyer, Louis Piquett, did not do well after his conviction for harboring Van Meter. Disbarred and ordered to pay a $10,000 fine, he entered Leavenworth on May 6, 1936, and was confined there until January 11, 1938. After his release Piquett worked in restaurants and tended bar in such places as Coburn's Tavern in Chicago. He stayed out of trouble and lived quietly with his wife. He was pardoned by President Harry S. Truman in January 1951, despite opposition from Hoover. When he died of a heart attack in Chicago on December 12, 1951, at the age of seventy-one, Piquett was hoping to get permission to practice law again.

Arthur O'Leary was able to avoid prison in return for his testimony that helped put Piquett behind bars. He is believed to have died in Dubuque, Iowa, around 1970.

Dr. Harold Cassidy committed suicide on July 30, 1946, at the Chicago home of a sister. Dr. Wilhelm Loeser later settled in Oklahoma City, where he died around 1956.[22]

Matt Leach lost his job as the head of the Indiana State Police in 1937 because of a lack of cooperation with the FBI. He wrote a book on the Dillinger case, but it was never published. Leach and his wife died on June 14, 1955, in an accident on the Pennsylvania Turnpike.[23]

Sergeant Martin Zarkovich overcame several handicaps, such as a liquor-smuggling conviction in 1930 and a demotion for not providing information about Dillinger to the governor of Indiana. After serving as chief of detectives he become police chief of East Chicago, serving from 1947 to 1952. He worked as a probation officer there until his death on October 30, 1969, at the age of seventy-one.[24]

In 1936 two high-ranking Secret Service officials, Joseph E. Murphy and Grady Boatwright, tried to look into Eddie Green's death to see if there was any merit to reports that he had been murdered in cold blood by the DOI. But Courtney Ryley Cooper, a crime writer close to J. Edgar Hoover, tipped him off about the investigation. Attorney General Cummings complained to Treasury Secretary Henry Morgenthau, and the two Secret Service officials were transferred to other positions. A .45-caliber bullet taken from Green's body was exhibited for many years in the Dillinger exhibit at FBI headquarters.[25]

Russell Lee Clark was assigned to the Ohio State Penitentiary's tailor shop. His mother, May; wife, Opal Long; sister, Dorothy Pierce; and his brother, Edward, often visited him. He was also visited by federal agents, but he said little to them.[26] Clark was one of the ringleaders of a strike by a thousand convicts in April 1935. He was placed in solitary confinement on bread and water.[27] In 1940 he and three other convicts made an attempt to escape—using a fake gun carved out of wood.[28]

Falling into obscurity, Clark spent more than thirty-four years in the Columbus penitentiary. Clark first came up for parole in April 1954, but his application was denied. He spent at least fourteen years of his sentence in solitary confinement.[29]

The Ohio State Penitentiary was a tough place to do time. First occupied in 1834, the facility spread over twenty-four acres. A report written in the 1930s stated:

> It is extremely doubtful if anywhere north of the Mason-Dixon Line general conditions respecting correctional methods are as deplorable and inadequate as in Ohio. . . . Hopelessly antiquated, shamefully overcrowded, and totally devoid of any constructive program . . . the archaic Ohio Penitentiary at Columbus probably has no equal in the United States. . . . Incomprehensible though it may seem, those responsible for the prisons are apparently willing to lock more than half the population in their cells day in and day out and forget them. They are willing to allow them to tick off the days on the cell walls, with no more inspiring or uplifting influence than cellmates as unregenerate as themselves.
>
> Overcrowding at the Ohio Penitentiary has reached a point where there is scarcely room to do anything more than jam the men into their cells the greater part of the day except for an occasional march in a "modified lock-step" about the sidewalks of the

yard for a few hours each day. Here is an institution which can accommodate properly not more than 2,000 men filled to overflowing with 4,400 prisoners of all kinds, ages and types.[30]

Clark was released in September 1968 after doctors found he had lung cancer and less than six months to live. He was taken by his sister Dorothy Pierce to Hazel Park, Michigan, where he died on December 24, 1968.[31]

By 1936, the days of America's so-called Robin Hood criminals were over. But they had been defeated at terrific cost. The Dillinger Gang alone had stolen at least $300,000 during its brief but prolific bank-robbing spree, and it cost law enforcement agencies throughout the country well over a million dollars to catch and/or kill the gang's members.[32]

The cost in human lives was also staggering. Eleven law enforcement officials fell to the gang's bullets, and perhaps as many as six citizens lost their lives as a result of the gang's activities.

In the end, eleven members of the Dillinger Gang were killed or executed and twenty-three were sent to prison.

Never again will the likes of the Dillinger Gang be seen in America.

Notes

Introduction

1. John Toland, *The Dillinger Days*. New York: Random House, 1963, 36.
2. William Helmer with Rick Mattix, *Public Enemies: America's Criminal Past, 1919-1940*. New York: Checkmark Books, 1998, xi-xiv.
3. Toland, *Dillinger Days*, 35-38.
4. Helmer, *Public Enemies*, 132.
5. Toland, *Dillinger Days*, 36.
6. G. Russell Girardin with William J. Helmer, *Dillinger: the Untold Story*. Bloomington, Ind.: Indiana University Press, 1994, 2.
7. Carl Sifakis, *The Encyclopedia of American Crime*. New York: Smithmark Publishers, Inc., 1992, 345-347.
8. Helmer, *Public Enemies*, 184-186.
9. Sifakis, *American Crime*, 345-347.
10. Ibid., 137-138.
11. Girardin, *Dillinger*, 4-6.
12. Toland, *Dillinger Days*, 294.
13. Sifakis, *American Crime*, 596-597.

Chapter 1

1. Roger A. Bruns, *The Bandit Kings from Jesse James to Pretty Boy Floyd*. New York: Crown Publishers, Inc., 1995, 176-178.
2. FBI Identification Order No. 1217 for John Dillinger, March 12, 1934.

3. John Toland, *The Dillinger Days.* New York: Random House, 1963, 5-7.
4. Report, L. E. Kingman, Jacksonville, Fla., April 11, 1934, DF 485, Sec. 11.
5. Robert Cromie and Joseph Pinkston, *Dillinger: A Short and Violent Life.* Evanston, Ill.: Chicago Historical Bookworks, 1990, 6-7.
6. Toland, *Dillinger Days,* 6-9.
7. Cromie and Pinkston, *Dillinger,* 9.
8. Toland, *Dillinger Days,* 9.
9. *Washington Herald,* May 8, 1934.
10. Letter, William G. Praed to Director, Oct. 21, 1959, DF, Sec. A129; Toland, *Dillinger Days,* pp. 9-10.
11. Cromie and Pinkston, *Dillinger,* 8.
12. Ibid., 10.
13. *Washington Herald,* May 8, 1934.
14. Toland, *Dillinger Days,* 11.
15. Rept., L. E. Kingman, Jacksonville, Fla., April 11, 1934, DF 485, Sec. 11.
16. Cromie and Pinkston, *Dillinger,* 10-12.
17. Tony Stewart, *Dillinger: The Hidden Truth.* Xlibris, 2002, 81-104.
18. Rept., L. E. Kingman, Jacksonville, Fla., April 11, 1934, DF 485, Sec. 11.
19. Toland, *Dillinger Days,* 12-14.
20. *New York Sunday Mirror,* Dec. 2, 1934.
21. Cromie and Pinkston, *Dillinger,* 15.

Chapter 2

1. Helen Wilson, *The Treatment of the Misdemeanant in Indiana.* Chicago: University of Chicago, 1938.
2. John Toland, *The Dillinger Days.* New York: Random House, 1963, 14-17.
3. Robert Cromie and Joseph Pinkston, *Dillinger: A Short and Violent Life.* Evanston, Ill.: Chicago Historical Bookworks, 1990, 15.
4. Mark Sufrin, "Dillinger," *American History Illustrated,* Feb. 1970, v. 4, no. 10, p. 37.
5. Indiana prison record of John Dillinger.
6. Cromie and Pinkston, *Dillinger,* 14-15.
7. Indiana prison record of John Dillinger.

Chapter 3

1. FBI Identification Order No. 1222 for Homer Van Meter, April 11, 1934.
2. Paul Maccabee, *John Dillinger Slept Here.* St. Paul, Minn.: Minnesota Historical Society, 1995, 209.
3. Memorandum for Mr. Clegg, April 7, 1934, DF 426, Sec. 10; *Fort Wayne (Ind.) Journal-Gazette,* Aug. 24, 1934.
4. *Fort Wayne (Ind.) Journal-Gazette,* Aug. 24, 1934.
5. John Toland, *The Dillinger Days.* New York: Random House, 1963, 20.
6. *Fort Wayne (Ind.) Journal-Gazette,* Aug. 23, 1934.
7. *Indianapolis Star,* Feb. 27, 1925.
8. *South Bend (Ind.) News-Times,* March 6, 7, 1925.
9. *Gary (Ind.) Post-Tribune,* Aug. 24, 1924.
10. Rept., Chicago, Aug. 25, 1934, V. W. Peterson, DF 3607, Sec. 59.
11. FBI Identification Order No. 1222 for Homer Van Meter, April 11, 1934.
12. Toland, *Dillinger Days,* 20.
13. *Chicago Tribune,* Jan. 6, 1926.

14. Toland, *Dillinger Days*, 18-21.
15. Ibid., 21.
16. Ibid.

Chapter 4
1. John Toland, *The Dillinger Days*. New York: Random House, 1963, 18.
2. *Indianapolis Star*, July 22, 1934.
3. Indiana prison record of Harry Pierpont; Indiana Central Hospital record of Harry Pierpont.
4. Rept., Cincinnati, N. B. Klein, June 13, 1934, DF 2008, Sec. 36.
5. Indiana prison record of Harry Pierpont; Indiana Central Hospital record of Harry Pierpont.
6. *Chicago Daily News*, Oct. 19, 1934.
7. Indiana Central Hospital record of Harry Pierpont.
8. Lori Hyde, "The Forgotten Harry Pierpont" (unpublished).
9. Indiana prison record of Harry Pierpont; Toland, *Dillinger Days*, 17-18.
10. Indiana Central Hospital record of Harry Pierpont.
11. Ibid.
12. Indiana prison record of Harry Pierpont.
13. Indiana Central State Hospital record of Harry Pierpont.
14. Mike McCormick, "The Dillinger Gang in the Wabash Valley, Part 2," *Terre Haute (Ind.) Tribune-Star*, July 5, 1998.
15. Indiana prison record of Harry Pierpont.
16. Toland, *Dillinger Days*, 18.
17. Ibid., 17-18.
18. McCormick, "Dillinger Gang, Part 2"; Toland, *Dillinger Days*, 107.
19. McCormick, "Dillinger Gang, Part 2."
20. *Marion (Ind.) Leader-Tribune*, Nov. 27, 1924.
21. Ibid., Dec. 24, 1924.
22. *Indianapolis Star*, March 12, 28, April 3, 1925.
23. Indiana prison record of Harry Pierpont; Toland, *Dillinger Days*, 17-18.

Chapter 5
1. Indiana prison record of John Dillinger.
2. John Toland, *The Dillinger Days*. New York: Random House, 1963, 17.
3. Robert Cromie and Joseph Pinkston, *Dillinger: A Short and Violent Life*. Evanston, Ill.: Chicago Historical Bookworks, 1990, 17.
4. Ibid.
5. Toland, *Dillinger Days*, 22-23.
6. Ibid., 26.

Chapter 6
1. John Toland, *The Dillinger Days*. New York: Random House, 1963, 24-27.
2. Indiana prison record of Harry Pierpont.
3. Toland, *Dillinger Days*, 31.
4. Ibid., 31-32.
5. Ibid., 32.
6. Ibid., 32-33.
7. *Fort Wayne (Ind.) Journal-Gazette*, Aug. 24, 25, 1934.

Notes

Chapter 7
1. *Detroit Free Press*, Aug. 29, 1935; Toland, *Dillinger Days*, 174.
2. Rept., Chicago, V. W. Peterson, Oct. 20, 1934, DF 4242, Sec. 70; 1910 Census.
3. Rept., Chicago, Earl Van Waggner, Jan. 15, 1934, DF, Sec. 54.
4. Rept., Chicago, V. W. Peterson, Oct. 20, 1934, DF 4242, Sec. 70.
5. *Detroit Free Press*, Aug. 29, 1935; Rept., Detroit, Nov. 26, 1934, DF, Sec. 76; 1910 Census.
6. *Detroit Free Press*, Aug. 29, 1935; Rept., Chicago, V. W. Peterson, Oct. 20, 1934, DF 4242, Sec. 70.
7. Rept., Detroit, Nov. 26, 1934, DF, Sec. 76.
8. *Detroit Free Press*, Aug. 29, 1935; Western Union, Chicago, Cowley to C. R. LaFrance, Oct. 5, 1934, DF, Sec. 68.
9. *Detroit Free Press*, Aug. 29, 1935.
10. Western Union, Chicago, Oct. 5, 1934, DF; Cowley to C. R LaFrance, DF. Sec. 68; *Detroit Free Press*, Aug. 29, 1935.
11. Rept., Detroit, Nov. 26, 1934, DF, Sec. 76.
12. *Grand Rapids (Mich.) Herald*, July 21, 22, 23, 1925.
13. *Detroit Free Press*, Aug. 29, 1935.
14. Rept., Chicago, V. W. Peterson, Oct. 20, 1934, DF 4242, Sec. 70.
15. *Grand Rapids (Mich.) Herald*, Dec. 23,1926; *Detroit Free Press*, Aug. 29, 1935.
16. *Grand Rapids (Mich.) Herald*, Jan. 4, 5, 1927.
17. *South Bend (Ind.) Tribune*, March 15, 16, 18, 1927; *South Bend (Ind.) News-Times*, March 15, 16, 17, 18, 19, 20, 1927.
18. Indiana prison record of John Hamilton; Toland, *Dillinger Days*, 27-28.
19. Rept., Chicago, V. W. Peterson, Oct. 20, 1934, DF 4242, Sec. 70; Rept., Detroit, March 28, 1934, DF 210, Sec. 6.
20. Rept., Detroit, Nov. 26, 1934, DF, Sec. 76; /Rept.?/, Oct. 6, 1934, DF, Sec. 76.
21. Memorandum for the file from H. E. Peters, Detroit, Oct. 17, 1934, DF 4232, Sec. 70.

Chapter 8
1. *St. Marys (Ohio) Evening Leader*, Sept. 26, 1934.
2. 1900 Census; Missouri prison record of Charles Makley (under the alias Charles McGray).
3. *Indianapolis Star*, July 22, 1934.
4. John Toland, *The Dillinger Days*. New York: Random House, 1963, 185.
5. Indiana prison record of Charles Makley; *St. Marys Evening Leader*, Sept. 22, 1934.
6. Indiana State Prison wanted poster of Charles Makley.
7. Robert Cromie and Joseph Pinkston, *Dillinger: A Short and Violent Life*. Evanston, Ill.: Chicago Historical Bookworks, 1990, 182; Toland, *Dillinger Days*, 120; *Chicago Herald and Examiner*, Sept. 10, 1934.
8. Cromie and Pinkston, *Dillinger*, 60.
9. *Kansas City Star*, Sept. 23, 1934.
10. Missouri prison record of Charles Makley (under alias Charles McGray).
11. Toland, *Dillinger Days*, 20.
12. *St. Marys (Ohio) Evening Leader*, Sept. 22, 1934; *Indianapolis Star*, June 6, 1928.

13. *St. Louis Globe-Democrat*, Jan. 6, 1926.
14. Ibid., Sept. 26, 27, 28, 1926.
15. *Indianapolis Star*, Oct. 1, 1926.
16. *Columbus (Ohio) Evening Dispatch*, Oct. 7, 1926.
17. *Kansas City Star*, Dec. 17, 1926; *Hammond (Ind.) Lake News*, June 5, 1928.
18. *Indianapolis Star*, March 25, 1927; *Cincinnati Enquirer*, June 9, 1927; *Indianapolis Star*, Nov. 2, 1927; *Decatur (Ind.) Daily Democrat*, March 27, 1928; *Mercer County (Ohio) Standard*, April 5, 1928.
19. *Hammond (Ind.) Lake News*, June 5, 6, 7, 8, 1928.
20. Indiana prison record of Charles Makley.

Chapter 9
1. *Chicago Herald and Examiner*, Sept. 11, 1934.
2. 1900 Census; Indiana prison record of Russell Lee Clark; Letter, Jayee to Courtney Ryley Cooper, June 26, 1936, DF, Sec. 117.
3. Letter, E. J. Connelley, SAC, Indianapolis, to SAC, Chicago, May 17, 1934, DF 1536, Sec. 29.
4. Indiana prison record of Russell Lee Clark.
5. Robert Cromie and Joseph Pinkston, *Dillinger: A Short and Violent Life*. Evanston, Ill.: Chicago Historical Bookworks, 1990, 181.
6. Letter, Jayee to Courtney Ryley, June 26, 1936, DF, Sec. 117.
7. G. Russell Girardin with William J. Helmer, *Dillinger: the Untold Story*. Bloomington, Ind.: Indiana University Press, 1994, 39; *Chicago Herald and Examiner*, Sept. 11, 1934.
8. Indiana prison record of Russell Lee Clark; Mike McCormick, "The Dillinger Gang in the Wabash Valley, Part 1," *Terre Haute (Ind.) Tribune-Star*, June 28, 1998.
9. *Indianapolis Star*, July 26, 27, 1927; Ibid., Aug. 9, 10, 1927; Ibid., Sept. 27, 1927.
10. Ibid., Dec. 9, 10, 11, 1927.
11. Indiana prison record of Russell Lee Clark; Cromie and Pinkston, *Dillinger*, 181.
12. Indiana prison record of Russell Lee Clark.
13. John Toland, *The Dillinger Days*. New York: Random House, 1963, 29-31.

Chapter 10
1. Indiana prison record of John Dillinger.
2. Robert Cromie and Joseph Pinkston, *Dillinger: A Short and Violent Life*. Evanston, Ill.: Chicago Historical Bookworks, 1990, 22.
3. Ibid., 22-23.
4. Ibid.
5. Cromie and Pinkston, *Dillinger*, 23-26.
6. Ron Rosner, "The Dillinger Era; a chronology of the Depression Era Outlaws" (unpublished).
7. John Toland, *The Dillinger Days*. New York: Random House, 1963, 63-71.

Chapter 11
1. Robert Cromie and Joseph Pinkston, *Dillinger: A Short and Violent Life*. Evanston, Ill.: Chicago Historical Bookworks, 1990, 31.
2. John Toland, *The Dillinger Days*. New York: Random House, 1963, 71.

Notes

3. Cromie and Pinkston, *Dillinger*, 31-36; *Muncie (Ind.) Star*, July 16, 1933.
4. Cromie and Pinkston, *Dillinger*, 36-37.

Chapter 12

1. G. Russell Girardin with William J. Helmer, *Dillinger: the Untold Story.* Bloomington, Ind.: Indiana University Press, 1994, 289-290.
2. Girardin, *Dillinger*, 289-291; *Chicago Times*, Dec. 6, 1934.
3. Alvin Karpis with Bill Trent, *The Alvin Karpis Story.* New York: Coward, McCann & Geoghegan, Inc., 1971, 73.
4. Myron J. Quimby, *The Devil's Emissaries.* New York: A. S. Barnes and Company, 1969, 263; Girardin, *Dillinger*, 290.
5. *Chicago Tribune*, Nov. 20, 1993; *New York Times*, Nov. 13, 1926.
6. Quimby, *Devil's Emissaries*, 263; Rept., Chicago, V. W. Peterson, Nov. 8, 1934, DF, Sec. 74.
7. Rept., Chicago, V. W. Peterson, June 25, 1934, DF 2211, Sec. 39.
8. Girardin, *Dillinger*, 285.
9. Rept., Chicago, V. W. Peterson, Feb. 11, 1935, DF 5421, Sec. 91.
10. Letter, S. P. Cowley to Director, Nov. 5, 1934, DF, Sec. 74; Rept., Chicago, V. W. Peterson, Nov. 8, 1934, DF, Sec. 74.
11. Rept., Washington, D.C., Arthur McLawhon, Jan. 12, 1935, DF 5172, Sec. 85.
12. Quimby, *Devil's Emissaries*, 265.
13. Steven Nickel and William J. Helmer, *Baby Face Nelson: Portrait of a Public Enemy.* Nashville, Tenn.: Cumberland House, 2002, 32-37.
14. /Rept.?/, Oct. 6, 1934, DF, Sec. 76; Letter, S. P. Cowley to Director, Nov. 23, 1934, DF, Sec. 75.
15. Rept., Chicago, V. W. Peterson, Feb. 11, 1935, DF 5421, Sec. 91.
16. Lew Louderback, *The Bad Ones; Gangsters of the '30s and Their Molls.* Greenwich, Conn.: Fawcett, 1968, 206-207.
17. Rept., Chicago, V. W. Peterson, Feb. 1, 1935, DF 5333, Sec. 90.
18. Girardin, *Dillinger*, 299.
19. William Helmer with Rick Mattix, *Public Enemies: America's Criminal Past, 1919-1940.* New York: Checkmark Books, 1998, 161-162.
20. *Chicago Tribune*, Jan. 1, 1991, Oct. 4, 1930.
21. Helmer, *Public Enemies*, 165.
22. *Chicago Tribune*, Nov. 23, 1930; Quimby, *Devil's Emissaries*, 265-266.
23. Rept., Chicago, V. W. Peterson, July 12, 1934, DF 2622, Sec. 44; *Chicago Tribune*, Nov. 23, 1930.
24. Steven Nickel and William J. Helmer, *Baby Face Nelson: Portrait of a Public Enemy.* Nashville, Tenn.: Cumberland House, 2002, 48-53.
25. Letter, S. P. Cowley to Director, Nov. 5, 1934, DF, Sec. 78; Rept., Chicago, V. W. Peterson, Nov. 8, 1934, DF, Sec. 74.
26. Quimby, *Devil's Emissaries*, 260, 267; Letter, S. P. Cowley to SAC, Washington, D.C., Nov. 23, 1934, DF, Sec. 75; Joliet Prison record of Lester Gillis.
27. Nickel, *Baby Face Nelson*, 55-57; Teletype, St. Paul, 1934, DF 2374, Sec. 40.
28. Rept., Chicago, V. W. Peterson, Sept. 27, 1934, DF 4051, Sec. 67.
29. Quimby, *Devil's Emissaries*, 268-270.
30. Nickel and Helmer, *Baby Face Nelson*, 68-69.

Notes

Chapter 13

1. Jay Robert Nash, *Bloodletters and Badmen*, Rev ed. New York: M. Evans and Company, Inc., 1995, 465; G. Russell Girardin with William J. Helmer, *Dillinger: the Untold Story*. Bloomington, Ind.: Indiana University Press, 1994, 324-328.
2. Steven Nickel and William J. Helmer, *Baby Face Nelson: Portrait of a Public Enemy*. Nashville, Tenn.: Cumberland House, 2002, 95.
3. Ibid., 133.
4. *Fort Wayne (Ind.) Journal-Gazette*, Aug. 24, 25, 1934.
5. Rept., Chicago, V. W. Peterson, Sept. 6, 1934, DF 3789, Sec. 62.
6. John Toland, *The Dillinger Days*. New York: Random House, 1963, 50-51.
7. Ibid., 132.
8. *Indianapolis Star*, Aug. 24, 1934; Toland, *Dillinger Days*, 132; Robert Cromie and Joseph Pinkston, *Dillinger: A Short and Violent Life*. Evanston, Ill.: Chicago Historical Bookworks, 1990, 105.
9. Melvin Purvis, *American Agent*. Garden City, N.Y.: Doubleday, Doran & Co., 1936, 103.
10. *Indianapolis Times*, Aug. 24, 1934.
11. Rept., Chicago, V. W. Peterson, Feb. 1, 1935, DF 5333, Sec. 90.

Chapter 14

1. Don Lambert, "How Iowa Rubbed Out Dillinger's Ace Gunman," *Startling Detective Adventures*, Sept. 1934, 8.
2. 1900 Census; Rept., Omaha, O. C. Dewry, June 16, 1934, DF 2043, Sec. 37.
3. Letter, H. H. Clegg to Director, June 13, 1934, DF 1990, Sec. 36.
4. 1915 Iowa State Census of Council Bluffs, Iowa (Pottawattamie County Genealogical Society).
5. Rept., Omaha, O. C. Dewry, June 16, 1934, DF 2043, Sec. 37.
6. 1915 Iowa State Census of Council Bluffs, Iowa (Pottawattamie County Genealogical Society).
7. *St. Paul Daily News*, June 8, 1934.
8. Leavenworth prison record of Thomas Carroll.
9. World War I record of Thomas Carroll (Serial no. 1423840).
10. *Council Bluffs (Iowa) Daily Nonpareil*, June 7, 8, 1934.
11. Paul Maccabee, *John Dillinger Slept Here*. St. Paul, Minn.: Minnesota Historical Society, 1995, 226-227.
12. FBI Identification Order No. 1223 for Thomas Carroll, April 25, 1934.
13. District Court of Pottawattamie County, Iowa at Council Bluffs (November term, 1921). The State of Iowa vs. Tom Carroll, James Durick, and Dick Fernley.
14. FBI Identification Order for Thomas Carroll.
15. Iowa Prison record of Thomas Carroll.
16. FBI Identification Order for Thomas Carroll; *St. Paul Pioneer Press*, June 1, 1934.
17. FBI Identification Order for Thomas Carroll.
18. *Kansas City Star*, June 30, 1929; *St. Joseph (Mo.) News-Press*, June 8, 1934.
19. FBI Identification Order for Thomas Carroll; District Court of the United States for the Northern District of Oklahoma. U.S. vs. Frank Sloane, alias Thomas Carroll, et. al. Case no. 1565 (1927).
20. *St. Joseph (Mo.) News-Press*, June 8, 1934; *Kansas City Star*, June 30, 1926.

21. FBI Identification Order for Thomas Carroll.
22. *Kansas City Star*, Feb. 28, 1927.
23. Ibid., March 24, 1927.
24. FBI Identification Order for Thomas Carroll; Missouri Prison record of Thomas Carroll; Rept., St. Paul, J. J. Waters, Oct. 12, 1934, DF 4178; Maccabee, *John Dillinger*, 226-227.
25. FBI Identification Order for Thomas Carroll; Leavenworth Prison record of Thomas Carroll.
26. Maccabee, *John Dillinger*, 227-230.
27. Letter, H. H. Clegg to SAC, Kansas City, June 7, 1934, DF 1951NR15, Sec. 35; U.S. National Archives, Central Plains Region, Kansas City, Mo., RG:21. Subgroup USAC (St. Paul, Minn.), Criminal case 6004.
28. Maccabee, *John Dillinger*, 229.

Chapter 15
1. Paul Maccabee, *John Dillinger Slept Here*. St. Paul, Minn.: Minnesota Historical Society, 1995, 62.
2. Memorandum for the Director from S. P. Cowley, April 4, 1934, DF, Sec. 8.
3. FBI Summary Report on Edward Green, July 23, 1936.
4. 1900 Census; Ramsey County, Minnesota, District Court, State of Minnesota against Eddie Green and John Doe, Nov. 4, 1922. (Minnesota Historical Society).
5. Maccabee, *John Dillinger*, 210.
6. Ramsey County District Court.
7. FBI Summary Report on Edward Green.
8. Ramsey County District Court.
9. *St. Paul Pioneer Press*, Dec. 24, 1921.
10. Ramsey County District Court. .
11. Maccabee, *John Dillinger*, 210; FBI Summary Report on Edward Green.
12. *St. Paul Pioneer Press*, Sept. 24, 25, 1922.
13. Ramsey County District Court.
14. FBI Summary Report on Edward Green; Maccabee, *John Dillinger*, 210.
15. FBI Summary Report on Edward Green.
16. William Helmer with Rick Mattix. *Public Enemies: America's Criminal Past, 1919-1940*. New York: Checkmark Books, 1998, 179-180; *Kansas City Star*, Jan. 29, 1933.
17. Maccabee, *John Dillinger*, 127-129; Alvin Karpis with Bill Trent, *The Alvin Karpis Story*. New York: Coward, McCann & Geoghegan, Inc., 1971, 75-79.
18. Maccabee, *John Dillinger*, 127-129.
19. FBI Summary Report on Edward Green.
20. Maccabee, *John Dillinger*, 167.
21. FBI Summary Report on Edward Green.
22. Maccabee, *John Dillinger*, 164.
23. FBI Summary Report on Edward Green.
24. *Minnesota Star*, April 4, 1934.

Chapter 16
1. John Toland, *The Dillinger Days*. New York: Random House, 1963, 72-73.
2. G. Russell Girardin with William J. Helmer, *Dillinger: the Untold Story*. Bloomington, Ind.: Indiana University Press, 1994, 25.

Notes

3. Toland, *Dillinger Days*, 72-73.
4. Ibid., 73-74.
5. Robert Cromie and Joseph Pinkston, *Dillinger: A Short and Violent Life.* Evanston, Ill.: Chicago Historical Bookworks, 1990, 41.
6. Girardin, *Dillinger*, 24.
7. Cromie and Pinkston, *Dillinger*, 41-44.
8. Ibid., 47-50.
9. Toland, *Dillinger Days*, 106; *Indianapolis Star*, Sept. 7, 1933.
10. Toland, *Dillinger Days*, 103-104.
11. Cromie and Pinkston, *Dillinger*, 50-51.
12. Toland, *Dillinger Days*, 132.
13. Ibid., 106-108.
14. Ibid., 74-76.
15. Cromie and Pinkston, *Dillinger*, 39-40.
16. Ibid., 52-53; Toland, *Dillinger Days*, 105-109.

Chapter 17
1. John Toland, *The Dillinger Days*. New York: Random House, 1963, 113-115; *Indianapolis Star*, Sept. 27, 1933.
2. Robert Cromie and Joseph Pinkston, *Dillinger: A Short and Violent Life.* Evanston, Ill.: Chicago Historical Bookworks, 1990, 178.
3. Toland, *Dillinger Days*, 114-118.
4. *Indianapolis Star*, Sept. 27, 1933.
5. Cromie and Pinkston, *Dillinger*, 62.
6. G. Russell Girardin with William J. Helmer, *Dillinger: the Untold Story*. Bloomington, Ind.: Indiana University Press, 1994, 29-30.
7. Cromie and Pinkston, *Dillinger*, 63-64.
8. Toland, *Dillinger Days*, 119-121.
9. Cromie and Pinkston, *Dillinger*, 65-67.
10. Ibid., 69-71; *St. Marys Evening Leader*, Oct. 4, 1933.
11. Toland, *Dillinger Days*, 125-126.

Chapter 18
1. John Toland, *The Dillinger Days*. New York: Random House, 1963, 111-112; Robert Cromie and Joseph Pinkston, *Dillinger: A Short and Violent Life*. Evanston, Ill.: Chicago Historical Bookworks, 1990, 55-56.
2. Cromie and Pinkston, *Dillinger*, 68.
3. Ibid., 68-69.
4. Ibid., 73-77; Toland, *Dillinger Days*, 128-132; *Lima (Ohio) News*, Oct. 13, 1933.
5. Cromie and Pinkston, *Dillinger*, 90.
6. Ibid., 79-80.

Chapter 19
1. Memorandum for Mr. Edwards, Aug. 23, 1934, DF (DF 97-57-1), *Grand Rapids (Minn.) Herald* Aug. 19, 1933.
2. Steven Nickel and William J. Helmer, *Baby Face Nelson: Portrait of a Public Enemy.* Nashville, Tenn.: Cumberland House, 2002, 125-126.
3. Paul Maccabee, *John Dillinger Slept Here*. St. Paul, Minn.: Minnesota Historical Society, 1995, 229-230; *St. Paul Pioneer Press*, Oct. 24, 1933.

Notes

Chapter 20

1. Carl Sifakis, *The Encyclopedia of American Crime*. New York: Smithmark Publishers, Inc., 1992, 207-208.
2. Robert Cromie and Joseph Pinkston, *Dillinger: A Short and Violent Life*. Evanston, Ill.: Chicago Historical Bookworks, 1990, 119; *Chicago Herald and Examiner*, Sept. 10, 1934.
3. Jay Robert Nash, *Bloodletters and Badmen*, Rev ed. New York: M. Evans and Company, inc., 1995, 208.
4. *Chicago Herald and Examiner*, Sept. 10, 1934.
5. Sifakis, *American Crime*, 206-207.
6. /Rept.?/, Oct. 6, 1934, DF, Sec. 76.
7. Nash, *Bloodletters*, 208-209; Rept., H. H. Clegg, May 25, 1934, DF 1712, Sec. 32.
8. Cromie and Pinkston, *Dillinger*, 119.
9. G. Russell Girardin with William J. Helmer, *Dillinger: the Untold Story*. Bloomington, Ind.: Indiana University Press, 1994, 39; *Chicago Herald and Examiner*, Sept. 11, 1934.
10. Girardin, *Dillinger*, 39.
11. *Chicago Herald and Examiner*, Sept. 11, 1934.
12. Letter, SAC, Detroit to Director, May 14, 1936, DF File 6705, Sec. 111; Memorandum for the Director from S. P. Cowley, June 2, 1934, DF File, Sec. 33; Rept., St. Paul, D. L. Nicholson, July 16, 1934, DF file, Sec. 44.
13. John Toland, *The Dillinger Days*. New York: Random House, 1963, passim.
14. Cromie and Pinkston, *Dillinger*, 78-79.
15. Toland, *Dillinger Days*, 132-133.
16. Cromie and Pinkston, *Dillinger*, 83-85.
17. Toland, *Dillinger Days*, 136.
18. Nash, *Bloodletters*, 210.
19. *Chicago Tribune*, Oct. 24, 1933.
20. Cromie and Pinkston, *Dillinger*, 84-85.
21. Cromie and Pinkston, *Dillinger*, 81.
22. Letter, Smith to Hughes, Oct. 14, 1933, DF file 2; Letter, Robinson to Hoover, Oct. 18, 33, DF 4.
23. *Evansville (Ind.) Courier*, Oct. 25, 1933.
24. Letter, E. J. Connelley to Hoover, Oct. 29, 1933, DF file 9.
25. Memorandum, E. J. Connelley to Hoover, Oct. 25, 1933, DF file; Claire Bond Potter, "Guarding the Crossroads: The FBI's War on Crime in the 1930s." (Ph.D. dissertation, New York University, 1990), 160-161.
26. Cromie and Pinkston, *Dillinger*, 88.
27. Ibid.
28. Toland, *Dillinger Days*, 142-147.
29. *Chicago American*, Nov. 17, 1933.
30. Sifakis, *American Crime*, 207-208.
31. Nash, *Bloodletters*, 208.
32. Cromie and Pinkston, *Dillinger*, 88.
33. Toland, *Dillinger Days*, 146-151.
34. Cromie and Pinkston, *Dillinger*, 118.

Notes

Chapter 21
1. Paul Maccabee, *John Dillinger Slept Here.* St. Paul, Minn.: Minnesota Historical Society, 1995, 229-231.
2. Letter, D. M. Ladd, SAC to SAC, San Antonio, Aug. 15, 1934, DF, Sec. 57.
3. *San Antonio (Texas) Express*, Dec. 12, 1933; Rept., Gus Jones, June 5, 1934, San Antonio, Texas, DF 1829, Sec. 34.

Chapter 22
1. *Chicago Herald and Examiner*, Sept. 11, 1934.
2. *Denver Post*, Sept. 24, 1934.
3. Robert Cromie and Joseph Pinkston, *Dillinger: A Short and Violent Life.* Evanston, Ill.: Chicago Historical Bookworks, 1990, 104-105.
4. Ibid., 120.
5. Ibid., 124.
6. Ibid.
7. Cromie and Pinkston, *Dillinger*, 129-130.
8. Ibid., 132.
9. William B. Breuer, *J. Edgar Hoover and His G-Men.* Westport, Conn.: Praeger Publishers, 1995, 138-139.
10. John Toland, *The Dillinger Days.* New York: Random House, 1963, 153-154.
11. Cromie and Pinkston, *Dillinger*, 126-127.
12. Toland, *Dillinger Days*, 153-154.
13. *Chicago Herald and Examiner*, Sept. 11, 1934.

Chapter 23
1. G. Russell Girardin with William J. Helmer, *Dillinger: the Untold Story.* Bloomington, Ind.: Indiana University Press, 1994, 52.
2. Letter, D. M. Ladd, SAC, St. Louis, to SAC, Detroit, Aug. 15, 1934, DF file.
3. Robert Cromie and Joseph Pinkston, *Dillinger: A Short and Violent Life.* Evanston, Ill.: Chicago Historical Bookworks, 1990, 131.
4. Letter, Clegg to Hoover, April 13, 1934, DF file 560.
5. John Toland, *The Dillinger Days.* New York: Random House, 1963, 157-159.
6. Toland, *Dillinger Days*, 174-176.
7. Rept., St. Paul, D. L. Nicholson, July 16, 1934, DF file.
8. Cromie and Pinkston, *Dillinger*, 135-136.
9. Toland, *Dillinger Days*, 176-182.
10. Cromie and Pinkston, *Dillinger*, 141-146.
11. Toland, *Dillinger Days*, 187-188.
12. Cromie and Pinkston, *Dillinger*, 154-155.

Chapter 24
1. G. Russell Girardin with William J. Helmer, *Dillinger: the Untold Story.* Bloomington, Ind.: Indiana University Press, 1994, 62-63.
2. John Toland, *The Dillinger Days.* New York: Random House, 1963, 195-196.
3. Ibid., 196.
4. Ibid., 206.
5. Robert Cromie and Joseph Pinkston, *Dillinger: A Short and Violent Life.* Evanston, Ill.: Chicago Historical Bookworks, 1990, 150-151.

Notes

6. Ibid., 156-157.
7. Toland, *Dillinger Days*, 206-207.
8. Cromie and Pinkston, *Dillinger*, 159.
9. Claire Bond Potter, "Guarding the Crossroads: The FBI's War on Crime in the 1930s." (Ph.D. dissertation, New York University, 1990), 166.
10. Cromie and Pinkston, *Dillinger*, 158-159.
11. Girardin, *Dillinger*, 76-80.
12. Toland, *Dillinger Days*, 209.

Chapter 25

1. Steven Nickel and William J. Helmer, *Baby Face Nelson: Portrait of a Public Enemy.* Nashville, Tenn.: Cumberland House, 2002, 115-117.
2. *New York American*, Feb. 11, 194.
3. Jay Robert Nash, *Bloodletters and Badmen*, Rev ed. New York: M. Evans and Company, inc., 1995, 466.
4. Paul Maccabee, *John Dillinger Slept Here.* St. Paul, Minn.: Minnesota Historical Society, 1995, 159; Ibid., 213-214.
5. *Indianapolis Times*, Aug. 24, 1934.
6. Rept., Chicago, V. W. Peterson, May 8, 1934, DF 1297, Sec. 24; Maccabee, *John Dillinger*, 167; Ibid., 215.

Chapter 26

1. G. Russell Girardin with William J. Helmer, *Dillinger: the Untold Story.* Bloomington, Ind.: Indiana University Press, 1994, 83-88.
2. Robert Cromie and Joseph Pinkston, *Dillinger: A Short and Violent Life.* Evanston, Ill.: Chicago Historical Bookworks, 1990, 164.
3. Ibid.
4. Ibid., 165; *Tulsa (Okla.) Daily Works*, March 4, 1934.
5. Cromie and Pinkston, *Dillinger*, 165-166.
6. Ibid., 170-172.

Chapter 27

1. William B. Breuer, *J. Edgar Hoover and His G-Men.* Westport, Conn.: Praeger Publishers, 1995, 157-158.
2. Robert Cromie and Joseph Pinkston, *Dillinger: A Short and Violent Life.* Evanston, Ill.: Chicago Historical Bookworks, 1990, 167-165.
3. *Chicago Tribune*, March 4, 1934; Cromie and Pinkston, *Dillinger*, 168-170.
4. G. Russell Girardin with William J. Helmer, *Dillinger: the Untold Story.* Bloomington, Ind.: Indiana University Press, 1994, 95.
5. *Lima (Ohio) News*, Feb. 14, 1934.
6. Cromie and Pinkston, *Dillinger*, 158.
7. Ibid., 172.
8. Ibid., 178-182.
9. John Toland, *The Dillinger Days.* New York: Random House, 1963, 243-244.
10. Cromie and Pinkston, *Dillinger*, 182.
11. *Fort Wayne (Ind.) Journal-Gazette*, Aug. 24, 1934.

Chapter 28

1. John Toland, *The Dillinger Days.* New York: Random House, 1963, 216.
2. Connelley to Hoover, April 28, 1933, DF 9; Memorandum to Nathan from

Notes

Hoover, March 6, 1934, DF; Claire Bond Potter, "Guarding the Cross-roads: The FBI's War on Crime in the 1930s." (Ph.D. dissertation, New York University, 1990), 160-161.

3. Helmet, *Public Enemies*, 210.
4. Paul Maccabee, *John Dillinger Slept Here*. St. Paul, Minn.: Minnesota Historical Society, 1995, 211.
5. Toland, *Dillinger Days*, 219.
6. Maccabee, *John Dillinger*, 210.
7. FBI Summary Report on Edward Green.
8. Maccabee, *John Dillinger*, 215.
9. FBI Summary Report on Edward Green.
10. Letter, H. H. Clegg to Director, April 13, 1934, DF, Sec. 12.
11. Toland, *Dillinger Days*, 220-224; Bryan Burrough. *Public Enemies: America's Greatest Crime Wave and the Birth of the FBI, 1933-34*. New York: The Penguin Press, 2004, 244-47.
12. *Tulsa Daily World*, March 7, 1934, March 10, 1934.
13. Toland, *Dillinger Days*, 224-239; Burrough, *Public Enemies*, 250-257.
14. Maccabee, *John Dillinger*, 222.
15. Myron J. Quimby, *The Devil's Emissaries*. New York: A. S. Barnes and Company, 1969, 271.
16. Toland. *Dillinger Days*, 243.

Chapter 29

1. Paul Maccabee, *John Dillinger Slept Here*. St. Paul, Minn.: Minnesota Historical Society, 1995, 213.
2. Rept., St. Paul, D. L. Nicholson, July 16, 1934, DF, Sec. 44.
3. Maccabee, *John Dillinger*, 219.
4. Rept., St. Paul, D. L. Nicholson, July 16, 1934, DF, Sec. 44.
5. John Toland, *The Dillinger Days*. New York: Random House, 1963, 242-247.
6. Robert Cromie and Joseph Pinkston, *Dillinger: A Short and Violent Life*. Evanston, Ill.: Chicago Historical Bookworks, 1990, 185-189.
7. Rept., St. Paul, D. L. Nicholson, July 16, 1934, DF, Sec. 44.
8. Rept., St. Paul, D. L. Nicholson, July 20, 1934, DF 2767, Sec. 46.
9. Steven Nickel and William J. Helmer, *Baby Face Nelson: Portrait of a Public Enemy*. Nashville, Tenn.: Cumberland House, 2002, 190.
10. Rept., St. Paul, D. L. Nicholson, July 20, 1934, DF 2767, Sec. 46.

Chapter 30

1. Paul Maccabee, *John Dillinger Slept Here*. St. Paul, Minn.: Minnesota Historical Society, 1995, 234-236; St. Paul News, April 4, 1934; Memorandum, Clegg to Director, April 4, 1934, DF 402, Sec. 10.
2. Maccabee, *John Dillinger*, 234-236; *St. Paul Pioneer Press*, April 8, 1934; Memorandum, S. P. Cowley to Director, April 19, 1934, DF 1584, Sec. 30.
3. Letter, D. R. Clark, April 7, 1934, DF 331, Sec. 8.
4. Maccabee, *John Dillinger*, 236.
5. Memorandum for the Attorney General from Director, June 27, 1934, DF, Sec. 39.

Notes

Chapter 31
1. John Toland, *The Dillinger Days*. New York: Random House, 1963, 253-257.
2. Rept., Detroit, A. A. Muzzey, May 22, 1935, DF, Sec. 105.

Chapter 32
1. G. Russell Girardin with William J. Helmer, *Dillinger: the Untold Story*. Bloomington, Ind.: Indiana University Press, 1994, 297.
2. Ibid., 145.
3. Rept., V. W. Peterson, May 3, 1934, DF 1291.
4. Girardin, *Dillinger*, 145.
5. Letter, D. M. Ladd, SAC, St. Paul, to Director, July 13, 1934, DF 2655, Sec. 44.
6. Robert Cromie and Joseph Pinkston, *Dillinger: A Short and Violent Life*. Evanston, Ill.: Chicago Historical Bookworks, 1990, 208.
7. Girardin, *Dillinger*, 146.
8. John Toland, *The Dillinger Days*. New York: Random House, 1963, 264.
9. Letter, D. M. Ladd, SAC, St. Paul, to Director, July 13, 1934, DF 2655, Sec. 44.
10. Toland, *Dillinger Days*, 263-265.
11. Cromie and Pinkston, *Dillinger*, 211.
12. Toland, *Dillinger Days*, 264.
13. Cromie and Pinkston, *Dillinger*, 211.
14. Toland, *Dillinger Days*, 264-272.
15. Rept., V. W. Peterson, May 3, 1934, DF 1291.
16. Toland, *Dillinger Days*, 268-272.
17. Cromie and Pinkston, *Dillinger*, 213.
18. Toland, *Dillinger Days*, 272-275.
19. Cromie and Pinkston, *Dillinger*, 213-215.
20. Cromie and Pinkston, *Dillinger*, 216.
21. Toland, *Dillinger Days*, 276-277.
22. Toland, *Dillinger Days*, 279-280.
23. Memorandum for the Director from Clyde Tolson, June 15, 1934, DF 3352, Sec. 55; Letter, D. M. Ladd, SAC, St. Paul, to Director, July 13, 1934, DF 2655, Sec. 44.
24. Cromie and Pinkston, *Dillinger*, 221.
25. Toland, *Dillinger Days*, 287-291.
26. Ibid., 291-292; Memorandum for the Director, RE: Alvin Karpis and Edward George Bremer, Oct. 21, 1935, DF 6506, Sec. 112.
27. Toland, *Dillinger Days*, 286.
28. Girardin, *Dillinger*, 150-151.

Chapter 33
1. Myron J. Quimby, *The Devil's Emissaries*. New York: A. S. Barnes and Company, 1969, 277.
2. G. Russell Girardin with William J. Helmer, *Dillinger: the Untold Story*. Bloomington, Ind.: Indiana University Press, 1994, 158-163.
3. John Toland, *The Dillinger Days*. New York: Random House, 1963, 293; Ibid., 299-300.
4. *Chicago Tribune*, April 28, 1934; William Helmer with Rick Mattix. *Public

Notes

Enemies: America's Criminal Past, 1919-1940. New York: Checkmark Books, 1998, 213; Rept., Detroit, D. E. Hall, Aug. 22, 1934, DF 3565, Sec. 58.

5. Robert Cromie and Joseph Pinkston, *Dillinger: A Short and Violent Life.* Evanston, Ill.: Chicago Historical Bookworks, 1990, 236-238.
6. Teletype, Ladd to Director, July 6, 1934, DF, Sec. 43.
7. Toland, *Dillinger Days*, 302-304.
8. Letter, H. H. Clegg to Director, June 30, 1934, DF 2144, Sec. 38.
9. Memorandum for the Director from E. A. Tamm, June 14, 1934, DF 2006, Sec. 36.
10. Letter, H. H. Clegg, St. Paul, to Director, June 29, 1934, DF, Sec.42.
11. Rept., O. C. Dewry, June 16, 1934, Omaha, DF 2043, Sec. 37; *Omaha (Neb.) World Herald*, June 8, 1934; Paul Maccabee, *John Dillinger Slept Here.* St. Paul, Minn.: Minnesota Historical Society, 1995, 231-232.
12. *Omaha (Neb.) World Herald*, June 8, 1934; Memorandum for Mr. Tamm from the Director, June 8, 1934, DF.
13. *Waterloo (Iowa) Daily Courier*, June 8, 1934.
14. Helmer, *Public Enemies*, 216; Ron Rosner, "The Dillinger Era; a chronology of the Depression Era Outlaws" (unpublished).
15. Maccabee, *John Dillinger*, 232.
16. *Omaha (Neb.) World Herald*, June 8, 1934.
17. *Waterloo (Iowa) Daily Courier*, June 8, 1934.
18. *Omaha (Neb.) World Herald,* June 8, 1934.
19. *St. Paul Daily News*, June 12, 1934.
20. Ibid.
21. Press Release of the Attorney-General on Rewards on Dillinger and Nelson, June 23, 1934, DF, Sec. 39.
22. Don Lambert, "How Iowa Rubbed Out Dillinger's Ace Gunman," *Startling Detective Adventures*, Sept. 1934, 67.
23. Toland, *Dillinger Days*, 305-306.

Chapter 34
1. Robert Cromie and Joseph Pinkston, *Dillinger: A Short and Violent Life.* Evanston, Ill.: Chicago Historical Bookworks, 1990, 244.
2. Teletype, St. Paul, July 1, 1934, DF 2374, Sec. 40.
3. Rept., Chicago, V. W. Peterson, Sept. 27, 1934, DF 4051, Sec. 67.
4. John Toland, *The Dillinger Days*. New York: Random House, 1963, 307.
5. *New York Times*, March 3, 1934; Jay Robert Nash, *Bloodletters and Badmen*, Rev ed. New York: M. Evans and Company, inc., 1995, 133; *Chicago Tribune*, March 4, 1934.
6. *Chicago Tribune*, July 23, 1934.
7. Malcolm Logan, "Glorifying the Criminal," *Scribner's Magazine*, v. 90, July 1931, 43-46.
8. Ibid.
9. Paul Gregory Kooistra, "American Robin Hoods: The Criminal as Social Hero." Ann Arbor, Mich., University Microfilms International, 1982. (Ph.D. Dissertation, University of Virginia), 275.
10. Harold Rissmiller, Reading, Pa., to FDR, May 15, 1934, DF 1332.
11. Jesse T. Kennedy to FDR, Nov. 22, 1933, DF 41.
12. William Helmer with Rick Mattix, *Public Enemies: America's Criminal Past, 1919-1940.* New York: Checkmark Books, 1998, 217.

13. Telephone memorandum from Rorer, March 31, 1934. DF 380.
14. Steven Nickel and William J. Helmer, *Baby Face Nelson: Portrait of a Public Enemy.* Nashville, Tenn.: Cumberland House, 2002, 289-297.

Chapter 35

1. John Toland, *The Dillinger Days.* New York: Random House, 1963, 314-315.
2. Robert Cromie and Joseph Pinkston, *Dillinger: A Short and Violent Life.* Evanston, Ill.: Chicago Historical Bookworks, 1990, 240-242.
3. G. Russell Girardin with William J. Helmer, *Dillinger: the Untold Story.* Bloomington, Ind.: Indiana University Press, 1994, 206.
4. Cromie and Pinkston, *Dillinger,* 242-243.
5. Toland, *Dillinger Days,* 315-316.
6. Steven Nickel and William J. Helmer, *Baby Face Nelson: Portrait of a Public Enemy.* Nashville, Tenn.: Cumberland House, 2002, 304.
7. Cromie and Pinkston, *Dillinger,* 247-248.
8. Nickel and Helmer, *Baby Face Nelson,* 305-306.
9. Toland, *Dillinger Days,* 307-319.
10. Memorandum for the Director from E. A. Tamm, Aug. 1, 1935, DF 6310X, Sec. 108.
11. Toland, *Dillinger Days,* 317-327.
12. Melvin Purvis, *American Agent.* Garden City, N.Y.: Doubleday, Doran & Co., 276.
13. Cromie and Pinkston, *Dillinger,* 251.
14. Girardin, *Dillinger,* 226.
15. Cromie and Pinkston, *Dillinger,* 254.
16. Ibid., 261.
17. Girardin, *Dillinger,* 306-307.
18. Ibid., 254-261.
19. *New York Times,* Jan. 2, 1991.
20. Cromie and Pinkston, *Dillinger,* 256-257.
21. William B. Breuer, *J. Edgar Hoover and His G-Men.* Westport, Conn.: Praeger Publishers, 1995, 181.
22. Carl Sifakis, *The Encyclopedia of American Crime.* New York: Smithmark Publishers, Inc., 1992, 210-211; Letter, Ernest T. Wallinder to Federal Bureau of Investigation, April 30, 1957, DF 7358, Sec. 128.
23. "Dillinger—a Nazi," by Albert Brandt, DF-A. Sec. A58.
24. Girardin, *Dillinger,* 312-313.
25. *New York Times,* July 25, 1934.
26. Letter, N. J. L. Pieper, SAC, San Francisco to Director, Jan. 22, 1938, DF 6976, Sec. 122.
27. "Why Not Shoot Dillinger," DF-A, Sec. A13.
28. Claire Bond Potter, *War on Crime: Bandits, G-Men and the Politics of Mass Culture.* New Brunswick, N.J.: Rutgers University Press, 1998, 153.

Chapter 36
1. William Helmer with Rick Mattix, *Public Enemies: America's Criminal Past, 1919-1940.* New York: Checkmark Books, 1998, 220-221.

Notes

2. Paul Maccabee, *John Dillinger Slept Here.* St. Paul, Minn.: Minnesota Historical Society, 1995, 240-241.
3. Memorandum for the Director, Aug. 10, 1934, DF 3300; Memorandum for Mr. Tamm, Aug. 13, 1934, DF, Sec. 55.
4. Bryan Burrough. *Public Enemies: America's Greatest Crime Wave and the Birth of the FBI, 1933-34.* New York: The Penguin Press, 2004, 481
5. Maccabee, *John Dillinger*, 242-246.
6. *St. Paul Pioneer Press*, Aug. 24, 1934.
7. *Fort Wayne (Ind.) Journal-Gazette*, Aug. 28, 34.
8. Maccabee, *John Dillinger*, 204; Teletype to Director from Ladd, Oct. 9, 1934, DF 4136, Sec. 69.
9. G. Russell Girardin with William J. Helmer, *Dillinger: the Untold Story.* Bloomington, Ind.: Indiana University Press, 1994,260.
10. *Kansas City Star*, Sept. 22, 1934.
11. *Indianapolis Star*, Sept. 24, 1934.
12. John Toland, *The Dillinger Days.* New York: Random House, 1963,335.
13. *St. Paul Dispatch*, Oct. 15, 1934.
14. *Washington Star*, Oct. 17, 34; *New York Times*, Oct. 17, 1934.
15. *Chicago Daily News*, Oct. 19, 34.
16. *Chicago Daily Times*, Oct. 22, 34.

Chapter 37

1. Steven Nickel and William J. Helmer, *Baby Face Nelson: Portrait of a Public Enemy.* Nashville, Tenn.: Cumberland House, 2002, 338.
2. Myron J. Quimby, *The Devil's Emissaries.* New York: A. S. Barnes and Company, 1969, 279-283; Rept., Chicago, V. W. Peterson, Dec. 6, 1934, DF 5070, Sec. 83.
3. Ibid.
4. Bryan Burrough. *Public Enemies: America's Greatest Crime Wave and the Birth of the FBI, 1933-34.* New York: The Penguin Press, 2004, 481.
5. Nickel and Helmer, *Baby Face Nelson*, 353-370.
6. Quimby, *Devil's Emissaries*, 282-284.
7. Ibid.
8. Ibid, 288.
9. Memorandum for the file, Nov. 11, 1934, DF 4377, Sec. 73; Robert Cromie and Joseph Pinkston, *Dillinger: A Short and Violent Life.* Evanston, Ill.: Chicago Historical Bookworks, 1990, 264.
10. Memorandum for the Director, Aug. 10, 1934, DF 3300, Sec. 54.
11. Letter, M. H. Purvis to Director, Aug. 20, 1934, DF 3537, Sec. 58.
12. Memorandum for Identification Division, Unit Five from Hoover, Sept. 12, 1935, DF, Sec. 109; *Chicago Daily News*, Aug. 31, 1935; Rept., Chicago, S. K. McKee, Sept. 12, 1 1935, DF 6384, Sec. 109.
13. William Helmer with Rick Mattix, *Public Enemies: America's Criminal Past, 1919-1940.* New York: Checkmark Books, 1998, 231.

Epilogue

1. Henry Allen, "Hoover," *Washington Post*, March 23, 1993, B1-B2.
2. Paul Maccabee, *John Dillinger Slept Here.* St. Paul, Minn.: Minnesota Historical Society, 1995, 262-265.
3. Nathan Douthit, "Police Professionalism and the War Against Crime in

Notes

the United States, 1920s-30s," in George L. Mosse, ed., *Police Forces in History*. Beverly Hills, Calif.: Sage, 1974, 330.

4. G. Russell Girardin with William J. Helmer, *Dillinger: the Untold Story*. Bloomington, Ind.: Indiana University Press, 1994, 269.
5. Ibid.
6. Helmer, *Public Enemies*, 278.
7. Allen, "Hoover," B1-B2.
8. Ovid Demaris, *The Director: An Oral Biography of J. Edgar Hoover*. New York: Harper's Magazine Press, 1975, 83.
9. Girardin, *Dillinger*, 264-267.
10. Ron Rosner, "The Dillinger Era; a chronology of the Depression Era Outlaws" (unpublished).
11. Rept., Chicago, V. W. Peterson, June 5, 1934, DF 221, Sec. 39.
12. Letter, SAC, Detroit to Director, Oct. 30, 1935, DF 6512, Sec. 113.
13. Girardin, *Dillinger*, 267.
14. John Toland, *The Dillinger Days*. New York: Random House, 1963, 340.
15. Girardin, *Dillinger*, 328.
16. Rosner, "Dillinger Era."
17. Office Memorandum, SAC, Minneapolis to Director, May 17, 1955, DF 7261, Sec. 127.
18. Rosner, "Dillinger Era."
19. *Milwaukee Journal*, Aug. 10, 1941.
20. Rosner, "Dillinger Era."
21. U.S. National Archives. Central Plains Region, Kansas City, Mo., RG:21., Subgroup USAC (St. Paul, Minn.). Criminal case 6004.
22. Girardin, *Dillinger*, 267.
23. Toland, *Dillinger Days*, 341.
24. Girardin, *Dillinger*, 267-268.
25. Office Memorandum to L. B. Nichols from E. C. Kemper, July 23, 1953, DF 7138, Sec. 125.
26. Letter, Jayee to Courtney Ryley Cooper, June 26, 1936, DF, Sec. 117.
27. *Toledo (Ohio) Blade*, April 19, 1935.
28. *Detroit Free Press*, Aug. 14, 1968.
29. Ellen Poulsen, *Don't Call Us Molls: Women of the John Dillinger Gang*. Little Neck, N.Y.: Clinton Cook Publishing Corp., 2002, 409.
30. Osborne Association. "The Report of a Survey on Correctional Institutions, Parole and Probation for the Sherrill Commission Survey of Ohio State Government." New York /1935?/, 3, 18-20.
31. *Columbus (Ohio) Citizen Journal*, Feb. 12, 1969.
32. Girardin, *Dillinger*, 256-260.

Selected Bibliography and Sources

BOOKS

Burrough, Bryan. *Public Enemies: America's Greatest Crime Wave and the Birth of the FBI.* New York: The Penguin Press, 2004.

Cook, Fred J. *The FBI Nobody Knows.* New York: Macmillan, 1964.

Cooper, Courtney Ryley. *Ten Thousand Public Enemies.* Boston: Little, Brown, 1935.

——. *Here's to Crime.* Boston: Little, Brown, 1937.

Corey, Herbert. *Farewell, Mr. Gangster!* New York: D. Appleton-Century, 1936.

Cromie, Robert, and Joseph Pinkston. *Dillinger: a Short and Violent Life.* New York: McGraw-Hill, 1962.

Edge, L. L. *Run the Cat Roads.* New York: Dembner Books, 1981.

Gentry, Curt. *J. Edgar Hoover: The Man and His Secrets.* New York: W. W. Norton, 1991.

Girardin, Russell G., with William Helmer. *Dillinger: the Untold Story.* Bloomington, Ind.: Indiana University, 1994.

Notes

Helmer, William, with Rick Mattix, *Public Enemies: America's Criminal Past. 1919-1940*. New York: Checkmark Books, 1998.

Hoover, J. Edgar. *Persons in Hiding*. Boston: Little, Brown, 1938.

Louderback, Lew. *The Bad Ones: Gangsters of the '30s and Their Molls*. Greenwich, Conn.: Fawcett, 1968.

Maccabee, Paul. *John Dillinger Slept Here: A Crook's Tour of Crime and Corruption in St. Paul, 1920-1936*. St. Paul, Minn.: Minnesota Historical Press, 1995.

Matera, Dary. *John Dillinger: The Life and Death of America's First Celebrity Criminal*. New York: Carroll & Graf Publishers, 2004.

Nash, Jay, and Ron Offen. *Dillinger Dead or Alive?* Chicago: Henry Regnery Company, 1970.

Nickel, Steven, and William J. Helmer. *Baby Face Nelson: Portrait of a Public Enemy*. Nashville, Tenn.: Cumberland House, 2002.

Potter, Claire Bond. *War on Crime: Bandits, G-Men, and the Politics of Mass Culture*. New Brunswick, N.J.: Rutgers University Press, 1998.

Poulsen, Ellen, *Don't Call Us Molls: Women of the John Dillinger Gang*. Little Neck, N.Y.: Clinton Cook Publishing, 2002.

Powers, Richard Gid. *G-Men: Hoover's FBI in American Popular Culture*. Carbondale, Ill.: Southern Illinois University Press, 1983.

Purvis, Melvin. *American Agent*. Garden City, N.Y.: Doubleday, Doran, 1936.

Quimby, Myron. *The Devil's Emissaries*. New York: A. S. Barnes, 1969.

Ruth, David E. *Inventing the Public Enemy: The Gangster in American Culture*, 1918- 1934. Chicago: University of Chicago Press, 1996.

Stewart, Tony. *Dillinger: The Hidden Truth*. /n. p./, Xlibris, 2002.

Summers, Anthony. *Official and Confidential: The Secret Life of J. Edgar Hoover*. New York: G. P. Putnam, 1993.

Toland, John. *Dillinger Days*. New York: Random House, 1963.

Whitehead, Don. *The FBI Story: A Report to the People*. New York: Random House, 1956.

PRIMARY SOURCES
FBI John Dillinger File
Various prison records.
Various court records.

Index

Index

Index

Index

Index

Index

Index